THE ILLUSTRATED TIMELINE OF
MEDICINE

HISTORY TIMELINES

THE ILLUSTRATED TIMELINE OF
MEDICINE

GILL DAVIES

ROSEN
PUBLISHING®
New York

This edition published in 2012 by:

The Rosen Publishing Group, Inc.
29 East 21st Street
New York, NY 10010

Library of Congress Cataloging-in-Publication Data

Davies, Gill.
The illustrated timeline of medicine/Gill Davies.
    p. cm.–(History timelines)
Includes bibliographical references and index.
ISBN 978-1-4488-4796-9 (library binding)
1. Medicine–History–Juvenile literature. 2. Medical innovations–History–Juvenile literature.
I. Title.
R133.5.D38 2012
610.9–dc22

2011008266

Manufactured in the United States of America

CPSIA Compliance Information: Batch #S11YA: For further information, contact Rosen Publishing, New York, New York, at 1-800-237-9932.

First published by Worth Press Ltd, Cambridge, England 2011 www.worthpress.co.uk

CONTENTS

Healing the Sick, a fresco by Domenico di Bartolo in the Sala del Pellegrinaio (Hall of the Pilgrim), Hospital Santa Maria della Scala, Siena.

Standing back and surveying the development of humankind on Earth, it could be said that virtually nothing has affected human history so much as disease. We have evolved in intimate connection with all manner of microscopic pathogens that have proved severe health risks. Above all, civilization has had its disadvantages for human health, bringing with it a multitude of new diseases, associated with settlement, agriculture, and animal husbandry.

Many of the worst diseases have arisen from proximity with animals. Cattle provided the pathogen pool with tuberculosis and viral poxes like smallpox. Pigs and ducks gave humans their influenzas, while horses brought rhinoviruses and hence the common cold. Measles—still killing a million children a year—is the result of canine distemper jumping between dogs or cattle and humans. Moreover, cats, dogs, ducks, hens, mice, rats, and reptiles carry bacteria like *Salmonella*, leading to fatal human infections such as hepatitis, whooping cough, and diphtheria. Current fears over the relationship between bovine spongiform encephalopathy

The Hippocratic Oath written in the form of a cross in a 12th-century Byzantine manuscript.

Detail from *The Triumph of Death* by Pieter Breughel the Elder.

An engraving by William Cheselden, from the *Osteographia*, or "*The Anatomy of the Bones*," 17th century.

(BSE), and the human Creuzfeld-Jacob Disease (CJD) remind us how vulnerable mankind has always been to infections transferred from animals.

The city, hub of civilization, has become the nucleus of disease. The towns of Renaissance Europe were riddled with typhus, typhoid, and plague. The industrial cities of the 19th century harbored tuberculosis, the "white plague." While mankind was at the hunter-gatherer stage, disease was insignificant. With the coming of civilization, cities, and the world population explosion that has occurred over the last ten thousand years, epidemics and pandemics have come to play a major part on the stage of world history.

Many of the turning points in human affairs can be put down less to the best-laid plans of humans than to misadventures with microorganisms. For example, the collapse of the feudal system in the Middle Ages was in large measure the result of the devastating invasion of Europe by bubonic plague. In the 1340s, the Black Death killed up to one-third of Europe's entire population, a calamity on a scale unimaginable nowadays except in the context of nuclear war.

Or take the conquest of the New World by the Old, initiated by Columbus's voyage across the Atlantic in search of the "Indies" in 1492. The victory was due less to the guns or guile of the *Conquistadores* than to the fact that the Spanish invaders were carrying with them the pathogens of disease to which *they* had some acquired immunity but to which New World natives had none at all. It is believed that by 1600 up to 90 percent of the American Indians had died in successive disease onslaughts, and the fabric of native life fell to pieces. It was thus disease rather than military might that vanquished the New World. Ironically, Columbus's men may have brought back with them one New World disease—that is, syphilis—that was to prove the scourge of Europe, coloring the gloomy religious and artistic culture of the time.

Operating theater at Jefferson Medical College, Philadelphia, c. 1870.

A poster for the prevention of tuberculosis.

Disease, in other words, has played a major part in human history, albeit one that most historians have generally ignored or downplayed. Humans have, of course, attempted to fight back—to prevent and, above all, to master disease through a variety of means including religion and magic, but above all, medicine. Healing has been practiced throughout recorded time. There is archeological evidence, from as far afield as France, South America, and the Pacific, that as early as 3000 BCE trephining or trepanning was being performed, cutting a small hole in the skull with a flint, presumably to allow the escape of evil spirits. Our first written records of medicine as an art and practice come from Mesopotamia and Egypt. Medicine as a rational science developed in that "Greek miracle" erupting around the Eastern Mediterranean from around 500 BCE. Hippocrates, the so-called "father of medicine," was an older contemporary of Plato.

Chickens being vaccinated against bird flu in Afghanistan.

What this timechart presentation, juxtaposing the history of disease and the development of medicine, makes so clear is that the battle was for long wholly unequal. Disease was rampant and medicine, however worthy, was for thousands of years a weak reed, ineffectual in saving the lives of those afflicted or at getting to grips with the real understanding of disease and its causes.

For most of the history of humankind, the story of medicine has been, at best, one of very slow and partial improvements in the understanding of the cause and cure of disorders. The workings of the human body in sickness and in health began to make considerable strides from the Renaissance onward with the rise of anatomy, physiology, and pathology, but, in the short term, those advances did little to restore the health of the sick. Only recently have scientists and doctors developed the skills, tools, techniques, and drugs that reliably save lives. Certain traditional medical procedures, like bloodletting, were almost certainly positively harmful. It is often said, not entirely facetiously, that it wasn't until after 1900 that a visit to the doctor was likely to leave you in a better state of health. In surgery it was only in the 19th century that it became possible to perform any ambitious surgical interventions, for example opening up the stomach or the chest. Until then, even attempts to set compound fractures often proved fatal, since lethal infections would set in. Only in the 20th century have we acquired drugs that are truly effective in fighting disease—the sulfa drugs pioneered in the 1930s and the antibiotics that came in during the Second World War. This timechart history shows very clearly how unequal the warfare between microbes and humans has been through most of history.

The other thing visible at a glance by this timechart presentation is the great complexity of medicine. There are some human endeavors—mathematics, for example, or perhaps theoretical physics—in which progress occurs as a result of the brilliant intuitions or experiments of a tiny elite of geniuses, working largely in their heads. Medicine, however, is not like that at all. Medicine requires the confluence and cooperation of all manner of different activities, occupations, and crafts, and the alliance of theoretical knowledge with practical skill.

The improvements in medicine in the Victorian era, for instance, depended upon the concatenation of multiple developments occurring on a broad front. Hospitals had to emerge as locations where, at one and the same time, sufferers were treated, students were taught their trade, and the crowded ranks of the sick could stimulate systematic study of disease itself (in the last resort, through the conduct of postmortems in the morgue). Universities had to be reformed so as to become powerhouses of new basic sciences—biology, chemistry, microscopy—and housing the specialized laboratories that stimulated so many discoveries. The medical professional had to be reformed, ensuring high-quality training and the elimination of quackery. Nursing had to be professionalized. A new type of public health had to be created to control the "filth diseases" rampant in industrial towns. And, not least, the state had increasingly to intervene to regulate and promote health and fund the treatment of the sick. All these diverse factors had to be present for medical progress to occur.

Within medicine, as the charts indicate, one development triggers another in a kind of (generally unplanned) chain reaction. Take surgery. Before the 19th century, the "cutter's art" was stymied by two key obstacles: pain and infection. Luckily, around 1800, the chemist Humphry Davy, pioneering the science of gas chemistry, experimented with nitrous oxide (laughing gas) and discovered its anesthetizing properties. During the next generation, that gas, along with ether and chloroform, began to be tried out in America. Ether was used surgically in Paris and in London in December 1846—the Scots-born Robert Liston amputated a diseased thigh from a patient under ether, pronouncing "This Yankee dodge, gentlemen, beats mesmerism hollow." The newspaper

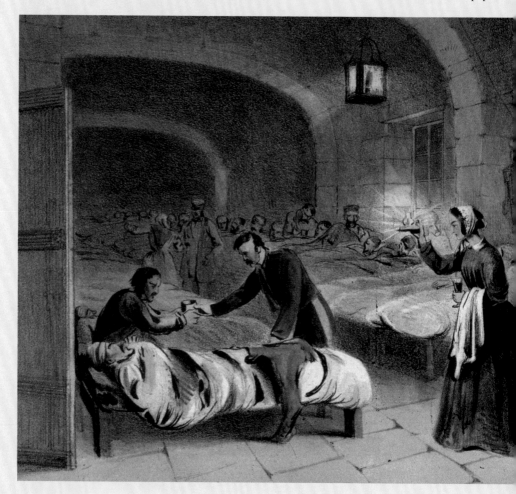

headlines sang "Hail Happy Hour! We Have Conquered Pain." And then the key event came on April 7, 1853: Queen Victoria took chloroform for the birth of Prince Leopold. "The effect was soothing, quieting, and delightful beyond measure," Her Majesty recorded in her journal.

Meanwhile, microscopists were establishing how inflammation, infection, and putrefaction were related to the microorganisms revealed squirming under their lenses. This gave surgeons a clue as to why so many of their patients died of post-operative sepsis. Effective antiseptic techniques were then pioneered in the 1860s in Glasgow by Joseph Lister. Thereafter it became possible to open up the human body, not just *painlessly* but *safely*. The door had been opened to modern surgery.

It can thus be seen that medicine is an infinitely complex jigsaw puzzle in which everything is interlocking. And, historically, the links between events have often been complicated, oblique, and totally unpredictable. The value of the timechart's presentation is that such connections are made visible at a glance. The flow of time is also made clear: The great stream of biological evolution itself, lethal pandemics, large-scale social change, and the parts played by individual pioneers, from

Florence Nightingale on her rounds at the field hospital in Scutari, Turkey. She reduced the Crimean War hospital death rate from 42 percent to 2 percent.

Hippocrates, through Vesalius, up to Pasteur, and the doctors and scientists alive today.

The history of medicine is a heroic story, in so far as it has been a gallant fight against death. But it has been a far from complete triumph. For millennia, disease humbled the powers of the doctors, and it would be foolishly short-sighted of us nowadays—however tremendous the achievements of recent medical science—to think that this situation has irrevocably changed. Evolutionary theory teaches us the law of the survival of the fittest. Bacteria and viruses have always shown themselves to be survivors. The saga of medicine is an ongoing struggle.

Roy S. Porter
MA, PhD (Cantab), FBA, Hon. FRCP
Professor of the Social History of Medicine
The Wellcome Institute for
the History of Medicine
London

Above: Trephined (trepanned) skulls are the first evidence of surgery. Smooth healed bone edges indicate that some, at least, of the victims survived their ordeal, and multiple holes that repeated operations were not unknown.

Right: Witch doctors in Lassa, Africa.

Facing page: A surgical procedure in a modern operating theater.

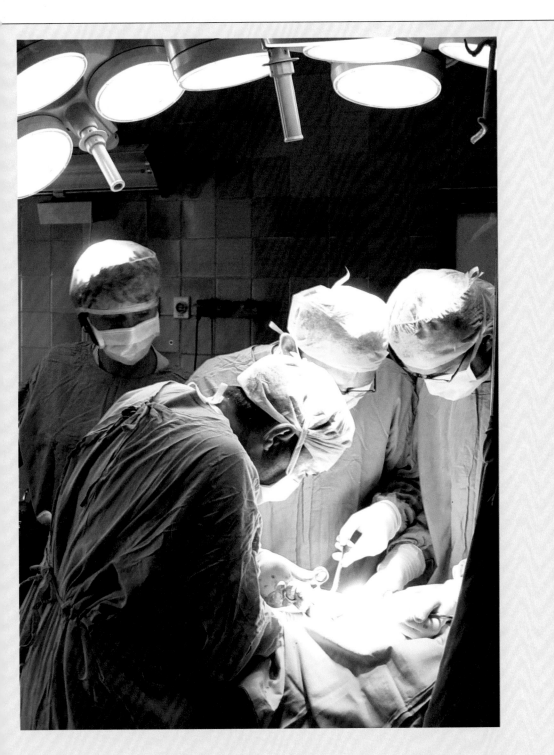

W e cannot be sure exactly which diseases ravaged early prehistoric humans, but, once the written recording of events began, those diseases that killed large numbers of the population have been noted appropriately.

The patterns have changed—with each age and community subject to the weaknesses of its own social structure, hygiene, and areas of ignorance. But prevention or cure has not necessarily advanced hand in hand with greater knowledge. And even as treatment has improved and certain diseases checked to some degree, so new ones seem to emerge to confound the scientists.

The number of diseases that have swept through communities during the history of humankind is vast. Within the confines of this short account, there is only space to look briefly at a few. However, the Bibliography refers to several books that can provide much more information for those who wish to know more.

A COURT FOR KING CHOLERA.

Right: "A Court for King Cholera," *Punch* magazine, 1852.
Below: A color-enhanced scanning electron micrograph showing *Salmonella typhimurium* (red) invading cultured human cells.

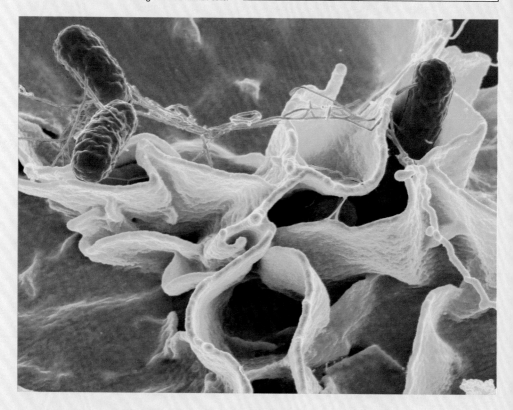

ST. ANTHONY'S FIRE

Outbreaks of a disease called St. Anthony's Fire were frequent in the Middle Ages from 591 onward.

It is difficult to be certain precisely what disease this was, but modern scholars presume it to be what is now called ergotism, a kind of fungal poisoning transmitted by eating infected grain. This can cause reddening and blistering of the skin—hence the fiery associations!

Many of the sick were in France: In monastic hospices where the patients were treated, victims appealed to the saints for help. These included Saint Anthony of Thebes, a legendary hermit and monk who lived in the desert—and, in later times, Saint Anthony of Padua, depicted above.

TIMELINE OF MEDICINE

Ancient man seems to have suffered arthritic deformities, TB of bones and joints, bone cancer, and serious dental infections.

Prehistory

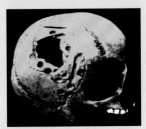

Trepanning, cutting a small hole in the skull with stones and flints. Skulls with up to 5 holes found. Excised rounds of skull worn as amulets. Still practiced for relief of intracranial pressure.

Trepanning (trephining), the earliest known surgery.

ANCIENT EGYPT
Records indicate the pulse was important in assessing patients. Wounds should also be probed.

10,000–2000 Written evidence of Egyptian medicine in ancient texts.

MESOPOTAMIA
10,000–2000 Herbal medicines used in Mesopotamia.

5000 Nomadic hunter-gatherer tribes become agrarian and settle in more stable communities, improving health and longevity, but trade spread diseases increase.

5000 The earliest recorded reference to oral disease is from an ancient Sumerian text that describes "tooth worms as a cause of dental decay."

ANCIENT EGYPT
5000–2500 Believed evil spirits entered body through mouth, nose, or ears and devoured vital substances.

5000–2500 Burns treated by swabbing with milk from mothers of male babies. Isis called upon to help (she used her milk to heal her son's burns).

5000–2500 Magicians utter spells over patients to attack diseases or their agents. Priestly medicine.

MESOPOTAMIA
3500 Early medicine recorded on baked clay tablets in cuneiform writing. Highly regulated profession.

Spinalonga, the leper island near Crete.

LEPROSY

The leprosy bacillus was not discovered until 1873, but had been busy causing disease and great fear of infection throughout man's history. In 600 BCE, leprosy was recorded in India. Biblical leprosy is a form of "uncleanness" and in all probability has no connection with the disease of that name. Another translation error resulted in the further complication of *elephantiasis graecorum* (leprosy) becoming known as *lepra arabum*. The Arabs themselves recognized that elephantiasis was a different disease.

There are some who believe that leprosy was brought back from the East by the Crusaders to Europe but, whatever lay behind its appearance, leprosy was prevalent throughout the Middle Ages. By that time the clergy were seen as the means of salvation and healing.

However, sufferers were still isolated from the rest of the community, and often banned from towns altogether. From about the year 1000 lepers were excluded from normal society.

LEPROSY

Lepers were ostracized. Outcasts from society, they had to carry bells or clappers to indicate their presence and wear a yellow cross.

It is suggested that the disease may have been brought into the West by the returning Crusaders. Whether or not this is so, in 1179 the Church authorities had made it the responsibility of priests to identify lepers. Thousands of hospices (called lazar houses) were set up across Europe to care for the victims of this dreaded disease. After 1300, physicians rather than churchmen or local officials, were given greater responsibility for the identification of lepers, and the numbers appeared to decrease simultaneously. This may have been because isolation had slowed its spread or because the Black Death had so drastically reduced the population of Europe, as well as limiting travel and contact—but in fact the reasons are not known. Or it may have been that overzealous officials had made genuine mistakes in diagnosis.

It is suspected that a wide variety of skin diseases may have been mistakenly diagnosed as leprosy. Sometimes this may have happened from ignorance, or from less altruistic reasons of power-seeking.

Even in recent times the victims have been cut off from normal life. For example, Spinalonga, an island close to Crete, housed Greek lepers as recently as 1957.

For various reasons, leprosy declined in the later Middle Ages. Much later on, Armaeur Hansen studied the disease in Bergen, Norway, and he succeeded in isolating the leprosy bacteria in 1873. The first International Conference on the subject was held in Berlin in 1893, and, in 1921, the British established ninety-four leprosy asylums in India.

Nowadays leprosy can be treated successfully with chemotherapy. It no longer carries its certain threat of disfigurement and slow painful death.

Lepers had to announce their presence by ringing a bell.

CHINA

3000 Stone acupuncture needles found in Inner Mongolia date back to this time.

ANCIENT EGYPT

2900–2750 An Egyptian lower jaw shows two holes drilled through the bone, possibly to drain an abscessed tooth.

2,800 Imhotep is doctor to the pharaoh Zoser and given full status as a god in 535 BCE. The Greeks adopted him, changing his name to Imouthes, and identified him with Asclepius.

CHINA

2700 The Chinese use acupuncture to treat pain associated with tooth decay.

2698–2598 Huang-ti, the Yellow Emperor, legendary author of *Nei Ching*, a medical compendium that was the standard work for thousands of years.

ANCIENT EGYPT

2500 Egyptian records show many afflictions of the eye and arthritis in mummy skeletons, but dental decay rare except in the wealthy!

2500 Three sorts of disease: 1) that will be treated, 2) that will be attempted to treat (a difficult cure), 3) unable to be treated. Last category needs supernatural treatment. Incantation and power of positive thinking important.

The Yellow Emperor and Shennong, another legendary emperor and experienced herbalist.

2500 Use of lapis lazuli, opium and hemlock potions, herb teas, and many plant extracts in decoctions, macerations, pills, boluses, lozenges, electuaries, poultices, ointments, eye lotions, plasters, creams, inhalations, fumigations, suppositories, enemas. More than 500 substances.

2500 Use of raw ox liver for treating night blindness—unwittingly supplying vitamin A, a lack of which is associated with this problem.

ANCIENT INDIA—INDUS VALLEY CIVILIZATION

2500–1500 At first magic important element, but sorcerers become practitioners and scholars.

ANCIENT EGYPT

2500 Surgeons lance boils, perform circumcisions, deal with fractures, cut out cysts, use scalpels, knives, forceps, probes, and red-hot irons to cauterize wounds.

2500 Surgical operations depicted upon tomb of pharaohs at Saqqara.

2500 Ptolemaic period raises ban on dissection.

2500 Mummification helps knowledge of anatomy. The Ebers Papyrus and Edwin Smith Papyrus of the first half of the 16th century BCE are important sources, refering to an earlier period. Edwin Smith Papyrus is earliest known surgical text.

Section of Ebers Papyrus.

2500 Doctors many and specialized—eye doctors, head doctors, stomach doctors.

2500 Anubis is conductor of the dead and patron god of embalmers.

CHINA

2000–500 Traditional medicine develops.

The god Anubis embalming the body of a pharaoh.

PLAGUE

Rat-borne plague is first thought to have emerged from the Himalayan borderlands between India and China. Pestilence struck the Roman Empire between 165 and 180 CE and may have been a mix of several diseases the soldiers carried back with them from Mesopotamia, but some sources claim it was predominantly smallpox. Then there was a second wave of pestilence, along with measles, in 251–266. At its height, this outbreak is believed to have killed 5,000 people a day in Rome.

The Plague of Justinian struck in 542, and the appearance of large buboes as swollen lymph nodes were clearly recorded. These can be egg-sized but may have swollen to the size of a apple. At any rate, Procopius reported that plague killed 10,000 people a day in Constantinople.

There were several plague outbreaks in Britain—one of which was clearly described by the Venerable Bede in 664.

Bubonic plague spread right across the world in the Middle Ages, carried, in the first instance, by fleas on the black rats that infested ships. Plague can be spread from person to person (by the bacteria in the coughs and sneezes of its human victims) when it reaches the lungs and causes pneumonic plague. It may have been called the Black Death

Robert Hooke's drawing of a flea, the kind that carried plague.

because of its symptoms: dark swollen lymph glands or simply because black is associated with horror. Bubonic plague raged between 1347 and 1351 killing some 75 million people—between 25 and 50 percent of the population in afflicted areas of Europe and the Middle East.

Quarantine was introduced by the Venetians at Ragusa in 1377. In some ports, ships had to wait forty days (*quaranta* being Italian for forty) before disembarkation was allowed.

During the 15th, 16th, and 17th centuries, plague recurred throughout Europe. It was endemic in England following the Black Death, but the first cases of the Great Plague appeared in London in 1664; it reached its peak in 1665 and killed a huge proportion of London's population (about 15 percent—some 80,000

The death toll from the Black Death outbreak in 1347–51 depleted Europe's population by about one-third—the most voracious plague ever.

people). At risk of spreading the disease, many fled the city. The dead were collected daily and taken away in handcarts to mass graves dug outside the city walls.

The disease spread widely over the country, but then its virulence seemed suddenly to subside. The Great Fire of London is often attributed with having killed the bacteria, but, in fact, it appears that it had "run its course" in other parts of the country as well—and its impact lessened in mainland Europe, too.

By the 1790s, Chinese commentators had observed that the disease was associated with the appearance of numbers of dying rats. Nonetheless, the ebb and flow of plague remains a mystery and may be associated with changing trade routes and density of rat populations. Several 20th-century outbreaks indicate that plague is still perhaps only "waiting in the wings"!

THE PLAGUE OF JUSTINIAN

Procopius of Caesarea described the course of this epidemic in detail in his History of the Wars *and claimed that, at its height, 10,000 died every day in Constantinople. This outbreak was of relatively brief duration, from 542 to the following year, but it was the first of three great pandemics, the second being the Black Death and the third the widespread epidemic of the 20th century. The plague spread through Italy to southern France and had reached Britain by 554. Meanwhile, it had also taken a severe toll in the Middle East and northern Africa. Mortality may have reached as many as 100 million and wiped out 25 percent of the population of the Roman Empire.*

ANCIENT GREECE AND ROME
2000–500 Homer describes medicine as "the noble art" in the *Iliad*.

CHINA
2000–1000 Chinese treat disease by balance and harmony of five elements: earth, water, fire, wood, metal, and between two opposing forces of Yin and Yang.

ASSYRIANS AND BABYLONIANS
1900–1800 Assyrians and Babylonians see the liver as the seat of life.

Babylonian clay model of a sheep's liver.

MESOPOTAMIA
1750 Code of Hammurabi. Earliest known regulations of medical practice.

ANCIENT INDIA
1500 Aryan invasion brings Sanskrit writings on pain-relieving herbs and wound surgery with descriptions of surgical instruments, "the most important of which is the hand."

ANCIENT EGYPT
1500 Paintings on the Physician's Tomb at Saqqara, Egypt, show men manipulating the feet and hands of others.

Code of Hammurabi inscribed on a polished stele c. 1792–90 BCE.

ANCIENT INDIA
1500 to 1000 *Charaka Samhita* and *Susruta Samhita*. Two basic texts of early Ayurvedic medicine. The latter prescribes 101 surgical instruments and 760 medicinal plants.

ANCIENT EGYPT
1160 The mummy of Rameses V, pharaoh in 1160 BCE, shows pockmarks on his skin as a result of smallpox.

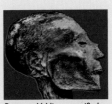

ANCIENT INDIA
800 BCE–1000CE Period of Brahminic medicine.

Rameses V: His mummified head shows signs of smallpox.

BLACK DEATH: FACTS
AND FIGURES

In Europe, some 25 million, one-quarter of the population, died.

75 million died worldwide.

In Florence, the death rate soared to 1,000 a day as the plague reached its zenith.

No other epidemic or war has taken so heavy a toll.

Doctors wore protective clothing, hoping to prevent plague infection. The beaked facepiece incorporated a sponge soaked in vinegar and aromatic substances.

The plague came from the East. During the three-year siege of Caffa in the Crimea, bodies of plague victims from the attacker's army were catapulted inside the walls. Some Italian merchants who had fled from the Tartars to seek refuge in Caffa survived this ordeal but then carried the pestilence back with them to Genoa when they sailed home. Black rats on the ships, and the fleas that bit them, soon spread the plague.

During 1675-84 plague raged in North Africa, Poland, Turkey, Hungary, Austria, and Germany. There were also plague attacks in :

PLAGUE ROUTE

1347: China and Turkistan - Crimea - Genoa - Sicily

1348: North Africa - Corsica - Sardinia - Italy - Spain - France

1349: Austria - Hungary - Switzerland - Germany - Low Countries - England

1350: Scotland - Scandinavia
There were mass burnings of Jews suspected of poisoning wells.

- Cologne in 1666-70
- Netherlands 1667-69
- Malta 1675 (11,000 died)
- Vienna 1679 (76,000 died)
- Prague 1681 (83,000)

And in Marseilles in 1720, 40,000 died in the city plus 10,000 in the surrounding area.

The pestilence struck down members of the nobility and royalty including King Alfonso XI of Castile and Joan, the daughter of Edward III of England.

PLAGUE IN 17TH-CENTURY LONDON

Year	Plague deaths	Total deaths
1603	30,578	38,244
1604	896	5,219
1605	444	6,392
1606	2,124	7,920
1607	2,352	8,022
1608	2,262	9,020
1609	4,240	11,785
1610	1,803	9,087
1611	627	7,343
1612	64	7,343
1625	41,313	63,001
1636	10,400	23,359
1637	3,082	11,763
1638	363	13,624
1647	3,597	14,059
1665	*68,596	
1666	2,000	

* Probably an underestimate.

SMALLPOX

It is possible that smallpox was rampant in 10,000 BCE, and it seems to have occurred in ancient Egypt. The mummy of Pharoah Rameses V (which dates back to 1160 BCE) shows typical pockmarks. In the 10th century CE, the Persian physician, Rhazes, described the disease, distinguishing it from measles. There was a veritable plague of smallpox, which devastated Europe in 1693 to 1694 when England's young Queen Mary II died as one of its victims. There were outbreaks in New England, too, and smallpox decimated the North American Indian tribes.

The Chinese inoculated against smallpox, placing pus from a mild case into a scratch on a healthy person. The Turks used a similar technique, which was noted by Lady Mary Wortley Montagu (wife to the British Ambassador in Turkey in the early 18th century). She brought the notion back with her to Britain, where its value was recognized and inoculation instigated—though at some risk to the first "guinea pigs" as the live virus, albeit selected from mild cases, could occasionally turn out to be a virulent strain.

Later, this procedure was made safer by Edward Jenner in 1798, when he discovered that milkmaids who had contracted cowpox developed resistance to smallpox. He used cowpox in his new-fangled "vaccinations," which soon became very popular and considerably reduced the presence of smallpox in Britain.

In 1967, smallpox was still a major threat, but, as vaccinations spread all around the world, its impact grew less and less, until in 1980, the World Health Organization was able to announce that it had been completely eradicated.

Initially, the concept of an injection derived from cowpox created some fear and ridicule—as this contemporary cartoon shows.

DISEASE AND PESTILENCE

Cholera personified—in the 1800s cholera spread from India through Mediterranean ports to reach Europe and North America.

CHOLERA

At one time cholera was confined to the East and still recurs annually as an epidemic in India. It was studied by the Dutch physician Jacobus Bontius in the Dutch East Indies in 1627. He described the disease accurately in 1642.

Cholera spread from India to China, where an outbreak in 1669 led to its full-fledged introduction into the Western World. There it flourished in towns and cities for the next two centuries or so, the ideal conditions for its spread to be found in these industrialized areas with crowded housing and poor sanitation. In 1831–32, cholera killed 5,000 in London and many thousands worldwide. Then another 50,000 succumbed in 1849–50. It was prevalent in the USA by 1836–38, and, during the American Civil War, some 50,000 died.

Queen Victoria's physician, John Snow, noted during an outbreak in Soho, London, in 1854, that cases centered around the Broad Street water pump. Local brewery workers who rarely drank water or those drawing water from a different pump did not appear to catch cholera. By simply organizing the removal of the Broad Street pump handle, Snow stopped the outbreak; there were no more new cases. Snow had proved that the disease spread through contaminated drinking water.

Nowadays it is largely kept at bay because of good standards of sanitation and water purification, but cholera still occurs regularly in the Far East and where primitive living conditions prevail. For example, in 2010 an outbreak occurred in Haiti where thousands of people were living in rough camps following a devastating earthquake.

TYPHOID

Typhoid symptoms are varied and not necessarily specific to typhoid alone, so it is difficult to ascertain its history precisely. Although a member of the salmonella family, typhoid is purely a human disease and is generally transmitted via polluted water and poor sanitation.

In the 18th century, there was a general belief that many diseases, including typhoid, were spread through filth and foul air. William Budd argued in 1839 that, although typhoid was certainly due to insanitary conditions, it was not just "in the air" but a contagious infection carried from one person to another. When, in

1847, he investigated one outbreak among students who had used a common well, his theories were further substantiated.

William Budd also distinguished typhoid from typhus, which is spread by human lice.

In 1901, Robert Koch discovered that typhoid could be

Bacteriologist Robert Koch discovered much about bacteria and established that apparently healthy people could be carriers of infection.

HEBREW

700–600 Hebrews believe disease comes as a punishment from God.

700–600 Pharmacy includes simple powders, ointments, perfumes, caraway, garlic, mandrake.

700–600 Circumcision so ancient a tradition that stone tools sometimes used even after metal ones in common use.

Hebrew ceremonial implements including circumcision knives.

ANCIENT GREECE AND ROME

639–544 Thales of Miletos. The first true scientist-philosopher of the Greeks who taught that water was the basic element.
A Greek cure for haemorrhoids: Cow sweat, ashes of dog's head, skin of a snake macerated in vinegar and rose honey. Cure for warts: Ashes of white dog's dirt and oil of roses. Belief that certain sacred dogs and snakes helped effect cures.

580–489 Pythagoras founds school at Croton. Earliest scientific studies of anatomy and physiology.

580–489 Alcmaeon of Croton discovers optic nerve and Eustachian tube of ear.

509 Etruscans pre-Roman. Were skilled dentists and mounted extracted teeth on gold bridges. Gold fillings and dental crowns unearthed.

Hippocratic Oath

There are many versions, one of which is given below:
I swear by Apollo the physician and by Asklepios, Hygeia, and Panacea, and all the gods and goddesses and call them to witness that... I will prescribe treatment to the best of my ability and judgement for the good of the sick, and never for a harmful or illicit purpose. I will give no poisonous drug, even if asked to, nor make any such suggestion; and likewise I will give no woman a pessary to cause abortion. I will both live and work in purity and godliness... I will... refrain from all deliberate harm or corruption, especially from sexual relations with women or men, free or slave. Anything I see or hear about people, whether in the course of my practice or outside it, that should not be made public, I will keep to myself and treat as an inviolable secret.

Hippocrates (460–377).

ANCIENT INDIA

500 Ayurvedic medicine can be traced back to 1000 BCE but its current form

200 Bas-relief from Bharut, India, shows a giant having his tooth extracted.

Typhoid Mary.

transmitted by seemingly healthy carriers. One such was "Typhoid Mary," an Irish-American cook on Long Island who was actually kept in jail for three years to prevent her from coming into contact with the general public. She is known to have caused at least forty-seven cases of typhoid and three deaths.

Vaccinations were used during the First World War and prevented the troops from being ravaged by the disease, despite their dreadful living conditions. Now antibiotics and greatly improved hygiene mean that typhoid has virtually disappeared from developed countries, but there still remain some 21 million cases of typhoid and nearly a quarter of a million deaths a year.

In the USA in 1900 there was an annual death rate of 30 per 100,000 population. In 1960, the total number of deaths was only twenty-one.

DISEASE AND PESTILENCE

TUBERCULOSIS

Prior to pasteurization, tuberculosis (TB) was sometimes transmitted to humans from cows through contaminated milk, but the bacilli are more generally passed from human to human by being carried in airborne droplets.

Historically, a form of tuberculosis has been described under the term "scrofula," which denoted a number of diseases that caused swollen glands. This was "The King's Evil" since it was believed that a royal touch could cure the disease.

During the 19th century reports suggest that a vast proportion of the British population suffered from the disease including a good number of children, but few died from a bovine infection. It was the pulmonary TB—rife in the 18th and 19th centuries and then called "consumption"—that was lethal. The mortality rates were very high, and it was the leading cause of death in European and American cities in the 19th century.

Bacteriologist Robert Koch identified the bacillus in the 1880s, but it was not until the 1920s that the BCG vaccine began to be used widely.

Vaccination (although often controversial) and understanding of hygiene have reduced the impact of the disease in the developed world, but it still appears hand in hand with poverty and in populations or territories where there has been no previous exposure. Because of their diminished immunity, AIDS victims are highly susceptible to the bacillus.

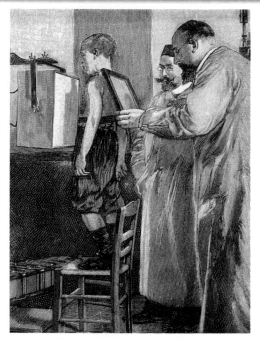
From the 1900s, X-rays became a powerful tool in early diagnosis of diseases such as tuberculosis.

SCURVY

Between 1600 and 1800 scurvy killed about one million sailors. It was first recognized specifically during the Age of Discovery. Long sea voyages without sources of fresh fruit and vegetables meant an inevitable deficiency of vitamin C in sailors' diets—after about three months the symptoms first appear, and they become life-threatening after seven to nine months.

In 1497 to 1499, it may be that as many as half of Vasco da Gama's crew died of scurvy on their voyage around South Africa to India. Magellan's crew, during their circumnavigation of the world (1519–22) also suffered badly but to some degree held the disease in check by their eating of wild celery and rats at Tierra del Fuego.

In due course, the disease would be better understood, and, by the end of the 16th century, the importance of citrus fruit was appreciated.

For centuries, taking scurvy grass was considered a preventive measure against scurvy. In fact, it is not a very good source of vitamin C.

SYPHILIS

Syphilis or the "Pox" is one of several venereal diseases, and it is sometimes difficult to ascertain which particular disease is being referred to in the earliest historical records.

It was certainly present in a mild form in Europe before 1492 but seems to have suddenly become deadly after Christopher Columbus's discovery of the Americas. It may be that an American strain returned with his crew or crossed with the European form, although this theory is now disputed. Perhaps the disease mutated in some way. Whatever the cause, a virulent outbreak spread across the face of Europe in 1493–94 and was a veritable plague until about 1530— and it has recurred ever since.

It was treated variously with substances such as mercury and guaiacum (from a Colombian timber) and was generally regarded as a symbol of immorality and vice by the end of the 18th century.

The use of penicillin and antibiotics mean that although the disease is still omnipresent, deaths from syphilis have greatly diminished since the 1940s.

Citrus fruits were proved to be both a preventive and a cure for scurvy.

British naval surgeon Edward Ives kept his crew supplied with cider, which seemed to help and, hearing of this, in 1747 James Lind conducted a controlled clinical trial using citrus fruit with one group of sailors, cider with another, and a mixture of substances with a third group—and so proved that citrus juice prevented the disease.

Later on British sailors would be referred to as "Limeys" because they were kept supplied with limes to maintain their vitamin C levels.

is from this date. Belief that the human body is a microcosm of the universe. The body substances (bone, flesh, fat, blood, semen, marrow) are the products of humors: Kaph (or phlegm), pitta (or bile), and vata (wind).

ANCIENT GREECE AND ROME
500–420 Hippocratic school of medicine flourishes. Earliest surviving writings of Hippocratic Corpus date from 420 BCE.
500–428 Anaxagoras believes that each element is composed of many small invisible particles or seeds, which were released from food by digestion and then reconstituted into components of the body—such as bone and muscle.

CHINA
479–300 *Nei Ching* manual of physic describes acupuncture, originated from work of 2600 BCE.

By 479 BCE, acupuncture had been used in China for many centuries.

ANCIENT GREECE AND ROME
c. 460 Empedocles's teaching leads to theory of the four elements: Earth, air, fire, and water.
460–377 Hippocrates, leader of medical school and guild in Cos, is regarded as the Father of Western Medicine.
430–427 Great plague of Athens.
400 Thucydides describes Athenian epidemic in his history.
384–322 Aristotle dissects many species and lays the foundations for embryology. He believes that careful observation, experimentation, and the study of cause and effect could lead to greater scientific knowledge.
370–288 Theophrastus of Eresos. Pupil of Aristotle. Author of *Enquiry into Plants*.

ANCIENT INDIA
4th century Surgery extensive inside and outside body. 121 different instruments. Repair of noses with "plastic surgery," cutting skin from forehead, leaving end near bridge of nose attached. It is sewed in place to nose stump. Wooden tubes inserted to keep artificial "nostrils" open.

MEASLES

Once Columbus had landed in America, the route was opened up for the exchange of diseases. Populations not previously exposed to a disease were particularly susceptible and, as the Spaniards arrived, measles struck in places like Brazil and Mexico.

Measles is primarily a childhood disease, but it does not entirely belong to the nursery, of course, and has been known to decimate adults and children alike in places such as Mexico, the Fiji islands, and Alaska, where previously unexposed and therefore vulnerable victims have succumbed in great numbers.

Its recorded history does not begin until the 10th century when the Muslim physician Rhazes described it, and then a century later, Avicenna, a Persian scientist, postulated that the rash was due to residual menstrual blood from the mother.

By the 16th and 17th centuries, physicians were better equipped to distinguish between measles and scarlet fever. Earlier, confusion had occurred because there was a less "clinical" approach, and physicians tended to analyze the types of people susceptible to particular diseases rather than concentrating on the close inspection of specific symptoms and signs.

It was not until the 19th century that outbreaks in colonies and settlements created a catastrophic death toll. The deaths were in part due to the disease and its complications but also to exhaustion and starvation, because when whole communities were taken ill en masse, there was no one to care for the young, sick, or elderly.

During a severe outbreak in the Faeroes in 1846, when 6,100 of the population of 7,864 contracted measles, Peter Ludwig Panum of Denmark conducted a thorough research into the pattern of the disease. This proved that once the distinctive measles rash appeared, the contagious "flu-like" stage had already been passed, so quarantine was ineffective.

Ever a disease of war, spread by the mobilization of soldiers and the close confines of military camps, from the American Civil War to World War I, it became clear to the various military medical authorities that the best protection was still exposure in childhood until such time as vaccines became available. A vaccine created from the modified live measles virus has been in use widely since the 1960s and considerably lessened the impact of measles and its side effects as a disease of childhood.

INFLUENZA

Spread by a virus, influenza is highly contagious but is often only of brief duration and—unless respiratory complications set in—is rarely fatal. Particularly susceptible are the very young and the old who are most likely to develop associated bronchitis or pneumonia, but there have been outbreaks that have become worldwide pandemics and exacted a heavy death toll. Hippocrates described an epidemic in the fifth century BCE that may have been influenza. There was certainly one clearly described in 1610.

In 1781-82, Russian flu swept over Europe from the east and again in 1889—when it reached all the populated continents and killed about 250,000 in Europe.

Generally sweeping universally, influenza was so-named because 18th-century Italian physicians believed its spread was *influenced* by the stars.

In 1918, almost the entire northern hemisphere was blanketed by the disease in a single month; it became one of the most severe killer diseases in history. Latest examinations of the records estimate that some 30 million may have died in a matter of a few months, with some fifty times that figure being taken ill. In the USA 548,000 died and perhaps as many as 20 million in India in this most catastrophic of outbreaks. The death toll in one year was higher than that of the entire First World War.

In the 1930s, new electron microscopes enabled scientists to photograph and better distinguish the various strains of the virus, and at last vaccines were able to be developed. There was an epidemic of Asian influenza in 1957, which began in China and then circled the globe, becoming more virulent as it did so, with respiratory complications increasing by the time it reached America. However, the prompt and widespread use of the specific flu vaccine ahead of the arrival of the disease reduced its severity and lessened mortality rates in the States.

Although each year the World Health Organization attempts to predict the likely

ANCIENT GREECE AND ROME
3rd century Alexandria has 700,000 volumes in library founded by Ptolemy I and a publicly funded research institute in its museum. The library was partially destroyed by fire in 48 BCE.

ANCIENT INDIA
3rd century Although not proven, some evidence suggests that Indians may have known malaria came from mosquito and plague carried by rats.

CHINA
c. 3rd–2nd century Deformities of the skeleton are mentioned in Chinese writings. It is not clear whether these abnormalities are the result of rickets.

CHINA
c. 280 Ts'ang Kung begins to study medicine. He writes 25 case histories—the only records of this kind in Chinese literature for 1,500 years. Describes cancer of stomach, cystitis, urinary retention, arthritis, paralysis, aneurysm, haemoptysis, and renal disease.

ANCIENT GREECE AND ROME
280 Herophilus of Chalcedon (330–260) BCE. First true anatomist.

Asclepius, Greek god of medicine.

ANCIENT INDIA
274 The early Indian doctors make house calls. Trained doctors from the Taxila and Benaras schools work with physician priests, who combine their skills with religious treatment. In 274 BCE, hospitals for the care of sick come into existence; the nursing attendants are men.

ANCIENT GREECE AND ROME
234–149 Marcus Porcius Cato, farmer, lawyer, soldier, consul, and censor. Collects recipes for medical treatment.

form of seasonal flu so that vaccines can be prepared in advance, new strains still create panic. For example, the influenza A H5N1 virus, commonly called "bird flu" or "avian flu," caused a global alert when it first passed from birds to humans in 1997, and similarly the new mutation H1N1, or "swine flu," sparked worries around the world when it became pandemic in 2009-10.

DISEASE AND PESTILENCE

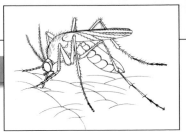

MALARIA

Malaria is caused by the parasitic protozoa, *Plasmodium*, which is carried by the females of certain mosquito species and injected into humans when bitten by these insects. It is still rife in tropical Africa, Asia, and Central and South America.

Mosquitoes carry the parasitic protozoa, *Plasmodium*, that spreads malaria.

Malaria leaves no marks on bones, so it is hard to trace its history in ancient times. We do know that it has been ubiquitous in warm climates for centuries, and, in 2700 BCE, a medical book, *Nei Ching*, described the swollen spleen and cycle of fever that would seem to be typical of malaria. In 1600 BCE, Sumerian and Vedic writing show malaria was prevalent then.

Several times malaria battered the defenses of the Roman Empire more powerfully than any military force had done.

There were severe outbreaks in Columbia in 1493. In 1630, the Countess of Chinchón was treated with an infusion from the bark of a Peruvian tree now named after her, and its active ingredient, quinine, has since been used universally for treating cases of malaria.

Although long associated with marshy areas and with several 19th-century investigators linking it to parasites, malaria's association with the mosquito was not properly understood until the beginning of the 20th century.

In the 20th century, with its increasing scientific "manipulation" of the natural world, it had been believed that the draining of marshy areas and the use of DDT on stagnant water would eradicate most of the malaria-carrying mosquitoes and, therefore, the disease itself, but the subsequent withdrawal of DDT and the development of resistant species has meant that malaria is still very much in evidence.

A U.S. soldier demonstrates DDT-hand spraying equipment while applying the insecticide.

YELLOW FEVER

In the jungle areas of Africa and America, this was long regarded as a non-lethal disease of childhood, as indeed it was until the arrival of non-immune Europeans into these parts of the world. The slave trade in turn introduced yellow fever to new areas and unprotected victims. Carried by mosquitoes through a chain of insect-monkey-insect or insect-man-insect, the disease is caused by a flavivirus and attacks the liver, causing severe yellow jaundice—hence the name yellow fever.

After its first appearance in Barbados in 1647, it spread through American ports and into some European ports, including Lisbon, Barcelona, and Swansea. Its impact in the Caribbean area was fearsome. In 1655, of 1,500 French soldiers in St. Lucia, only 89 survived. In time, ships had to fly the warning Yellow Jack flag if stricken, and, in the 1850s, there were several severe outbreaks in New Orleans.

As was the case with a number of diseases then, many physicians believed that yellow fever was an illness that arose from the fetid air in streets where dead animals lay rotting and human waste accumulated to create horrid vapors.

Eventually (following Ronald Ross's researches in malaria) in 1899 Walter Reed, an American physician, suggested that yellow fever was also carried by mosquitoes. Carlos Finlay, a physician in Cuba, had proposed a similar notion in the 1880s, but he transferred mosquitoes fed on yellow fever patients to uninfected volunteers after only three to five days—too short a time for the virus to have fully developed in the carrier, so he was unable to prove his theories.

In due course, volunteer soldiers were split into two groups. One set was exposed to the soiled bedding and clothing of yellow fever victims; the second set to mosquitoes known to have already bitten yellow fever patients. Only those unfortunates in the second group contracted the disease, so the mosquito agency was established. The Reed Commission also established that yellow fever was caused by a virus.

Facing page: The outbreaks of yellow fever repeatedly spread from tropical regions through ports such as New Orleans (here shown as it was in 1884).

219 Arrival of Archagathus, traditionally first Greek doctor to arrive in Rome. He is granted Roman citizenship and a public surgery.

ANCIENT GREECE AND ROME

200 Just before this period, Archagathis, a Greek Roman citizen, founds first European pharmacy shop near the Forum in Rome. Sells remedies, dresses wounds, opens a surgery and hospital.

A Roman pharmacy.

150 Attitudes to surgery Under the Hippocratic Oath, using knives and the cutting of patients "for the stone" had been forbidden to the respected, educated physicians or doctors, so surgeons were the less-educated "craftsmen" who actually undertook these grisly tasks. Later, the Church would also strongly oppose dissection and surgery, and it was not until the 13th century that the two medical fields were regarded as a whole and equally respected.

100 Julius Caesar supposedly delivered by Caesarian section. Asclepiades introduces humane treatment of mentally deranged. Some treatments based on interpretations of dreams.

Birth of Julius Caesar, reputedly by Caesarean section in about 120 BCE, depicted in a medieval manuscript.

In Havana and the Panama Canal area, William Crawford Gorgas spearheaded the control of mosquitoes through swamp drainage, oiling of the breeding sites, using insecticides, and screening sick rooms. By the 1930s, a vaccine had been created. Yellow fever slithered back to the confines of the jungle but is not entirely defeated. It still flares up now and then in tropical cities.

POLIO

Until 1955, American families were terrified of the childhood disease poliomyelitis, usually just called polio, and sometimes known as infantile paralysis.

This infectious disease or virus attacks the nervous system, and although the majority of infected individuals do not show any symptoms, up to 2 percent of cases are severe and devastating. In these, the virus enters the bloodstream and then the nervous system, destroying motor neurones and leading to muscle failure, paralysis, and even death. In the 1940s and early 1950s, it was so common in the USA that it seemed to be a modern-day plague, leaving about one child in 5,000 killed or crippled. In the U.S., it tended to occur in annual summer epidemics, with nearly 58,000 cases in 1952, the worst year of the outbreak. That year 3,145 people in the U.S. died from polio, and 21,269 survived with some degree of paralysis.

Among its victims was Franklin D. Roosevelt, who caught polio in 1921 (at the age of 39), lost the use of his legs, but went on to become

A physical therapist assists polio-stricken children while they exercise their lower limbs. After the polio vaccination was introduced in 1955, the number of those stricken by the disease dropped radically within 5 years.

U.S. president. Paralysis of the legs is characteristic of spinal polio, the most common form of the paralytic condition. Another common sight in hospitals was that of children in an "iron lung," a huge artificial ventilator that kept children breathing until their muscles recovered enough for them to respirate unaided.

Although polio was known throughout history, there did not appear to be any major epidemics until the late 19th century, when regular outbreaks sparked off an intensive search for a cure. Karl Landsteiner identified the polio virus in 1908, and three separate types of the polio virus were later identified. Since exposure to the virus gives immunity, most researchers worked on a weakened but "live" virus, looking to develop a strain that would give only a mild infection, and therefore bestow future immunity.

Jonas Salk of the University of Pittsburgh looked instead at using a "killed" or deactivated form of the virus as an antigen, a substance that would trigger the production of antibodies against any later exposure to the disease. After a national test involving two million children, he announced a successful vaccine in 1955.

Salk became a popular hero, particularly since he refused to take any personal profit from his discovery, and vaccination programs have now led to the almost complete disappearance of polio in most of the world. However, it is still present in India, Afghanistan, Pakistan, and Nigeria. Infected individuals from those areas can carry the infection elsewhere, and, in 2011, an outbreak in the Republic of Congo caused at least 179 deaths.

The number four

The number four assumes an almost magical significance in medical thinking—derived from the balance of the four seasons, the four elements (water, air, fire, and earth), the four qualities (moist, dry, hot, and cold) and the four humors of the body.

FLEGMAT ♓ ♈ SANGVIN

♏ ♉

♋ ♑ ♒ ♊

♐ ♌

MELANG COLERIC ♍

The four humors dominated medicine from Greek times right through the Medieval period and even extended into the 19th century. These were sanguine (blood), choleric (yellow bile), melancholic (black bile), and phlegmatic (phlegm)—the four fluids of the body, which had to be kept in balance to retain health.

100 Asclepiades of Bithynia. Scholars think that almost everything about Asclepiades remains controversial, but he is undoubtedly successful. He holds a mechanistic view of the body. Rejects strong drugs in favor of wine, baths, and massage. Recommends exercise. Credited in Rome with an ability to arouse the almost dead.

99–55 Lucretius, Roman prefect. He describes epidemic in *De Rerum Natura*, containing exposition of doctrines of Epicurus.

80 Mithridates VI, King of Pontus (120–63 BCE), experiments with poison antidotes. His composition for Theriac contains 41 ingredients.

46 Julius Caesar grants Roman citizenship to all doctors practicing in Rome.

23 Antonius Musa cures Emperor Augustus of serious illness with his cold water treatment. Doctors granted immunity from taxes.

ANCIENT GREECE AND ROME

14–37 CE *De Medicina* (On Medicine) written by Cornelius Celsus (8 volumes), who was not a doctor of medicine but knew about clamping veins to prevent hemorrhage, describes goiter, cataract, tonsillectomy, and plastic surgery. Advises cleaning wounds and defines acute inflammation. We learn an enormous amount about Roman medical thought and practice. Earliest scientific medical work in Latin. Lost for centuries and rediscovered in Siena in 1426.

23–79 Life of Pliny the Elder (Caius Plinius Secundus), great Roman naturalist: His *Natural History* (37 books) describes drugs obtained from animal, vegetable, and mineral sources.

40–90 Pedanius Dioscorides, a respected army surgeon in time of Nero, writes five-volume *De Materia Medica*, 600 remedies—undisputed authority on plant medicines for over 1,500 years.

Pharmacy: Theriac, a compound of 61 ingredients including viper meat and opium, was a universal antidote. Said to have been invented by Andromarchos (c. 54) of Crete, physican to Nero.

69–79 Vespasian frees doctors from military service.

79 Plague follows eruption of Vesuvius. 200 different instruments, including vaginal speculum, found at Pompeii. Limited anatomical knowledge.

96 Aqueducts carry clean water. (There are sophisticated latrines in

Roman toilets, Ephesus.

14–37 CE Julius Caesar, military genius and shrewd politician, encouraged Roman citizenship and allowed all doctors in Rome to become Roman citizens.

AIDS

The HIV (human immunodeficiency virus) attacks and takes over human immune system cells called CD4 lymphocytes. An individual can be HIV positive for years with mild or no symptoms, until the virus manifests itself. As HIV multiplies, it gradually and irrevocably damages the immune system. AIDS (acquired immunodeficiency syndrome) is the most advanced stage of HIV virus infection. At this point, the defensive capabilities of the immune system are severely compromised, rendering it easy prey to "opportunistic" infections. The ultimate result is death. There is no known cure or vaccine for AIDS.

HIV is believed to be a descendant of SIV (simian immunodeficiency virus), found in wild monkeys in sub-Saharan Africa. It is believed to have crossed over to humans through butchered meat. In the human body, it developed as a new strain. From Africa, the virus traveled to Haiti and then to the USA, from where it spread to the rest of the world.

Initially believed to be a sexually transmitted disease among homosexuals, it was soon found to afflict heterosexuals, too—today, the latter far outnumber the former. HIV is transmitted via bodily fluids. These are blood, semen, vaginal fluid, and mother's milk. In order for AIDS to develop, the virus has to get into the bloodstream. This usually happens because of unsafe sex, through infected needles used for injections or drug use, and at any time from when a baby is in the womb up to the breast-feeding stage. Other modes of delivery could be shaving razors, tattooing, and body piercing.

At the end of 2007, about 33 million people worldwide were estimated to be infected by HIV. Ninety-five percent of these live in the developing world. The worst affected region is sub-Saharan Africa, which accounts for almost 70 percent of known cases. Since 1981, AIDS has claimed 25 million lives.

Billions of dollars have been pumped into the battle against AIDS. Now, simple and accurate tests can detect HIV presence in the body. While the frantic search for a cure continues, the present method of treatment is antiretroviral (ARV) therapy. ARV drugs work by restricting the amount of HIV in the blood, thereby delaying the onset of AIDS and allowing the patient to live relatively normally for as long as possible. Costs of drugs have been brought down, and efforts at making them available to affected areas have had modest success. Meanwhile, massive awareness programs have focused on preventive measures and on clearing up misconceptions. On the other hand, the campaign has been impeded by regional politics, social prejudices, corruption, poor management, and poverty.

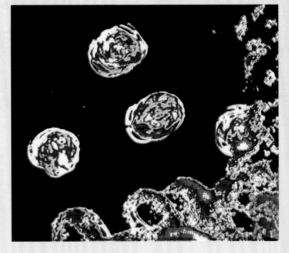

AIDS virus.

forts.) System of drains and canals. Controls on conditions of food sales in markets. Orders specify burial and cremation, hygiene in public baths.

98–117 Rufus of Ephesus writes on gonorrhoea, anatomy, kidney disease, and bedside medicine in *On the interrogation of the patient.*

c. 98–138

Soranus of Ephesus, Roman founder of obstetrics. His fame rests on his *Diseases of Women*, a text used for 15 centuries. He advises

Soranus of Ephesus is regarded as the "Father of Obstetrics."

contraception, using cotton, ointments, or fatty substances. Describes obstetric chair and vaginal speculum, diagnosis of difficulties in labor. Writes *Signs of Fractures* and *On Acute Chronic Diseases.*

CHINA

2nd century Warlord Kuan Yun drinks wine and plays chess while his surgeon, Hua T'o, cuts and scrapes out a poisoned arrow wound right down to the bone. When later he tries to treat his lord's headache with trepanning, Kuan Yun is worried the surgeon might have been bribed to murder him and has him executed.

190 Hua T'o, the famous Chinese surgeon, employs anesthesia using an effervescent powder dissolved in wine. Said to have removed a gangrenous spleen using this method. Surgical advance stopped after his time because of Confucian interdict on mutilation of the human body.

ANCIENT GREECE AND ROME

131–201 Galen, born at Pergamum. His first surgical appointment is to the gladiators there.

Galen giving a public lecture in Rome.

He studied medicine at Alexandria, went to Rome about 162 CE, and wrote extensively on anatomy, physiology, and practical medicine, stressing the humoral theory and the Hippocratic doctrine.

158 Galen becomes surgeon to gladiators.

165–169 Antonine Plague.

HEBREW

2nd–6th century The Talmud or book of the law transmitted orally (Mishna), contains information on diseases and Jewish surgery.

CHINA

c. 200 Doctor Zhang Zhongjing writes a massive medical book, containing all the medical remedies and treatments known. The book recommends a preparation (ephedrine, in 1928) made from the horsetail plant to ease asthma.

280 Wang Shu-ho composes the 12-volume *Mei Ching* (Book of Pulse). He argues that examining the pulse is the fundamental action of medicine and draws a comparison between the human body and a chord musical instrument. Likening the different pulses of the body to the

Chinese pulse chart.

chords, he claims that harmony or discord within an organism can be established by reading the pulse.

ANCIENT GREECE AND ROME

Guilds purchased texts and send them to military forts, so medical knowledge spreads to every corner of the Roman Empire.

3rd century Martyrdom of saints Cosmas and Damian. Legend of their grafting a dead Ethiopian's leg on a patient dying of cancer.

200 Medical licensing introduced.

251–266 Plague of Cyprian.

302 Eusebius, Bishop of Caesarea, describes Syrian epidemic of smallpox.

325–403 Oribasius. Provides a treatise on the treatment of fractures by mechanical appliances, including screw traction and elaborate multiple-pulley systems. Composes a medical and surgical encyclopedia.

357–377 First great Christian hospital at Caesarea founded by Saint Basil, where the sick,

TIMELINE OF AIDS

Late 19th century–1950: HIV passes on to humans from African monkeys.

1950–60: Earliest known AIDS cases.

1970s: AIDS reaches USA.

1980–85: Disease is recognized. Virus discovered. First HIV antibody test approved.

1986–87: First AIDS cases in Asia. First anti-HIV drug approved. USA denies entry to HIV+ foreigners. Discriminatory attacks on a few HIV+ individuals.

1991: 10 million infected with HIV worldwide.

1993: Thailand's AIDS control budget increases almost 2,000 percent to $44 million.

1996: AIDS researcher Dr. David Ho is *Time* magazine's Man of the Year.

1997: 22 million infected worldwide. 6.5 million dead.

1998: 5,000 volunteer in the U.S. for first human trial of an AIDS vaccine.

1999: 20 years after the epidemic started, AIDS is fourth biggest killer worldwide.

2000: U.S. declares HIV/AIDS a national security threat, convinced that the global epidemic could bring down governments, trigger ethnic conflicts, and undo free-market democracies.

2001: China finally admits that the disease is a serious domestic problem. All 189 UN member countries sign a Declaration of Commitment on HIV and AIDS.

2002: In parts of Africa, HIV is killing teachers faster than they can be trained. Fusion inhibitor drugs offer new treatment. First 20-minute HIV test approved.

2003: Upsurge in heroin traffic in central Asia boosts drug addiction and HIV infection. Price cut on ARV drugs for poor countries. Thailand reduces incidence of HIV. Only 1 percent of 4.1 million HIV+ people in sub-Saharan Africa are receiving AIDS treatment.

2004: PEPFAR, a $15 billion AIDS program for 12 African countries, initiated by USA.

2006: Rock star Bono creates Product Red. Large multinationals sell merchandise under this brand to raise money for AIDS. *Lancet* publishes special issue with a red cover. One-a-day pill for HIV infection approved for sale.

2008: Scientists Françoise Barré-Sinoussi and Luc Montagnier, discoverers of HIV, awarded Nobel Prize for medicine.

2009 The first signs of a potential AIDS vaccination is shown by a trial of 16,000 volunteers in the U.S., suggesting a new vaccine is 31 percent effective at preventing infection.

2010 By now HAART, or highly active anti-retroviral drug combination therapy, has given a person with AIDS a life expectancy of 69 years, compared to a prognosis of only five years after diagnosis in 1996. The drugs are expensive, however, and not widely available in many countries.

I HAVE AIDS
Please hug me

I can't make you sick

J. keeler

AIDS HOTLINE FOR KIDS
CENTER FOR ATTITUDINAL HEALING
19 MAIN ST., TIBURON, CA 94920, (415) 435-5022

One of the most recognized AIDS posters ever produced.

the leprous, the poor, and the stranger could receive care and medical assistance. By 500, Edessa, a town of 8,000–10,000 souls, has three small hospitals, supplemented in emergencies by beds erected in public colonnades.

CHINA

Chinese knowledge of substances to use for treatment is vast, and pharmacists hand down knowledge of texts.

ANCIENT GREECE AND ROME

Cupping used by virtually all Roman doctors. A heated bell-shaped metal vessel is placed on the skin to raise a blister and to draw out the "vicious humor." Cupping and venesection are also in Arab-Islamic medicine.

c. 397 Fabiola founds first hospital in Western Europe. Eastern hospitals become even larger and more complex.

502–575 Aetius of Amida (reign of Justinian I). Describes ligatures, traumatic aneurysms, and diphtheria in his *Tetrabiblon*.

> **Hospitals** Ephesus in **420** had one with over 75 beds—Jerusalem in **550** had one with 200 beds—St. Sampson in Constantinople was even larger—Edessa had a women's hospital by **400**—Some big hospitals at Antioch and Constantinople were divided by **600** into male and female wards.

ANCIENT GREECE AND ROME

525–606 Alexander of Tralles. Skilled physician. Masterpiece *Twelve Books on Medicine*.

TURKEY

541–544 Plague of Justinian. Mediterranean countries.

WORLD

541–749 First plague pandemic (spreads to many nations).

SWITZERLAND

570 Marius, Bishop of Avenches, introduces the term "variola" (smallpox pustules or pock marks).

FRANCE

581 Gregory of Tours describes smallpox epidemic at Tours.

590 Pandemic of St. Anthony's fire (ergotism).

CHINA

6th century Castration of eunuchs practiced. To reduce pain, a hot decoction of pepper pods is applied first to the genitals.

6th century Precious stones are believed to have medical powers—jade and pearl—but ginseng root is considered equally powerful.

Growth of Hospitals and Universities

FRANCE

542 Nosocomia founded at Lyons by Childebert I and at Arles by Caesarius. Nosocomia are hospitals associated with a cloister for the care only of the sick.

SPAIN

580 Hospital at Merida founded by Bishop Masona.

ANCIENT GREECE AND ROME

610 Hospital of St. John the Almsgiver at Ephesus.

An early hospital: Hôtel-Dieu in Paris, France.

ARABIA

707 Teaching hospitals appear in Damascus. The state builds and administers hospitals across the empire.

BRITAIN

794 St. Albans Hospital in England.

FRANCE

962 Hospice of Great St. Bernard.

1145 Hospital of the Holy Ghost founded at Montpellier by William VIII of Montpellier.

ITALY

1080–1200 School of Salerno now a center of knowedge. Five-year courses of study before practice. Anatomical dissection on animals.

c. 1150 Medical school at Bologna established.

Pharmacy is the science of preparing and using drugs. From time immemorial, the skills of pharmacy have involved the cultivation of plants that have continually been used as a major source of drugs. Minerals and animal products have also been implemented—and, more recently, the list has included synthesized chemical compounds.

This is an ancient art, practiced in one form or another since primitive man first extracted juice from plants to help healing or to soothe wounds. There are many references in the Bible to ointments and medications. Moreover, many of the products used at the time of the ancient Greeks, and some from as long ago as ancient Egypt (like the castor oil plant), still prove to have useful properties today.

However, many very strange concoctions were also employed by the ancients and included such exotic ingredients as crocodile droppings, lapis lazuli, opium, hemlock potions, pounded pine, prunes, wine dregs, lizard dung, sulphur, cow and goat milk, honey and wax, lion fat, castor, human and dog excrement, cattle urine, and poppy seeds in beer.

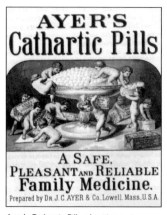

AYER'S
Cathartic Pills

A SAFE,
PLEASANT and RELIABLE
Family Medicine.
Prepared by Dr. J. C. AYER & Co., Lowell, Mass., U.S.A.

Ayer's Cathartic Pills advertisement.

An apothecary's shop in the Middle Ages.

ROLE OF THE PHARMACIST

An apothecary's tools.

The role of the pharmacist was at one time undertaken by the healers themselves, who prepared their own medications. In due course the areas of responsibility became separate. Even the physician-priests of Egypt were divided into two types: those who tended the sick and those who remained in the temples to prepare remedies for the patients. Egyptian prescriptions were made up in proportion to fractions based on the Eye of Horus. The Hearst Papyrus (c. 1550 BCE) is inscribed with some 250 prescriptions.

According to legend, Asclepius (who was the Greek god of healing) delegated the duty of compounding his remedies to his daughter, Hygeia, the goddess of health, who thence became his apothecary.

The Arabian influence in Europe during the eighth century CE further separated the role of pharmacist and physician. Then, during the Middle Ages in Europe, there was a distinct separation between the roles of the physician and apothecary. The physician dealt with the patient and prescribed, while the apothecary supplied and dispensed medicines.

BRITAIN
1123 St. Bartholomew's Hospital (London) founded by Rahere.
1132 Holy Cross Hospital founded at Winchester.

ANCIENT GREECE AND ROME
600 Aaron, a Christian priest, describes smallpox in his *Pandectae*. This vague reference is cited in the vivid description of smallpox by Rhazes in his *Continens* (860–932).
625–690 Paul of Aegina. Discusses tracheotomy, tonsillectomy, catheterization, lithotomy, and many other surgical procedures.

IRELAND
675 Monastic records of smallpox.

FRANCE
829 Trotula, a respected female practitioner of Salerno (**c. 1150** Trotula's *Book on Midwifery* is a composite work mainly written by men).

ARABIA
850–920 Isaac Judaeus. *Book on Foods and Simple Remedies, Book on Urine, Book on Fever*. Famed for *Regimen Sanitatis Salernitaneum*.

PERSIA
860–925 Razi, or Rhazes, writes about 200 books on medicine, logic, philosophy, theology, natural sciences, alchemy, astronomy, and mathematics. His compendium translated into Latin is known as the *Continens*. Celebrated alchemist. Considered to have been the greatest physician of the Islamic world.

The physician Rhazes.

SPAIN
936 Abu'l Qasim al Zahrawi (Albucasis). Eminent Muslim surgeon writes first illustrated book on surgery and introduces the use of red-hot iron to cauterize wounds.

BRITAIN
10th century Belief in elves is widespread in Northern Europe, and Anglo-Saxons believe

PHARMACY: AN ANCIENT ART

HERBALS

In the first century CE, the first Western herbal book was written by a Greek army surgeon, Dioscorides, and was a *materia medica*.

The Chinese have a long record of using drugs, with books on roots and herbs appearing as early as the third millennium BCE, when the legendary Shen Nong listed some 365 drugs and medicinal herbs.

Juliana Anicia, daughter of a Roman emperor, put together one of the earliest herbals before 512 CE, while John Gerard compiled much herbal lore into his *Herball*, published in 1597—with a new and improved edition in 1653.

Nicholas Culpeper published his famous *Herbal* in 1653, and it has remained in print ever since.

The World Health Organization of the United Nations began publishing the *Pharmacopoeia Internationalis* in the early 1950s.

John Gerard's *Herball*, published in 1597, is still a popular book today.

THE ROLE OF WOMEN

In feudal times, the lady of the manor was often deemed responsible for the health of the family and those who served them—so accumulated knowledge was passed on from mother to daughter. Many effective herbal remedies were developed and dispensed by her ladyship to help the sick. She would grow the herbs in her garden, and these included sage, mint hyssop, thyme, parsley, marjoram, and bay. There were many wise old women, midwives, and faith healers—who all prescribed herbs. Much of this knowledge was passed on orally except among the more educated wise women, the nuns, and lay sisters, who kept records of their herbal cures.

Sadly, during the Middle Ages and right up until the 18th century, there was a great fear of black magic and witchcraft, and some of the wise women, despite the fact that their knowledge and cures were helping their neighbors, were regarded with suspicion. The better their remedies, the more likely these were to be seen as spells, so the unfortunate women were sometimes regarded as evil and persecuted.

GROWING KNOWLEDGE

Arab medical practitioners had accumulated an enormous store of information about herbs and medicines. Rhazes (864–925), the Persian physician and medical author, introduced many new herbs to the Western world. Later, the Normans established "spicers" into the households of places that they conquered, including Great Britain. The spicer's role was to add the right spices to improve or disguise the dubious flavor of the preserved winter meat. In time, the role of these spicers evolved into that of the herbalist and apothecary.

Herbs and spices were ingredients for traditional medicines.

Medieval monks grew herb gardens in order to have the vital ingredients at hand to prepare their cures. Apothecaries also became skilled specialists.

38

THE FIRST THERAPIES

The earliest primitive treatments of pain, injury, or disease would have been instinctive reactions such as:
- *Rubbing an injured area*
- *Exerting pressure to slow or stop bleeding*
- *Sucking skin stung by an insect*
- *Using warmth to make a patient comfortable*
- *Extracting thorns*
- *Using cold to deaden pain.*

Bone needles have been found in Palaeolithic deposits, so we know it would have been possible to stitch wounds together then, but perhaps ancient tribes used the method still practiced in primitive cultures where a wound is held together and then ants or termites applied. Once the insects' powerful jaws secure the wound edges together, their bodies are removed but the jaws left in place to continue to seal the wound while it heals.

Protector figures such as the Egyptian goddess Isis, seen here with her son Horus, were called upon to help cure illness.

As civilizations developed, so healers became part of the structure of society. Witch-doctor, priest, and healer often were one and the same person, especially in pre-Columbian and early African societies.

that elves would attack them with a shower of arrows, thus producing sudden illness in humans.

PERSIA
980–1037 Ibn Sina or Avicenna. Arab physician and philosopher is "The Prince of Physicians" in Baghdad. His great work is *Canon of Medicine*.

Crusaders sack Jerusalem.

INDIA
Pre-11th century Traditionally Indians are inoculated against smallpox with pus from a smallpox skin boil.

ITALY
1020–1087 Constantine the African. Medieval medical scholar who translated Greek and Arabic medical works into Latin, a development that profoundly influenced Western thought.

SPAIN
1094–1162 Ibn Zuhr or Avenzoar. Eminent Arab physician born in Seville. Chief medical work *Altersir* or *Theisir*, a treatise on clinical medicine.

PALESTINE
1096–1099 Crusaders: Bring diseases back with them, including leprosy.
1099 Order of St. John of Jerusalem founded when Crusades reach the Holy City. Brotherhood of the order cares for pilgrims. Later gives rise to the St. John Ambulance Association.

A leper announcing his presence.

FRANCE
1131 Council of Rheims forbids monks to practice medicine for money.

SPAIN/EGYPT/PALESTINE
1135–1204 Moses Maimonides. A famous pupil of Averroes of Cordoba, becomes Saladin's physician.

PHARMACY: AN ANCIENT ART

A CHANGING WORLD

The discoveries of the Americas and wider exploration of the world in general, and its resources, led in turn to the discovery of new plants and fresh sources of herbs and drugs. However, it seems that these new, exciting possibilities were not tapped as fully as they might have been, and, although some plant substances were imported, many potentially useful drugs were not introduced into Europe from the New World.

Meanwhile, a law enacted by the city council of Bruges in 1683 forbade physicians to prepare medications for their patients. This was now stipulated to be the prerogative of the pharmacist alone.

In America, Benjamin Franklin, founder and first president of the Pennsylvania Hospital, appointed an apothecary to the hospital, and this underlined the two separate "entities" of physician and pharmacist.

VIPERS AND TOADS

There was a great trade in vipers in the Middle Ages, as their blood, once dried, was the major ingredient of theriac, an important drug used from the 11th to the 17th century. It was supposed to cure all manner of things, including syphilis and plague.
(Today, Russell's viper venom is used to help hemophiliac blood to clot.)
Other popular drugs included unicorn horn (which was taken from narwhal whale tusks) and toad stones. These were supposedly extracted from a toad's head!

Above: Theriac was an enormously popular cure-all for six centuries and was often kept in special ornamental jars. Although essentially made from various herbs, a vital ingredient was a powder made from dried vipers—so it could be a profitable enterprise to collect snakes and sell these to apothecaries.

CHEMISTRY

A German pharmacy in 1838.

While the natural world provided sufficient ingredients for the herbalist in the Middle Ages, as more towns sprang up and spread, meadows and forest vanished, and it became necessary to produce more drugs for an increasing urban population from diminishing resources.

Apothecaries' shops were established, each covering its own district, to supply local needs. Plants were bought in from the countryside and foreign ingredients and medicines imported from farther afield.

Meanwhile, the work and study of alchemists (whose aim was to turn base substances into gold) contributed much to the knowledge of the time. In practical terms, they perfected the techniques of distillation and the isolation of acids, alcohol, and metals and, in their approaches to research, exposed new concepts in chemistry, opening up routes of knowledge that would eventually lead to biochemistry and chemotherapy.

As understanding of chemistry grew and the constituent elements of the plants used was better understood, so pharmacy took on a more scientific role. Chemical compounds and formulas were appreciated and implemented.

TURKEY
1136 The charter of the Pantokrator Hospital at Constantinople, an exceptionally well-funded royal foundation.

ITALY
1139 Lateran Council renews interdict of Rheims.
1140 King Roger II of Sicily restricts medical practice to licentiates.

SYRIA
1160 Great Islamic hospital at Damascus.

CZECHOSLOVAKIA
1161 Jewish physicians burned in Prague on charge of "poisoning wells."

GERMANY
1163 Hildegard von Bingen, an abbess who was supposed to have healing powers, writes medical books on holistic healing and natural history.

BRITAIN
1167–68 Migration of students to Oxford to form a *studium generale*, an institute whose excellence was recognized by the Holy Roman Empire or the Vatican.

Leper having his sores bathed in a lazar house.

Growth of Hospitals and Universities

ITALY
1158 University of Bologna founded.

FRANCE
1180 University of Montpellier founded.

1181 Montpellier declared a free school of medicine by William VIII, Count of Montpellier.

BRITAIN
1197 Hospital of St. Mary Spital in London.

ITALY
1198 Hospital movement inaugurated by Innocent III.

FRANCE
c. **1200** University of Paris founded.

BRITAIN
c. **1200** University of Oxford founded.

ITALY
1204 Innocent III opens Santo Spirito in Sassia Hospital.
1204 University of Vicenza founded by migration of students.

BRITAIN
1215 St. Thomas's Hospital founded by Peter, Bishop of Winchester.
1217 Cambridge. Some evidence of teaching.

ITALY
1222 Foundation of University of Padua.

FRANCE
1223–1226 2000 lazar houses in France.

ITALY
1224 Frederick II issues law regulating the study of medicine and founds University of Messina.
1224 Frederick II founds University of Naples.

ITALY
1170 Roger of Palermo completes his *Cyrurgia Rogerii* (Roger's Surgery). Roger's enlarged edition known as *The Practice* is re-edited by his pupil Roland of Parma about 1250 as *Libellus de Cyrurgia* (Roger's Surgery).
1179 Church authorities say lepers must be identified and segregated.

PALESTINE
1191 Teutonic Order approved by Clement III.

GERMANY
1193–1280 Albertus Magnus. Dominant figure in learning of science.

EUROPE
13th century Crusaders bring back the Turkish

Infertile women would ask the goddess Tauret, depicted as a hippopotamus, for help.

ANCIENT EGYPT

As disease was regarded as the work of the gods or evil spirits, there is no clear dividing line between religion and medicine in ancient Egyptian medicine. Drugs and incantations were used in equal measure, but this is not to denigrate the abilities of the Egyptian doctors who were famous for their skills and whose medications were highly prized throughout the Mediterranean world.

As early as 2,600 BCE there were "specialists" who might be seen as the equivalents of present-day doctors, surgeons, vets, gynecologists, and dentists!

Surviving medical papyri provide us with much information on Egyptian medicine, with descriptions of ailments and treatments dealing with everything from contraception ("use excrement of crocodile mixed with sour milk") to hippopotamus bites!

EGYPTIAN PREGNANCY TEST

The first pregnancy test is also described, using barley and emmer, which the woman should "moisten with her urine every day. . . if both grow, she will give birth."

Modern experiments show that the urine of a woman who is pregnant allows the barley to grow, whereas that of a woman who is not pregnant will prevent the barley growing—so there is some scientific support for this ancient test.

THEOPHRASTUS PHILIPPUS AUREOLUS PARCELSUS

Paracelsus (1493–1541) was a physician from Switzerland whose theories encouraged the search for the active constituents of medicinal plants and promoted chemical remedies and the more specific application of appropriate drugs. He also investigated painkillers. Paracelsus helped to improve and reform pharmaceutical practice and increase understanding of chemistry. In due course, in Britain, pharmacists and druggists replaced the apothecary (who became a medical practitioner), drugs began to be manufactured and advertised, and an ever-expanding new industry was launched—the first proprietary pharmaceutical products appearing in the 1890s.

Paracelsus.

Bath, leading to the establishment of no fewer than 32 public baths in Paris.

ITALY
1204 Latin Crusaders sack Constantinople.
1210–1277 Gugliemo Salicetti or Saliceto. Important Italian surgeon who wrote many books. Unusual for his time, he insists that medicine and surgery are closely linked.
1214 Ugo Borgognoni made city physician of Bologna.
1221 Holy Roman Emperor, Frederic II decrees that no one should practice medicine unless publicly approved by the masters of Salerno.
1231 Gregory IX issues bull *Parens scientiarum* authorizing faculties to govern universities.
1231 Frederick II issues law authorizing a quinquennial dissection at Salerno.

SPAIN
1235–1350 Raymond Lull. A medieval alchemist.

FRANCE
c. 1240 Arnold of Villanova (d. 1311). A medieval alchemist who translates Galen and Avicenna. He states, "Use three physicians still, first Doctor Quiet, next Doctor Merryman, and Doctor Diet."

Growth of Hospitals and Universities

SPAIN
1243 University of Salamanca founded by Ferdinand III of Castile.

BRITAIN
1244–45 University of Oxford chartered by Henry III.
1247 Hospital of St. Mary of Bethlehem founded as a priory by Simon Fitzmary.
1249 University College (Oxford) founded by William of Durham.

ITALY
1246 University of Siena founded.

TURKEY
c.1250 First Islamic medical schools in Turkey.

SPAIN
1254 Alphonso the Wise founds University of Seville.

FRANCE
1257 Sorbonne founded at Paris.

BRITAIN
1253 University College, Oxford, founded.
1263 Balliol College (Oxford) founded.
1264 Merton College (Oxford) founded.

ITALY
1266 University of Perugia founded.

BRITAIN
1284 Peterhouse (Cambridge) founded.

EGYPT
1284 Mausuri hospital founded in Cairo.

ITALY
1288 St. Maria Nuova hospital founded in Florence.

FRANCE
1289 University of Montpellier (1181) chartered by Nicholas IV as a *studium generale*.

SPAIN
1300 University of Lerida founded by James II.

FRANCE
1305 Clement V charters Universities of Orleans and Angers.

ITALY
1305 City Hospital of Siena established.

PORTUGAL
1309 University of Coimbra chartered by King Diniz of Portugal (reconstituted 1772). This is an important school of medicine.

ITALY
1312 University of Palermo founded.
1318 University of Treviso chartered by Frederick the Fair.

BRITAIN
1318 Recognition of Cambridge as *studium generale* or *universitas* by papal bull of John XXII.

FAMOUS GREEKS

A fresco depicting Asclepius, the Greek god of healing and medicine, with the god Hermes and the three Fates.

Asclepius (or Aesculapius) is Homer's blameless physician and is now regarded as the god of medical art. Legend relates that he was the son of Apollo, brought up by Chiron who instructed him in healing. Later stories claim that he was no such thing—but a competent physician of Epidaurus, killed by a thunderbolt from Zeus because his success was enabling humans to escape death. However, an intercession from Apollo to Zeus obtained a place for Asclepius amongst the heavenly stars.

Asclepius had four daughters. One, Hygeia, gave her name to our modern term for cleanliness—hygiene; and another, Panacea, whose name means "heal-all," gave her name to the term now used for a universal remedy.

Hippocrates of Cos (460–377 BCE) is regarded worldwide as the Father of Western Medicine. He is credited with developing the humoral theory of Empedocles of Sicily, which stated that a perfect balance was desirable for health. The Hippocratic School taught of the healing power of nature and the importance of physical observation and the art of prognosis. It also taught the forecasting of the outcome of an illness by physical signs.

Aristotle 384–322 BCE. A pupil of Plato and teacher of Alexander the Great. He dissected many species, studied insect and animal behavior, and laid the foundations for embryology. Some sources claim that he may even have suggested evolution. His main importance to medicine was his belief that scientific methodology (e.g., careful observation, experimentation, and study of cause and effect) could lead to greater scientific knowledge.

PRE-COLUMBIAN MEDICINE

The medical practices of native tribes in the Americas, in particular Mexico and Peru, remained secret until the European invasions in the 16th century. However, even in ancient times it seems there were some sophisticated ideas and surgery.

There was a mix of religious and magical practices and extensive use of hallucinogenic plants such as hallucinogenic mushrooms.

Double-headed serpent, an Aztec symbol associated with fertility.

Midwives checked fetal positions, watched the mother's diet, and supervised birth. They gave infusions to speed up birth—including one from oppossum tail, which induced a violent delivery.

Herophilus of Chalcedon 330–260 BCE. The first true anatomist, Herophilus realized the brain was the seat of learning and feelings and clearly described its structure—one part of skull was named after him. He distinguished arteries from nerves, sensory from motor nerves. He described the heart as a pump, named the prostate and duodenum. Alexandrian doctors discovered the use of ligatures to tie off blood vessels so they could undertake some basic operations, repairs, and amputations.

Marcus Porcius Cato 234–149 BCE. Farmer, lawyer, soldier, consul, and censor. Lived to be 85. Collected recipes for medical treatment. Recommended cabbage leaf juice for many things: wounds, tumors, ulcers, dislocations, bruising, pain-killing. Also mentioned wormwood and wine. Cato provided an early "home remedy" type of instruction in his book *On Agriculture.* He believed that it should be part of the knowledge of every household.

ITALY
1320 University of Florence founded.
1321 John XXII issues bull establishing medical school at Perugia.

FRANCE
1332 John XXII charters University of Cahors as a *studium generale.*

ITALY
1338 Exodus of students to Pisa.
1339 Benedict XII charters University of Grenoble as a *studium generale.*

BRITAIN
1340 14,000 students at Oxford.

ITALY
1343 Clement VI charters University of Pisa as *studium generale.*

SPAIN
1346 Clement VI charters University of Valladolid (*studium generale,* 1418).

BRITAIN
1347 Pembroke Hall (Cambridge) founded.
1350 Trinity Hall (Cambridge) founded.

ITALY
1240 Emperor Frederick II issues three regulations that separate the profession of pharmacy from medicine, institutes government

GALEN *131–201 CE*

One of the most important figures in the history of medicine, Galen was born at Pergamum in Asia Minor, now Bergama in Turkey. His first surgical appointment was to the gladiators there. He traveled widely and studied medicine at Alexandria. He went to Rome about 162 CE and later entered the imperial service. He wrote extensively on anatomy, physiology, and practical medicine. His medical writings stressed the humoral theory and the Hippocratic doctrine. He claimed to have written 125 books, and his teaching dominated the revival of medical thinking and influenced its practice for many centuries after his death.

RHAZES
865–923 OR 932 CE

Arabian teaching schools helped to preserve for posterity much of the work of the Greeks and to encourage excellence in physicians.

One of the greatest physicians of the Arab world, Rhazes, was born a Persian Muslim in the city of Rayy, where he became chief physician in a new hospital before taking up a similar appointment in Bagdad. He was always very generous to the poor and willing to treat them.

As well as being a doctor, Rhazes was also an alchemist and an intellectual—a philosopher with a remarkably agile mind. He wrote many books on Greek, Syrian, Arabic, and Indian medicine and added information on his own experience and ideas. His works include accurate clinical descriptions of smallpox and measles and explain his use of catgut for suturing wounds and his atomic theory of matter.

Despite his intellectual aspirations, he advised that, "All that is written in books is worth much less than the experience of a wise doctor."

Rhazes introduced new herbs to the West.

HILDEGARD VON BINGEN (c. 1098–1179)

Hildegard von Bingen was a visionary healer born in Germany who was sent to study with her abbess aunt when aged only eight. From an early age she appeared to have the gift of spiritual healing. In due course she became an abbess herself and began to write medical books, including *Causae et curae* (Causes and Cures), which discussed holistic healing, and *Physica*, a natural history covering humans, plants, and animals. She had a wide influence in the Middle Ages.

Saints Cosmas and Damian performing the "Miracle of the Transplanted Leg."

THE SAINTS

Between 800 and 1000, many saints were associated with cures, with the saints Cosmas and Damian becoming patron saints of medicine.

St. Blasius—throat and lung
St. Apollonia—teeth
St. Erasmus—abdomen
Saints Lucia and Triduana—the eyes

IBN SINA OR AVICENNA
980–1037

Avicenna, the notable Persian physician and philosopher who had already achieved brilliance by the age of 18, eventually became known as Islam's Prince of Physicians. He believed that logic was more important than firsthand investigation and created a splendid illuminated work, the *Canon of Medicine*, which was a veritable encyclopedia of medicine that was translated and used throughout Europe until the 1500s. It included information on diagnosis (such as urine samples and taking the pulse) and prescriptions to be used for preventive measures.

supervision of pharmacy, and obliges pharmacists to take an oath to prepare drugs reliably. Dissection encouraged and surgery and pharmacy regulated.

1250 Roland of Parma edits the *Surgery of Roger of Salerno.*

FRANCE
1260–1320 Henri de Mondeville, surgeon to Philip the Fair, advocates cleanliness when treating wounds and "the avoidance of pus." He describes many surgical procedures, including plastic surgery.

ITALY
1266 Teodorico Borgognoni or Theodoric (1205–96) teaches new treatment of wounds.

Herbs were a major source of medication during the medieval period.

1267 Council of Venice forbids Jews to practice medicine among Christians.

1270 Spectacles introduced by Venetian glassmakers at Murano. 1285 Salvino degli Armati makes spectacle lenses by spinning crown glass.

1275 Saliceti completes first known treatise on regional surgical anatomy; prefers using knife to cautery, which had replaced surgery since Roman times and was the most common procedure.

BRITAIN
1290 Jews expelled from Britain. Three hundred fifty years pass before they're allowed to return.

ITALY, FRANCE
1295–96 Guido Lanfranchi completes his treatise on surgery, *Cyrugia Magna.*

FRANCE
1300–68 Guy A de Chauliac. Great surgeon and leader.

Today there are many alternative approaches to treatment and healing, beyond the confines of conventional medicine as practiced by the orthodox practitioner. Many of these are complementary to the treatment offered within the medical profession—but such medication or therapy is best pursued following consultation with a doctor. For many years, medicine in the Western world has been dominated by pharmaceutical drugs and, in recent times, the technology of medicine—but this is now changing, and an integrated approach, drawing on both conventional and complementary methods, is becoming acceptable. Some doctors have undertaken training in certain complementary therapies in order to be able to offer both kinds of treatment to their patients.

The ancient Egyptians pressed flowers to extract their juices for medicinal purposes.

The history of these therapies goes back a very long way. Herbal-based treatments were once the main source of treatment, while acupuncture is a very ancient skill, practiced in China for thousands of years. Conventional medicine emphasizes a diagnostic approach and focuses on specific problems and symptoms whereas, in general, complementary medicine is more holistic. It treats the whole person and encourages self-healing.

ACUPUNCTURE

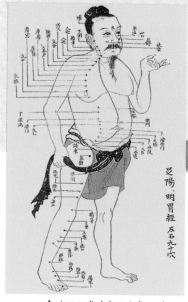

Ancient medical charts indicate the "acupoints" into which fine needles may be inserted, according to the specific treatment.

One of the best known Eastern therapies, acupuncture, involves inserting fine sterile needles into particular locations on the body. A treatment for disorders and pain relief in the East, it is now widely accepted in the Western world as a means of pain relief and anesthesia.

Ancient stone acupuncture needles found in Inner Mongolia date back to 3,000 BCE. It has been practiced widely in China for 2,500 years.

Doctors and missionaries in the 17th century introduced acupuncture into Europe. The World Health Organization has named some forty conditions that can be treated with acupuncture.

AROMATHERAPY

Herbal oils have been used in many cultures throughout history. Essential oils were used to embalm the dead in ancient Egypt and recorded by the ancient Chinese as medicinal. They were also described in the Bible. The oils may be massaged into the body through the skin or inhaled through the nose. In 1000 CE, Persian physician Avicenna developed distillation. The Crusaders introduced his methods into Europe. In the Middle Ages, essential oils were widely used as medicines. In 1910, French chemist René Maurice Gattefossé used lavender oil on his burned hand and discovered that it healed quickly with little scarring. His studies led to other French doctors, such as Dr. Jean Valnet, exploring the use of essential oils. Essential oils were used to treat wounded soldiers in World War II. There has been a recent surge of interest in the effects of aromatherapy and a growing body of practitioners. It is popular as a therapeutic and a useful relaxing technique.

AYURVEDIC MEDICINE IN INDIA

Ayurvedic medicine can be traced back to 1,000 BCE. Its practitioners believed the human body's substances to be the products of humors: Kaph (or phlegm), pitta (or bile), and vata (wind). The point of equilibrium depended on age, sex, temperament, climate, nutrition, and the nature of daily activities.

The books on ayurvedic medicine, Caraka Samhita (*primarily medical*) *and* Susruta Samhita (*primarily surgical*), are the two basic texts of Ayurvedic medicine. Both were written about the fifth century BCE. The classical understanding of Ayurvedic medicine combines a physical system of tubes, valves, and burners with an alchemical system for ingestion, digestion, and excretion. A proper balance is necessary for good health, taking the environment into consideration. The Ayurvedic approach reached its modern form by 1,000 CE.

Lord Brahma, the Creator, to whom Indian medicine is attributed.

ITALY
1302 First judicial postmortem (Bologna).

FRANCE
1304 Henri de Mondeville (*c.* 1260–1320) teaches anatomy at Montpellier. He studied medicine at Montpellier, Paris, and Bologna.

Surgical procedures from
Henri de Mondeville's *Cyrurgia*.

1306–20 Henri de Mondeville (1260–1320) writes his *Cyrurgia*. Development of the first proper French surgery.

EUROPE
14th century By now most Turkish Baths in England have become brothels.

BRITAIN
c. 1307–90 John of Arderne writes surgical treatises, collected after his death.

ITALY
1315 Anatomical dissection by Mondino de Luzzi (*c.* 1270–1326) at Bologna University.
1316 Mondino writes first "modern" text book on anatomy *Anathomia*. 40 editions published. It remains a standard text until Vesalius, two centuries later.

GERMANY
1316 City surgeon works at Lübeck for 16 marks ($4) per year.

ITALY
1317 John XXII issues bull *Spondent pariter* against alchemy and other magical practices.
1326 John XXII issues bull *Super illius specula* against practice of magic.

FRANCE
1328 City Physician at Strasbourg.

ITALY
1333 Public medico-botanical garden at Venice.

49

Samuel Hahnemann.

HOMEOPATHY

Homeopathy treats the patient as a whole. In 1810, a German doctor, Samuel Hahnemann, founded homeopathy on his therapeutic principle that "like cures like." Cinchona produces fever-like symptoms, and he therefore argued that what produces fever also cures fever.

Another completely separate principle of homeopathy is that of "infinitesimal dosage." This can be achieved only by vast dilution. This dilution is accompanied by violent shakings—an essential element known as succussion.

Hahnemann's ideas soon spread throughout Europe, Asia, and America. The term "homeopathy" is derived from the Greek words *homoios* and *pathos* meaning same and suffering, respectively. It remains a popular but controversial form of treatment.

Samuel Hahnemann's medicine box.

HERBALISM

Ancient civilizations in Egypt, Persia, China, India, and the Americas were using herbal remedies long before formal European medicine began. Their use declined a little with the surge of science in the 18th century. Now, however, modern clinical research confirms some of the claims made for herbal remedies.

Samuel Thomson set up herbal schools in the USA in the early part of the 19th century.

Modern Western herbalism is now available as a course of study at some universities.

Herbalists claim that the mix of ingredients in plants ("'herbal synergy") work as a group—for example, with one chemical perhaps counteracting or alleviating the side effects of another. This provides a more natural balance of chemicals than extracting and isolating, or synthesizing, one particular ingredient.

Most commonly used herbs are:
Chamomile
Garlic
Ginger
Lavender
Peppermint
Rosemary
Sage
Sandalwood
Tea tree
Clove oil
Eucalyptus

Some flowers used in cures are Lavender (above left) and Digitalis (above right).
Digitalis, from foxgloves, had long been used as a secret ingredient of herbal cures. Then, in 1785, William Withering made public its use for treating dropsy. It is still used today for heart conditions.

Feeling the pulse.

CHINESE MEDICINE

Early Chinese medicine was incredibly advanced, well developed long before that of the West—with the Yellow Emperor, Huang Ti's medical compendium Nei Ching (written in about 2,600 BCE) remaining as a standard work of reference for thousands of years. Its current form dates from an extensive revision done in about 800 CE by Wang Ping. One section deals entirely with acupuncture.

The Red Emperor, Shennong, had compiled the first medicinal herbal, Pen-tsao, in 2,800 BCE.

Sun Szu-miao (581–682) wrote a thirty-volume work called A Thousand Golden Remedies and headed a committee that created some 50 volumes on pathology.

The doctrines of Confucius had forbidden any violation of the body, so knowledge was based on observation and reasoning rather than actual dissection.

The Chinese believed in a system of humors similar to that of the West but with five elements, rather than four. They also believed emotions were contained within specific organs: anger and the soul in the liver, happiness in the heart, thought in the spleen, and sorrow in the lungs.

Feeling the pulse was an important element of diagnosis with one tome, Muo-Ching, taking ten volumes to describe all the various pulse characteristics.

They understood that "blood current flows continuously in a circle and never stops" and that this movement was under the control of the heart.

1345 *Anatomica* by Guido de Vigevano. He tries to improve status of surgeons by emphasizing their clinical and diagnostic qualities.

BRITAIN
1345 English pepperers, grocers, and apothecaries unite in Guild of St. Anthony.
1345 First apothecary shop in London.

The rich were buried in coffins, while the poorer victims of plague were thown into open pits and burned with lime.

The pestilence struck down members of the nobility and royalty, including King Alfonso XI of Castile and Joan, the daughter of Edward III of England.

EUROPE
1347–51 The Black Death, otherwise known as bubonic plague or "the pestilence," was the worst plague ever recorded, killing 75 million people between 1347 and 1351. Ports began to quarantine ships coming from plague areas, making them wait for 40 days before disembarking. This explains the word "quarantine"; *quarante* is Italian for "forty." It was black rats on the ships that carried the pestilence, via plague-ridden fleas, ashore. Humans caught the disease when they were bitten by a rat flea, and they could then spread it in the coughs and sneezes caused by the disease. The victim would be feverish, and the lymph glands under the arms, in the groin, and along the jaw line would swell.

EGYPT
1348 Black Death outbreak.

FRANCE
1363 Guy de Chauliac (1300–68), an influential surgeon and teacher, completes his *Chirurgia magna*.

BRITAIN
14th century The Church dominates education and the arts.

HYDROTHERAPY

Various uses and forms of water, especially natural hot springs, have been regarded as potential cures for various ailments in recorded history all around the world.

In Greece, temples to Asclepius, the god of medicine, were mainly raised near hot springs.

The Romans built complexes of baths for immersion in various temperatures.

Treatment with spa water—so popular in Roman times—enjoyed a huge revival in the 19th century.

During the 19th century, visiting spas to "take the waters" became very fashionable. The water could be taken both internally or externally.

Father Sebastian Kneipp (1821–97) was a Bavarian monk who founded modern hydrotherapy. Treatments included hot and cold baths, compresses, foot baths, sitz baths, steam baths, showers, and wraps. (A sitz bath is when the patient sits up to the waist in a hip bath with the feet in another, one hip bath containing hot water, and one cold. The patient keeps changing ends!)

Water alters the blood flow—cold water being stimulating and hot water relaxing—and both hot and cold water have a range of effects on the body systems that can be soothing and/or beneficial.

Steam baths and saunas induce sweating, which is believed to eliminate impurities from the body.

Today, aerated whirlpools, underwater massage, and exercise in water are also used as therapy.

NEW HEALING CONCEPTS

Whether or not he was a charlatan—and it has been suggested that some of his "performances" and theories were dubious—nonetheless **Franz Anton Mesmer** *(1634–1815) introduced the concept of mesmerism into the 18th century. He believed that a fluid was "permeating the entire universe and infusing both matter and spirit with its vital force." Convinced that the body was subject to similar fluids and that animal magnetism could to some extent control the flow of these fluids, he believed mesmerism could disrupt patterns of pain and nervous disorders.*

First in Austria and later in fashionable treatment rooms in Paris, Mesmer held group sessions where he was purported to have cured cases of hysteria. However, he underwent investigation by scientists and met much opposition, so he was forced to retire, but the subsequent emergence of suggestion and hypnotism does in retrospect perhaps lend his practices some credence.

Franz Joseph Gall *(1758–1828) was a German anatomist and physicist who was studying at Vienna when he invented the notion of phrenology, believing that the brain was made up of some thirty-seven different components that controlled particular temperaments. Seeming to reflect the magic number four of medieval humors, Gall claimed there were four such traits: vital, active, muscular, and nervous.*

Gall thought that the size and shape of these brain "organs" could be altered, thus affecting the personality. "Bump doctors'" traveled considerable distances across Europe to lecture and entertain— and to analyze people's heads by feeling the skull.

HYPNOSIS

A state of consciousness between sleep and wakefulness can be induced by a therapist using hypnosis, who may then work with patients in this state to cause physical or mental change.

Many ancient texts and tribal traditions include references to inducing trance-like states, with rhythmic dancing and drumming often being used to help achieve this.

The Austrian doctor Franz Mesmer (1734–1815) investigated the powers of "animal magnetism" and, through this research, began to use powers of suggestion to put patients into a trance and try to bring about cures. Whether or not he was a charlatan, the term "mesmerize" remains!

Scottish surgeon James Braid (1798–1860) induced hypnotic trances in patients in 1843 and coined the term "hypnosis" from the Greek word *hypnos* for "sleep."

James Esdaile (1808–59) performed operations in Calcutta using hypnosis for anesthesia.

Modern hypnotherapy is now accepted as a complementary therapy. However, no formal training in this area is given to medical students.

Caricature of Franz Joseph Gall, inventor of phrenology (the "science" of feeling head shapes).

ITALY
1374 Venetian Board of Health/Quarantine (*quaranta giorni*) established at Venice in 1403.

EUROPE
1377 Ragusa (now Dubrovnic) institutes quarantine.

Growth of Universities

CZECHOSLOVAKIA
1348 Clement VI charters University of Prague as a *studium generale*.

SPAIN
1354 Pedro IV founds University of Huesca.

ITALY
1355 Charles IV charters University of Arezzo (1215) as *studium generale*.
1357 Charles IV charters University of Siena (1246) as a *studium generale*.
1360 Innocent VI recognizes University of Bologna as a *studium generale*.
1361 University of Pavia chartered by Charles IV.

POLAND
1364 Casimir the Great charters University of Cracow.

AUSTRIA
1365 Duke Rudolph IV founds University of Vienna.

FRANCE
1365 University of Orange founded by Charles IV.

HUNGARY
1367 University of Fünfkirchen founded by King Louis of Hungary.

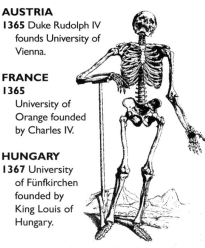

Caricature of a skeleton symbolizing perhaps the victory of medicine.

MASSAGE

Massage can be used to treat a countless number of disorders. As well as being soothing and relaxing, it can relieve pain, boost circulation, improve lymphatic and digestive disorders, and tone up the muscles.

There are many different techniques, and the art of massage goes back to the most ancient civilizations in Egypt, China, and India.

In ancient Greece, Hippocrates recommended "rubbing . . . to bind a joint that is loose, and to loosen a joint that is rigid."

Later, in Roman times, Julius Caesar had a daily massage to relieve the pain of neuralgia.

Physiotherapy was developed by Swedish gymnast, Per Henrik Ling, and was formally established in the UK in 1894 with the foundation of the Society of Trained Masseurs.

The Touch Research Institute in Miami, Florida, reports quite dramatic therapeutic effects from massage—such as premature babies gaining 47 percent more weight and astounding drops in the glucose levels of diabetic children.

The benefits of massage have been appreciated throughout medical history.

REFLEXOLOGY

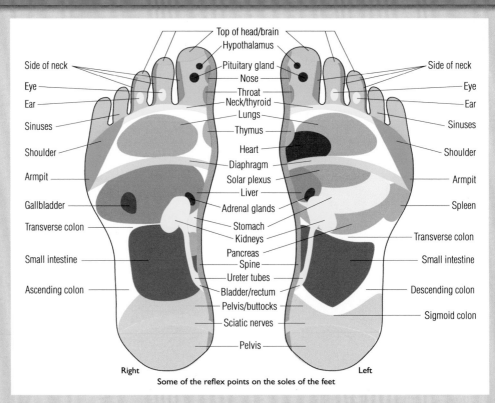

Top of head/brain
Hypothalamus
Side of neck
Pituitary gland
Side of neck
Eye
Nose
Eye
Ear
Throat
Ear
Neck/thyroid
Sinuses
Lungs
Sinuses
Thymus
Shoulder
Heart
Shoulder
Diaphragm
Armpit
Solar plexus
Armpit
Liver
Gallbladder
Adrenal glands
Spleen
Transverse colon
Stomach
Transverse colon
Kidneys
Small intestine
Pancreas
Small intestine
Spine
Ascending colon
Ureter tubes
Descending colon
Bladder/rectum
Pelvis/buttocks
Sigmoid colon
Sciatic nerves
Pelvis

Right

Left

Some of the reflex points on the soles of the feet

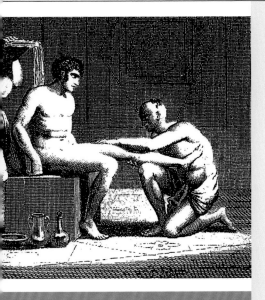

Reflexology involves massaging specific areas of the foot that are believed to connect in some way to particular organs or parts of the body. Practitioners believe this allows energy channels to flow freely so that damaged areas heal better.

Internal organs and stress-related disorders are the most likely to respond well to reflexology treatment. At present, there is little scientific evidence to substantiate these claims, but the massage is very relaxing and may well work in ways as yet not understood.

The treatment originated in China 5,000 years ago, and ancient Egyptian wall paintings show a form of manipulation of the feet being used in 2330 BCE.

American Dr. William Fitzgerald introduced zone therapy into the West in 1913.

An American therapist, Eunice Ingham, wrote books on reflexology in the 1930s, detailing reflex points on the hands and feet, while Doreen Bailey set up a reflexology practice and training courses in Britain in 1960.

There are over 7,000 nerve endings in each foot.

GERMANY AND FRANCE

1379 Clement VII charters Universities of Erfurt and Perpignan.

1386 Urban VI charters University of Heidelberg as a *studium generale*.

1388 Urban VI charters University of Cologne as a *studium generale*.

1389 Urban VI recharters University of Erfurt.

ITALY

1391 Boniface IX charters University of Ferrara as a *studium generale*.

AUSTRIA

1399 Beginning of Faculty of Medicine, University of Vienna.

GERMANY

1402 Boniface IX charters University of Würzburg.

ITALY

1404 University of Turin founded.

GERMANY

1409 Alexander V charters University of Leipzig as a *studium generale*.

FRANCE

1409 *Studium generale* at Aix in Provence.

BRITAIN

1411 University of St. Andrews founded by Bishop Henry Wardlaw as a *studium generale* or *universitas studii*.

ITALY

1412 University of Turin founded by Counts of Savoy (refounded 1431).

GERMANY

1419 Martin V charters University of Rostock.

GERMANY

1388 Salaried city veterinarian at Ulm.

SPAIN

1391 First dissection recorded in Spain.

1391 University of Lerida permitted to dissect a body every three years.

TIBETAN MEDICINE

Traditional medical systems have existed in Tibet for more than 2,500 years. These were based on the relationship between humans and nature. From the early centuries of the first millennium, Buddhism gained hold in Tibet and permeated all aspects of life, including medicine. During this time, other ancient systems of medicine, primarily Unani (Graeco-Islamic), Chinese, and Ayurvedic—the traditional system of India—also found their way into Tibet. Encouraged by open-minded rulers,

Above: The Medicine Buddha. (continued on page 58)

OSTEOPATHY

Osteopathy was "invented" by Dr. Andrew Taylor Still in the USA in 1874. He claimed that "all illnesses were due to malpositions of the spine and curable by manipulation." Modern osteopaths make more moderate claims and concentrate on their manipulative skills.

Osteopathy is widely practiced throughout America, Europe, Japan, and Australasia. This is now an established and respected therapy that seeks to relieve problems in the muscular-skeletal system through the means of touch, massage, and manipulation. Osteopathy aims to stimulate the body's own natural healing powers and to restore the balance of the body's framework. It is particularly relevant in the treatment of back pain, neck pain, and sports injuries but may also be used to relieve arthritis, headaches, and insomnia. The name derives from the Greek words for bone (*osteon*) and suffering (*pathos*).

It was an army doctor from Virginia, Dr. Andrew Taylor Still, who founded the American School of Osteopathy in 1892.

In 1917, Dr. John Martin Littlejohn founded the British School of Osteopathy, and Dr. William Garner developed cranial osteopathy during the 1930s.

Osteopaths have been licensed as doctors in the USA since 1972, while in the UK the Osteopath Act of 1993 granted osteopaths official recognition.

ITALY
c.1400 Milan institutes permanent health board.

EUROPE
1400 Epilepsy still seen as an infectious disease. A medical text of the time includes epilepsy in a list of contagious diseases.
1400–99 The Renaissance witnesses the rebirth of anatomy.

SPAIN
1400s Gold leaf is used as a dental filling material.
1409 Insane asylum at Seville.

ITALY
1410 Insane asylum at Padua.

BELGIUM
1424 First recorded regulations for midwives in Brussels.

SPAIN
1425 Insane asylum at Saragossa.

BRITAIN
1429 Grocers' Company (forerunner of Society of Apothecaries) given its charter.

GERMANY
1440 Printing press developed by Gutenberg. Movable type used for the first time in Europe.

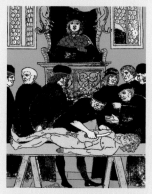

Mondino de Luzzi lectures at Padua while an assistant dissects a body.

57

they mingled with, and enriched the existing traditions. However, by the time Tibetan medicine was eventually codified as a system in the 11th century, it had been totally infused with the principles and philosophy of Buddhism. The most important school was founded in Lhasa in the late 17th century. The 1950s Chinese invasion of the country was an immense, almost crippling, blow. Tibetan institutions were actively suppressed and dismantled. Many doctors fled to other countries and managed to keep the system alive.

Tibetan medicine regards all aspects of health as a function of the effects of the forces of nature and of one's own spiritual bent. It recognizes four forces of nature. Earth, from which come stability and firmness, is the foundation of physical development. Water, the provider of moisture, is responsible for bodily fluids. Fire, through its heat, powers metabolic function. Wind expresses its movement as the body's circulatory processes, and to the existence of Space do all of these owe their very existence. At the spiritual level, the guiding principles are the Buddha's Four Noble Truths, which propound that the cause of all suffering is the illusory perception of the world by our senses, which once realized and corrected is the ultimate cure.

Three humors within the body, with which the natural and spiritual factors interact, control its physiological and mental processes. Imbalances and disturbances in any of these three humors cause illnesses. Wind handles blood, digestive and nervous circulation, and takes care of our worldview. Bile conducts metabolic and intellectual processes. The expression of strong emotions like anger and hatred fall in its domain. Phlegm enables lubrication and promotes memory and will. On the other hand, it can also be a cause of ignorance.

Diagnosis and treatment in Tibetan medicine is very person specific. Indicators of illness are looked for in urine, pulse, tongue, eyes, and pressure points of the body. Once the problem is determined, the first line of remedy addresses the ego. This is based on the fundamental Buddhist assumption that the root of all ill lies in the mind. Spiritual counseling is given, behavioral changes suggested, and meditation of different kinds, depending on the nature of the disorder, advised. Diet is considered next. The intake of food, also viewed as a combination of the qualities of the five elements, is to be adjusted as required. The actual administration of medicine comes after this. Tibetan medicine employs only natural substances. Most of these are herbs, but resins, minerals, soil, and precious metals—from which are created *Rinchen rilpo*, the seven types of precious pills—are also used. Formulations range from simple to the very complex, containing anywhere between three to as many as 150 different substances. Physical therapy is the fourth aspect of treatment. This includes massage, acupuncture, inhalation, moxibustion (burning of dried moxa herb on or above the skin at specific points), and cupping (applying inverted cups on the skin, with the aim to influence energy flows by varying the vacuum created inside).

Today, the future of the Tibetan system of medicine is delicately poised. While there is growing interest in the West, there is also an apprehension that Western approaches to its understanding and practice could lead to an "impurification" of the original form. Environmental changes, and the degradation of Himalayan and Tibetan ecologies, have placed pressure on herbal resources, though these are now being produced through cultivation. The relatively small pool of traditional masters and institutes of learning needs to be consolidated and ensured so that transmission of knowledge continues. The Tibetan Medical and Astrological Institute is situated in Dharamsala, India, which is the headquarters of the Tibetan Government in Exile. It has several branches. In addition, there are centers in Nepal, Bhutan, Bengal (India), and in Italy and the USA.

Above: A scoop of dried Tibetan *goji* berries, also called wolfberries.
Left: The Dalai Lama, Tibetan spiritual leader.

New Universities

ITALY
1422 University of Parma founded.

BELGIUM
1426 University of Louvain.

FRANCE
1431 University of Poitiers.
1437 University of Caën.
1441 University of Bordeaux.

ITALY
1445 University of Catania.

SPAIN
1450 University of Barcelona.

LUXEMBOURG
1450 University of Treves.

BRITAIN
1450 University of Glasgow founded as a
studium generale.

GERMANY
1456 University of Greifswalds.
1457 University of Freiburg.
1459 University of Ingolstadt founded; opened
in 1472.

SWITZERLAND
1460 University of Basel founded by citizens
of Basel.

FRANCE
1463 University of Nantes.

FRANCE and HUNGARY
1465 Universities at Bourges and Budapest.

SPAIN
1474 University of Saragossa.

DENMARK
1475 University of Copenhagen.

GERMANY
1476 University of Mainz.

BRITAIN
1494 University of Aberdeen.

SPAIN
1499 University of Alcala.
1501 University of Valencia.

GERMANY
1502 University of Wittenberg constituted as a
studium generale.

SPAIN
1504 University of Santiago.
1505 University of Seville.

GERMANY
1506 University of Frankfurt on the Oder.

SPAIN
1508 University of Madrid.

FRANCE
1518–1545 Collège de France (Paris).

SPAIN
1526 University of Santiago.
1531 University of Granada.

ITALY
1450 Niklaus Krebs of Cuss (Cardinal Cusanus)
suggests timing the pulse and weighing blood
and urine.
1450 Theophrastus translated into Latin. *Enquiry
into Plants.*

A page from the Gutenberg
Bible, the first book ever
printed with movable
type. Medical writers soon
took advantage of the new
technology and had their
texts printed.

UNANI MEDICINE

The term "Unani" derives from the Arab name for Greece, and the origins of Unani medical theories are traced back to Hippocrates (5th century BCE). From that time up to the 11th century, Unani developed into a distinct system of medicine, receiving, like Tibetan medicine did, from all the great medical traditions of the times: those from the Arab world, China, and India. In its mature form, Unani is credited to the Persian polymath Ibn Sina (1080–1137), author of the classic, *Canon of Medicine*, and one of the greatest physicians of the medieval world. Unani found its most favorable home under the Muslim rulers of India. After a subdued phase under the British, it was revived in the second half of the 20th century by the Indian government's formal recognition and support. India continues to be the enduring center of Unani. Besides this, it is studied in West Asia, North Africa, and has a miniscule presence in the West.

The essential philosophy of Unani is the concept of temperament. According to it, nature has bestowed every individual with a unique temperament. (This concept extends separately to age, particular organs and edibles, which have their own temperaments.) Like other ancient systems, Unani attributes disease to imbalances in the body's own physiology as opposed to the action of external causatives like viruses and bacteria. The physiological balance in the body is determined by four humors, namely, blood, phlegm, yellow bile, and black bile, responsible for sanguine, phlegmatic, choleric, and melancholic temperaments, respectively. The correct inter-humoral balance must be maintained for good health.

The Unani physician diagnoses illnesses by determining the existing

Above: Ibn Sina.
Left: Islamic medical text, c. 1500.

GERMANY
1452 Barber surgeons of Hamburg *(meister Bartscheerer)* incorporated.
1452 Ratisbon ordinance for midwives *(Regensburger Hebammenbuch)*.

Thomas Linacre.

1457 Gutenberg Purgation-Calendar printed (first medical publication).
1460 Heinrich von Pfolspeundt writes treatise on surgery.

BRITAIN
1460–1524 Thomas Linacre trains at Oxford and Padua. He develops close links between the English and the Italian schools. Makes new translations of classical medical works and becomes physician to kings Henry VII and Henry VIII.

Once the New World was discovered, plants from there, especially from the Tropics, proved to be a source of fresh medicines.

EUROPE
15th century The feudal system begins to diminish.
Mid-15th century New ideas are developed and pave the way for the coming Renaissance with its outpouring of new concepts and approaches to understanding and exploring the natural world.

Growth of Hospitals
ITALY
1456 Ospedale Maggiore at Milan founded.

BRITAIN
1492 Linacre Center's medical lectures at Oxford and Cambridge, England.

1505 Royal College of Surgeons of Edinburgh chartered.

MEXICO
1524 Cortes erects first hospital in city of Mexico.

ITALY
1533 Buonafede holds first chair of *materia medicia* at Padua.

Santa Maria della Scala Hospital, Siena, Italy, 1443.

state of humoral balance. This is done by considering several parameters, such as the patient's food intake, digestion, sleep and activity patterns, physical environment, and emotional state. Actual examination may be made of the pulse—analyzed at the wrist with three fingers, and its nuances are believed to provide several hundred kinds of information—urine, stool, color of the hair and eyes, and complexion. The Unani repertoire of treatment ranges from advice on dietary and lifestyle changes to minor surgery. Herbal preparations play a big role. The preference is to use single herbs or basic combinations in the raw, rather than multi-herb preparations. The majority of these are regarded

as food nourishment rather than as drugs, and all are possessed of properties characterized in various degrees as moist, dry, hot, or cold. Herbal treatment is administered in many forms. Orally, it is by way of water solutions, capsules, conserves, decoctions, and syrups. Internal cleansing is achieved through induced purging, vomiting, excessive sweating, and diuresis. Oils, ointments, salves, tinctures, and poultices are used for external applications. Usually practiced surgical procedures are few and minor. They include venesection and cauterization.

Above: A traditional hakim with his medicines.
Left: The Nigella flower.
Overleaf: The practice of meditation.

THE HAKIMS OF DELHI

Unani physicians are called *hakims* (Arabic for "doctor" or "wise one"). The Unani tradition was fostered in India by successive generations of hakims of the Sharifi (as they came to be called) family, who came to the country in the 16th century from Central Asia, with Babur, the first Mughal emperor. The Sharifi medical lineage continued into the 20th century. The most widely known of them was Hakim Ajmal Khan (1863–1927), who founded three great, currently functioning Unani institutions. Ajmal Khan's protégé, Salimuzzaman Siddiqui, conducted extensive research on the medicinal properties of plants. He is especially credited for isolating chemical compounds in the Rauwolfia serpentina plant, which are effective against a variety of nervous and psychosomatic disorders.

GERMANY
1462 Bloodletting-Calendar printed at Mainz.
1469–71 Ferrari da Grado's *Practica* printed.
1470 Medical treatises of Valescus de Taranta, Jacopo de Dondis, and Mattaeus Sylvaticus printed.
1471 Treatises printed of Mesue and Nicolaus Salernitanus (*Antidotarium*).

ITALY
1472 Bagellardo's treatise on paediatrics printed.
1473 Simone Cordo's *Synonyma medicinae* printed (first medical dictionary).
1474 Saliceto's *Cyrurgia* (probably first work on surgery) printed.
1476 Latin text of Saliceto's *Liber in scientia medicinali* printed (written 1275). He describes renal dropsy.
1478 First edition of Ketham's *Fasciculus medicinae* printed.
1478 First edition of *Celsus* printed at Florence in movable type (lost since the 1st century CE).

GERMANY
1478 Mondino's *Anothomia* printed at Leipzig.
1479 First edition of Avicenna's *Canon of Medicine* printed.

ITALY
1480 Latin text of *Regimen Sanitatis* printed. *Herbarium ofPseudo Apuleius* printed.

GERMANY
1484 Peter Schöffer's herbal *Latin Herbarius*.
1485 German *Herbarius*.

ITALY
1484 Innocent VIII authorizes burning of witches in bill *Summis desiderantes*.

BRITAIN
1485 Sweating sickness sweeps across parts of England, killing up to a third of the residents of the communities it visits.

PERSIA
1486 First Latin edition of Rhazes (Persian physician 860–925) printed.
1489 *Malleus malleficarum* (Witches' Codex) of Jacob Sprenger printed.

GERMANY
1489 168 bathhouses at Ulm.

1489 The spread of venereal diseases leads to the closing of communal baths even though few people have adequate water supplies to bathe or to wash properly.
1490 University of Heidelberg moves to Speyer on account of the plague. Galen (Greek physician 131–201 CE) first printed in Latin.

GERMANY
1491 Meidenbach's *Hortus (Ortus) Sanitatis*.

BRITAIN
1492 John of Gaddesden's *Rosa Anglica* printed.

ITALY
1492 Niceolos Leoniceno (1428–1524) corrects botanical errors of Pliny.

GERMANY
1493 Smallpox in Germany.

EUROPE
1493 Severe malaria outbreaks noted following discovery of the Americas.

SWITZERLAND
1493–1551 Paracelsus: Questions the classics and defies tradition; teaches in the vernacular rather than Latin; and advocates chemical therapies; is called the "Father of Pharmacology."

ITALY
1494 First Aldine edition printed: Press of Aldus Manutius, Italian printers.

EUROPE
1496–1500 European pandemic of syphilis.

ITALY
1496 Albrecht Dürer's (1471–1528, German) drawing of a syphilitic covered in sores

Baths at Leuk, Switzerland. Mixed bathing was popular in Germanic countries.

illustrates the importance of astrological influences on the epidemic.

FRANCE

1497–1558 Jean Fernel introduces the earliest division of medicine into the now standard disciplines of physiology and pathology. In his book *Universa Medicina* (Universal Medicine), published 1567, he also has a section on therapeutics. He is the first to describe appendicitis accurately.

Astrology influenced the treatment of syphilis.

ITALY

1498 Florentine *Ricettario* (first official pharmacopeia).

FRANCE

1499 Johann Peyligk (1474–1522) publishes anatomical drawings.

EUROPE

16th century At this time, the number of lepers in special hospitals is now very low. These hospitals are now frequently seized for other purposes.

16th century Typhus, diphtheria, smallpox, and measles become more common, as does the incidence of scurvy amongst sailors. Venereal diseases spread and many concoctions against it are sold by quacks.

ITALY

1500 Berengario da Carpi treats syphilis with mercurial ointments.

16th century For a period still steeped in superstition and mysticism, where many still believe in witchcraft and magic, it nevertheless gives rise to a great number of freethinkers whose work changes diagnosis and the understanding of the human body and disease—men such as Jean Fernel (see below), Vesalius—whose anatomy and surgery has enormous influence—and Paracelsus, who questions the classical teachings (see 1527).

WESTERN WORLD

16th century Theriac, made partly from dried vipers, is a popular antidote and will remain so until the 17th century.

BRITAIN

1500–99 Special institutions for the insane begin to appear.

1501 Magnus Hundt's *Anthropologium* published.

EUROPE

1501 *Morbus Hungaricus* (typhus) pandemic in Europe.

ITALY

1507 Benivieni's collection of postmortem sections printed.

1508 Guaiac brought from West Indies and tropical America used in medicine as wood or resin for syphilis, dropsy, and gout.

EUROPE

1510 Pandemic influenza in Europe.

FRANCE

1510–90 Ambroise Paré achieves fame as an army doctor and becomes a renowned master surgeon and the first to introduce the use of ligatures in amputations.

Preparing a potion against the plague, 1500.

ITALY

1510 Leonardo da Vinci draws the human body very accurately, showing muscles, blood vessels, lungs, and heart.

1513 Rösslin's *Roszgarten*—earliest printed text book for midwives.

16th century Printing spearheads the spread of knowledge during the Renaissance.

FRANCE

1514 Pierre Brissot revives Hippocratic teaching that blood-letting should be carried out near the lesion.

ITALY

1514 Gunshot wounds described in Vigo's *Practica*.

OTHER THERAPIES

Acupressure
Began over 3,000 years ago in China. Ancient system of massage to encourage "life energy" to flow through body.

Alexander technique
Began 1931. Improving posture and stance to relieve stresses on the body. Anthroposophical medicine began 1913 by Rudolf Steiner. A holistic approach encouraging the sense of self and a balance of mind and body.

Bach flower remedies
Began 1930s. Using healing powers of plants to keep mind and body in harmony.

Bates method
Early 20th century. Enhancing eyesight without lenses or surgery.

Biochemic tissue salts
Began 1870s. Using 12 mineral salts to supplement diet intake.

Bioenergetics
Began 1970s. Psychotherapy: Exercises to release physical tension and so relieve mental traumas and anxieties.

Chiropractice
Began 1895. Spinal manipulation: Used to treat spine, joints, and muscles and maintain the health of the central nervous system and organs.

Clinical ecology
Began 1940s. Identifying and avoiding irritants and allergies in the modern environment.

Cranio-sacral therapy
Began 1970s. Applying pressure to the cranium and spine to stimulate the membranes.

Feldenkrais method
Began 1940s. Manipulation and developing awareness of the body through movement.

Hellerwork
Began 1970s. Massage, body alignment, and release of tension.

Meditation
Began many thousands of years ago. Evolved through various major religions, introduced into Europe in 19th century, popularized 1960s. Profound relaxation to treat stress-related problems.

Megavitamin theory
(or Orthomolecular) *Began 1970s.* Treatment with large doses of vitamins, minerals, and amino acids.

Naturopathy
Began in ancient times, revived 1895. Using the power of the body to heal itself.

Rolfing
Began 1940s. Pressure and manipulation to bring body into appropriate vertical alignment. Improves breathing and suppleness.

Shiatsu
Began in ancient China, reached Japan 1,500 years ago, revived in Japan 19th/20th century. Massage and stimulation at key points to improve energy flow.

T'ai Chi Ch'uan
Began in 13th century by Taoist monks. Movement and breathing techniques to promote self-healing.

Tragerwork
Began 1975. Massage, movement, and relaxation techniques to reintegrate the body and mind.

Yoga
Began 5,000 years ago in India. Gentle exercise, postures, and breathing techniques.

Music, art, light, sound, and color are all also used in a variety of specialized therapies.

Midwives attending delivery on a birth stool, from Rösslin's *Roszgarten*.

BELGIUM

1514–64 Vesalius, a Flemish doctor, founds the "new anatomy" in Padua—a great teacher and writer.

GERMANY

1517 Gersdorff's *Field-Book of Wound-Surgery* published.

1518 Nuremberg ordinance regulating sale of food.

BRITAIN

1517 Linacre's translation of Galen published.

1518 Royal College of Physicians founded by Thomas Linacre and receives charter from Henry VIII.

ITALY

1521–23 Berengario da Carpi publishes anatomical treatises.

EUROPE

1520s It becomes accepted that syphilis was a sexually transmitted disease. Mercury treatment is still continued because syphilis begins to be viewed by ordinary people as a sign of sin, and the pain and danger posed by this treatment is regarded as a necessary punishment that the sinner must undergo. Aristocrats, however, feel they belong to the elite if they contract syphilis. They favor guaiacum as a cure. This is a more pleasant treatment than being "rubbed" with mercury, even if no more effective.

16th century The Reformation changes the role of the Church as countries become Protestant.

GERMANY

1522 Midwifery solely female province. A Doctor Wertt of Hamburg burns at the stake for impersonating a midwife. He wanted to study obstetrics!

1525 Complete works of Galen in Greek.

ITALY

1523–62 Gabriel Fallopius (or Fallopio): Works with Vesalius, teaches at Padua, and writes on anatomy. He describes tiny parts of inner ear and reproductive system—fallopian tubes named after him.

Gabriel Fallopius.

1525 First Latin translation of Hippocrates printed.

1526 First (Aldine) Greek text of Hippocrates published at Venice.

1526 First Greek translation of Hippocrates printed.

SWITZERLAND

1527 Paracelsus (1493–1541). He publishes a pamphlet outlining his revolutionary ideas and promising to free the decayed art of medicine from

Paracelsus

its worst errors; he burns books by Galen and Avicenna and popularized chemical remedies.

ITALY

1528 First Aldine edition of Paul of Aegina.

GERMANY

1528 Albrecht Dürer (1471–1528) treatise on human proportion published.

EUROPE

1529–30 Sweating sickness spreads over Europe.

FACTS ABOUT THE MIDDLE AGES

Christian establishments did much to care for the sick, providing practical help through the first charity hospitals and monastic infirmaries. This was where the local people sought help, and the monks or nuns provided herbal remedies and treated their illnesses. Herbal remedies were very important, and the monks kept their own herb gardens.

The casting out by the church of devils (believed to be the root cause of many mental and physical conditions) was an accepted treatment of such ailments as epilepsy.

Astrology played an important part in medical thinking, diagnosis, and treatment. The different signs of the zodiac were linked to specific parts of the body.

The establishment of guilds further separated surgeons from physicians. Because of the similar tools and knives they used, surgeons were linked with barbers, and physicians with apothecaries and artists because these three "professions" all used powders.

It was not deemed fit for men of the church to deal with obstetrics, so midwives practiced independently of established medicine, as did the barber surgeons and folk healers. Midwives would sometimes act as intermediaries when a woman patient was treated by a doctor.

Bloodletting was widely practiced, the release of blood being seen as beneficial as part of the humoral theory and the aim to maintain the correct balance of fluids.

Monks and nuns provided care for the sick, often in special infirmaries.

Medievial painting dipicting Guy de Chauliac examining patients.

GUY DE CHAULIAC
1300–1368

Guy de Chauliac was a student at Paris, Toulouse, and Montpellier, in France, and at Bologna, in Italy. Highly educated, he became a great surgeon and wrote books describing operations for bladder stones and hernias. Chauliac also suggested the use of traction and a system of weights and pulleys to keep broken leg bones properly stretched and in place while they repaired.

ITALIAN SCHOOLS OF MEDICINE

Salerno

The great school of Salerno in southern Italy was the first real medical school in Europe and had been of importance since the 11th century. It drew students and physicians from many countries and had women as students and on its teaching staff.

It was given great support in 1224 by Frederick II of Sicily, who decreed that all those practicing medicine required the approval of Salerno Medical School.

Roger of Salerno wrote a book called Roger's Surgery. This explained much about trephining and the treatment of fractures, dislocations, and wounds.

Surgical operations depicted in a 13th-century manuscript from Salerno.

Bologna 1158

The renowned medical school of Bologna University attracted many of the finest students and physicians from all over Europe. Here Theodoric de Lucca introduced the use of a small sponge soaked in opium and mandrake to be sucked or swallowed as an anesthetic. A particularly brilliant teacher there was Guglielmo Salicetti, and Bologna is where Mondino de Luzzi became a pioneer in anatomy.

By 1300, the Pope had given special permission for some human dissection to take place at Bologna, although monks and priests were still forbidden to practice any surgery.

Padua 1222

Padua developed from this background of excellence and was an offshoot of the Bologna school.

In the anatomy theater at Padua, hundreds of students could be taught at once and have a clear view of dissections or surgical procedures.

It was to remain an important research center for some 300 years.

In time, Montpellier in France would become a major European school of medicine.

ITALY
1530 Sarsaparilla introduced—dried roots of several tropical American plants; used as an emetic, to treat psoriasis and as a flavoring.
1532 Rabelais publishes first Latin version of the aphorisms of Hippocrates.
1534 Aldine edition of *Aetius* published.

GERMANY
1530 Otto Brunfels (1488–1534) publishes his atlas of plants, *Herbarium vivae eicones.*

FRANCE
1536 Ambroïse Paré (1517–90) performs excision of elbow-joint.

Virginia snakeroot.

THE RENAISSANCE

This was a time of new thinking, of reassessing the old values and beliefs and rejecting much that had been traditional for centuries. The invention of the printing press—and the subsequent spread of books and learning—freed education from the Church. This independent growth of learning spearheaded many revolutionary ideas. The Turkish capture of Constantinople in 1453 led to an influx of refugee scholars into the West who brought fresh ideas with them, while the opening up of new routes to India and America stimulated a greater understanding of the natural world.

As a result, many of the concepts laid down by Galen, which had been dominating medical thought and forestalling development since Roman times, were challenged. Now courageous physicians and surgeons like Paracelsus in Switzerland were able to reject the old and introduce the new. In 1527, Paracelsus even went so far as to burn books by Galen and Avicenna in order to underline his demand for new thinking.

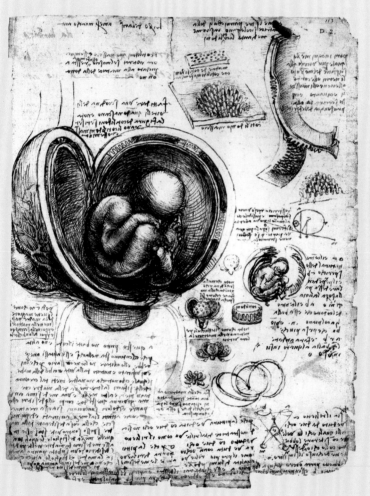

LEONARDO DA VINCI
1452–1519

Italian artist Leonardo da Vinci, in his search to understand human form, dissected over thirty corpses, despite restrictions against this. He made about 750 detailed drawings of the human body, exploring muscles, veins, arteries, and organs such as the heart and lungs. It was to be some two hundred years before all this work was published, so it is difficult to ascertain if he influenced contemporary medical thinking but his work reflects the fresh analytical scientific approach of the time— and his drawings have become excellent sources of reference ever since their publication.

Leonardo's drawing of the womb and fetus.

AMBROISE PARÉ
1510–1590

Paré, who became known as "the father of modern surgery," began his career as a barber surgeon in Paris in 1553. He was given the position of resident surgeon at the great medieval hospital there, the Hotel Dieu. Later, he became surgeon to Henry II of France and, in due course, the three kings who succeeded him.

This was a time of great unrest in France, and it was in his role as an army surgeon for some thirty years that Paré "made his name." He became an expert at treating battle wounds. Previously, amputations had been treated with hot pitch or boiling elder oil (with gunpowder) and cauterized to staunch the bleeding. Paré used egg yolk, rosewater, and turpentine instead of pitch, and introduced the use of ligatures. His patients recovered far better than those treated in the conventional way, and their wounds healed better. He swore "never again to so cruelly burn the poor wounded by gunshot" and stated, "I dressed the wound, and God healed him."

Paré made false limbs for the amputees and developed false eyes and false teeth.

Ambroise Paré

ITALY
1537–1619 Hieronymus Fabricius ab Aquapedente discovers much about valves in the veins.
1537 Dryander's *Anatomia* published.
1538 Vesalius (1514–64) publishes his *Tabulae anatomicae sex*.

SWITZERLAND
1537 Vesalius (1514–1564) graduates at Basel.

EUROPE
16th century More institutions are built to house the insane.

BRITAIN
1540 English barbers and surgeons unite as Company of the Barber Surgeons (would eventually become the Royal College of Surgeons in 1800).
1540 Henry VIII allows four dissections a year.

EUROPE
1540 After Mattioli had suggested internal use of mercury for syphilis in 1533, this becomes common practice.

Above left: Artificial hand design by Paré in 1575. Left: Paré tending to injured soldiers.

ANDREAS VESALIUS
1514–1564

Vesalius was born in Brussels, the son of an apothecary. He trained as a doctor in Louvain and Paris, where he practiced dissection on the hanged bodies of criminals stolen from the public gallows.

In due course, he moved to Padua where dissection was permitted and became professor of surgery and anatomy there when he was only twenty-three. His public dissections attracted huge numbers of students. Overall, his influence was enormous and transformed the university to become a center of excellence in medicine.

In 1543, his most famous work, *De Humani Corporis Fabrica* (The Workings of the Human Body), was published, with 300 illustrations of the human body drawn by Jan van Calcar and many misconceptions about the human body corrected, in particular precepts based on animal dissection and many of Galen's anatomical errors.

Eventually Vesalius became physician to Emperor Charles V.

THE IMPACT OF THE NEW WORLD

Christopher Columbus landed on the shores of the New World in 1492. This discovery of a new land and peoples opened up enormous potential as the unknown continent was also a source of new plants and medicines derived from them.

One discovery was the bark of Cinchona, an evergreen tree, which contains alkaloids, and some of these alkaloids are still used in drugs today. The bark was soaked to extract quinine, then known as "Peruvian bark" or "Jesuit's bark."

Columbus also brought back from America coca leaves (from which cocaine would later be extracted).

Guaiacum (extracted from a New World timber) became a popular treatment for venereal disease, which was prevalent in the Middle Ages. This new "cure" was often sold by street vendors.

It is understood that a mild form of syphilis was present in Europe prior to the discovery of the Americas, but, after Columbus returned from his voyage, a much more virulent form of the disease swept across Europe. This may have been a "new" disease from the New World, or syphilis may simply have had an increased virulence in the Old World. There is still controversy over the subject, but, whatever the reason, syphilis became a veritable plague, raging across Europe. It became such a large problem that, in 1495, Holy Roman Emperor Maximilian issued mandates against blasphemy, gambling, and godless behavior, since the new plague was seen as God's punishment for unseemly behavior.

Sweet coca leaves.

Guaiacum wood from the New World was sold by street vendors as a treatment for venereal diseases.

1540 Valerius Cordus discovers sulphuric ether.

BAVARIA
1542 Leonhard Fuchs (1501–66) publishes *De historia stirpium*, the most famous 16th-century herbal classifying medical plants.

ITALY
1543 Vesalius founds modern anatomy—*De humanis corporis fabrica* is one of the most influential medical books ever published.

BRITAIN
1545 *Boke of Children* by Thomas Phayre published: First English book on pediatrics.

FRANCE
1545 Paré (1517–90) improves amputation and treatment of gunshot wounds. Founder of orthopedics. Collected works published 1575.

Columbus brought back several new medical treatments from America, including cinchona. The bark of the cinchona tree (also known as Peruvian or Jesuit's bark) contains alkaloids, including quinine. It was soaked to extract a drug that reduced fever. Coca leaves (from which cocaine would be derived four centuries later) were chewed by the South American Indians as a painkiller.

GERMANY
1546 Valerius Cordus publishes first German pharmacopeia.

ITALY
1546 Girolamo Fracastoro (1483–1553) publishes work on contagious illnesses. He believes disease is carried by imperceptible seeds transmitted in the air or by contact.
1550 Hollerius prescribes spectacles for nearsightedness.

BRITAIN
1552 Caius's treatise on sweating sickness.

CHINA
1552–78 52 volume *Great Herbal* compiled by Li Shi-chen. It contains some 1,900 prescriptions.

SPAIN
1553 Michael Servetus, first to suggest transit of blood through lungs, burned at stake in Geneva because of his heresy.

BRITAIN
1554 Johannes Lange describes virgin's sickness (*morbus virgineus*), later called chlorosis, with symptoms of pallor and weakness. Marriage and motherhood are regarded as the cure.

FRANCE
1554 *Editio princeps of Aretaeus* printed at Paris. Aretaeus of Cappadocia (120–180 CE) writes vivid descriptions of many diseases.

SWITZERLAND
1554 Jacob Rueff's (German) new version of Rösslin's *Swangern frawen (De Conceptu)*; becomes popular book for midwives.

FRANCE, SWITZERLAND
1556 Wandering lithotomist, Pierre Franco, removes bladder stone through abdominal wall.

ITALY
1558 Cornaro publishes treatise on personal hygiene.

BRITAIN
1560 Sir John Harington born, translator of

Harvey shows a dissected deer heart to King Charles I and the young prince. Painting by Robert Hannah, 1848.

WILLIAM HARVEY
1578–1657

In 1628, William Harvey published *De Motu Cordis* (On the Motion of the Heart). This great book announced his proof of the circulation of the blood and contained precise descriptions of how the heart beats and the "mechanisms" of circulation.

The notion that blood moved within a contained system was a vast move forward in physiology and medicine.

It was not an entirely new idea, of course. In the second century, Galen had understood that blood moved to and fro, ebbing and flowing in the veins. Its transit through the lungs had been proposed by Michael Servetus (1511–53), and Andrea Cesalpino (1519–1603) had deduced there was some form of closed circulation system but had not worked out all the fine details or supplied convincing proof of this.

Educated first at Cambridge, England, William Harvey went to study at Padua under some of the great medical men of the time. Returning to London, he was elected to the London College of Physicians and in due course became court physician to King James I and King Charles I.

Based on experimentation with animals, observation, and dissection, Harvey concluded that the heart pumped some 144 ounces (4.3 liters) of blood a minute. Since this was continuously in one direction, the blood must be contained in a closed system. As well as arteries and veins, to complete the circuit, Harvey assumed the existence of capillaries, although these microscopic structures were not actually discovered until after his death.

Inevitably, there was considerable debate and controversy over Harvey's findings but his careful experimentation and precise explanations and logic made his claims the harder to refute.

Regimen Sanitatis Salernitanum and designer of a toilet that could be flushed. One is installed in the Queen's house at Richmond in 1596. They are not in general use in Britain until the 19th century.

GERMANY
1560–1634 Wilhelm Fabry von Hilden (Fabricus Hildanus), considered the father of German surgery, carries out amputations with a red-hot knife, claiming this reduces hemorrhage. He is the first to advocate amputation through healthy tissue above a gangrenous part, and first to classify burns.

1560 Maurolycus describes far- and nearsightedness and optics of the lens.

1561 Pierre Franco's treatise on hernia published.

ITALY
1561 Fallopius (Gabriele Falloppio) publishes first major work, *Observationes anatomicae*, greatly extending knowledge of anatomy, especially of female reproductive system (fallopian tubes are named after him), inner ear, cerebral arteries and nerves, eye muscles, tissues.

BRITAIN
1562 Witchcraft made a capital offense in England.

1563 Witchcraft a capital crime in Scotland.

1562–68, 1574–77, 1580–82 Pandemic influenza.

1565 Elizabeth I permits dissection of executed criminals.

Sweating sickness strikes in 1551.

ITALY
1564 Galileo born. He encourages careful measurement in medicine and science and develops the telescope.

1564 Eustachius discovers abducens nerve, thoracic duct, and suprarenal glands.

FRANCE
1564 Henri Estienne (Stephanus, 1531–98), and Jean de Gorris (Gorraeus 1505–77), each publish a medical dictionary.

SWITZERLAND
1567 Paracelsus's account of miners' diseases published.

1570 Felix Platter (1536–1614), one of first to distinguish between various mental disorders.

ITALY
1569–90 Gerolamo Mecuriale publishes many important works and text books.

1572 Geralamo Mercuriali's systemic treatise on skin diseases. Writes on medical gymnastics.

FRANCE
1575 Paré introduces artificial eyes.

SWITZERLAND
1576 Pare publishes tract on mineral waters.

Artificial hand devised by Paré 1575.

BRITAIN
1578–1657 Life of William Harvey, who would later demonstrate the circulation of blood.

EUROPE
1580s Witch-hunting becomes more widespread toward the end of the century.

ITALY
1580 Prospero Alpino introduces moxibustion from the Orient, a form of therapeutic healing as old as acupuncture, with the same points and meridians, but using powdered leaves of mugwort burned on the skin.

Administering moxibustion.

1581 Rousset's treatise on Caesarean section published.

SPAIN
1583–1600 Diphtheria (*garotillo*) epidemic.

GERMANY
1583 Georg Bartisch's *Augendienst (Opthalmodouleia)*—the first book on eye surgery published.

ITALY
1583 Cesalpino (1519–1603) classifies plants in his *De plantis*.

BRITAIN
1585 Guillemeau's treatise on diseases of the eye published.

In Britain during the 1600s, there were various sources of help:

1. A few highly qualified physicians who had been trained in medicine at universities charged very high fees. Control was in the hands of the College of Physicians in London.
2. Practitioners throughout the country prescribed medicines and performed surgery.
3. In cities, there were barber surgeons, trained by apprenticeship and examination.
4. Many towns had apothecaries, who were apprenticed, but learned simple treatments while working (they sold groceries as well as medicines).
5. Every fair had a stall set up by a tooth-puller, who sold herbs and who could do simple operations. They traveled around the country, setting up wherever there were enough people to make it worthwhile, and they did not charge much.
6. In villages, there were wise women and midwives who either charged very little or nothing to help their neighbors. They may have had herbal knowledge from a local teacher, but no formal teaching.

EXTRACTS FROM SAMUEL PEPYS' DIARY FOR THE YEAR 1665

April 30
Great fear of the sickness here in the City, it being said that two or three houses are already shut up. God preserve us all.

June 7
This day, much against my will, I did in Drury Lane see two or three houses marked with a red cross upon the doors, and "Lord Have mercy Upon Us:" writ there—which was a sad sight for me, being the first of that kind . . . that I ever saw.

June 17
Going in a Hackney Coach from Holborn, the coachman I found to drive very badly. At last he stopped, and came down hardly able to stand. He told me that he was suddenly taken very ill and almost blind, and that he could not see. So I got down and went to another coach, with a sad heart for the poor man and fear for myself, in case he had been struck with the plague . . . But God mercy upon us all.

June 21
I find all the town almost going out of town, the coaches and wagons being full of people going into the country.

Samuel Pepys (1633–1703): His diaries provide a clear account of the plague.

August 12
The people die so, that now it seems they carry the dead to be buried by daylight, the nights not being long enough to do it. And my Lord Mayor commands people to be inside by nine at night that the sick may leave their domestic prison for air and exercise.

17th-century dentist at work.

August 31
In the City died this week 7,496, and of them 6,102 of the plague. But it is feared that the true number of the dead this week is near 10,000; partly from the poor that cannot be taken notice of, through the greatness of the number, and partly from the Quakers and others that will not have any bell ring for them.

September 3
It is a wonder what will be the fashion after the plague is done, as to periwigs, for nobody will dare buy any hair for fear of infection, that it had been cut off the heads of people dead of the plague.

September 20
But, Lord! what a sad time it is to see no boats upon the river, and grass grows all up and down Whitehall court and nobody but poor wretches in the streets! And which is worst of all . . . the number of deaths from the plague has increased about 600 more than last week.

ITALY
1586 Giovanni Battista della Porta's (1536–1605) *De humana physiognomia* published. Pioneer of physiognomy, or facial character study.
1587 Aranzi gives first description of deformed pelvis.

SWITZERLAND
1589–91 First definitive collection of Aranzi's works published in Basel.

SPAIN
1590 José d'Acosta describes mountain sickness.

HOLLAND
1590 Invention of compound microscope by Hans and Zacharias Janssen.

EUROPE
1591 Pandemic plague outbreak.

ITALY
1594 First permanent operating theater built at Padua.
1595 Quercetanus uses calomel (mercurous chloride); it becomes a much-acclaimed purgative.
1595 *La Commare o Riccoglitrice (The Midwife)* by Scipione Mercurio is published, one of the earliest books to advise Caesarean section in cases of a contracted pelvis. The book also includes a picture of the "Walcher position."

GERMANY
1595 Libavius publishes first treatise on chemistry (*Alchymia*).
1595 City of Passau issues ordinance for midwives.

BRITAIN
1596 Harington's *Metamorphosis of Ajax* published—in which he describes his invention of the flushing toilet.

Toilet depicted in Harington's book.

FRANCE
1596 René Descartes born: Philosopher who regarded human body as a machine.

ITALY
1597 Gaspare Tagliacozzi (1546–99), a professor

HISTORY OF HOSPITALS

Hospitals are variously categorized. There are those at which patients are treated and sent back the same day (out-patient), and others at which they can stay for up to several days for longer treatment. General hospitals are "one-stop shops," offering treatment for all kinds of diseases and people, whereas specialized institutes offer care for specific ailments only, or for particular age groups. Some hospitals are attached to universities and research centers while others only provide medical care. There are large hospitals and small hospitals (clinics), and those run without a commercial motive, as well as those operated for profit. All of these evolved at different periods in history.

The earliest formal "facilities" for sick people are believed to have existed in ancient Egypt and Greece. These were temples, devoted to gods of healing like Saturn and Asclepius, where the afflicted were deposited in the hope of receiving divine help. Some scholars believe that clinics were attached to the temples. From Sri Lanka in Asia comes perhaps the earliest documentation, backed by architectural evidence, of a formal hospital. It was sited at the fifth-century BCE town of Mihintale.

Physician in hospital sickroom, woodcut print, 1682.

Two hundred years later, the compassionate emperor of India, Ashoka, had a series of hospitals constructed within his empire. For Rome, the stimulus was different. The armies of an expanding empire needed its soldiers to be in fighting condition. Where the legions marched, therefore, medical care units followed.

As the centuries advanced, the two main impulses for hospitals remained religious and military. Christianity made it the moral duty of its adherents to care for the sick and deprived. Monks and nuns operated infirmaries as part of their monasteries. These were enlarged and opened to the needy laity. Important ones were at Cappadocia, Monte Cassino, Lyon, and Paris. With the rise of Islam in the seventh century, the mobile military hospital spread on the back of the all-conquering Arab armies. But hospitals also received a major fillip from a more humane side of Islam, which prescribed charity toward all, irrespective of religion. During the reign of the Caliph Haroun-al Rashid, hospitals were attached to mosques. Baghdad became known as a center for readily available medical facilities.

A Benedictine monk. This order was noted for its healing abilities.

BIMARISTAN

In Persian, the word *bimar* means "sick." In their concept and functioning, bimaristans, or hospitals, in early medieval West Asia were ahead of their times. They offered a wide range of health care under one roof. Extensively staffed—including with female nurses—and well-organized, bimaristans boasted specialist physicians for different diseases. Apprentices were exposed during training to all aspects of hospital management. There were separate sections for men and women. Not only were all services gratis (free), poor patients at the time of discharge were given money to tide them over until the time they could earn for themselves.

of medicine at Bologna, publishes treatise on plastic surgery. Famous for rhinoplasty (nose reconstruction) and grafts for ears, lips, and tongues, but his operations are seen as impious and prohibited by the authorities.

1597 Codronchi's treatise on medical jurisprudence published.

1599 Ulisse Aldrovandi's *Historia animalium* published.

1600 *Foglietti* newspaper published in Venice.

17th century This was the period when modern chemistry and physics begin to take shape.

17th-century dentist at work.

WORLD
1600 Between 1600 and 1800, scurvy killed many sailors, possibly more than all the deaths from shipwrecks, naval warfare, and other diseases combined.

SWITZERLAND
1602 Physician, Felix Platter (1536–1614) publishes the first attempt at classification of diseases at Basel. Platter dissects more than 300 bodies.

BRITAIN
1602 William Harvey graduates at Padua. He begins to lecture on the circulation of blood.

1602 Fedeli publishes treatise on medical jurisprudence.

William Harvey.

ITALY
1603 Hieronymus Fabricius ab Aquapendente's *De Venarum Ostiolis* influences his pupil, William Harvey, in explaining circulation of the blood.

GERMANY
1604 Johann Kepler demonstrates inversion of optic image on the retina.

BELGIUM
1605 Verhoeven publishes the first ever newspaper at Antwerp.

MEXICO
1609 Jalap, a strong purgative from the fibrous roots of a climbing plant, introduced to Europeans.

FRANCE
1609 Louise Bourgeois (1563–1636), who had delivered French kings, publishes her observations on midwifery.

ITALY
1609 Santorio invents clinical thermometer.

1610 Cristoforo Guarinoni describes syphilitic gummata of brain.

1610 Minderer introduces ammonium acetate (*spiritus Minderei*).

1610 Galileo devises microscope.

SPAIN
1611 Villa Real and Vihus describe epidemic diphtheria (garotillo) in Spain.

ITALY
1616 Cesare Magati (1579–1647) treats gunshot wounds with plain water.

BRITAIN
1617 John Woodall's *Surgions Mate* features value of lemon or lime juice in scurvy prevention.

1617 Society of Apothecaries created by Royal Charter of James I: "Grocers are but merchants, the business of the apothecary is a mistery (sic) wherefore I think it be fitting they be a corporation of themselves."

1618 First edition of *London Pharmacopeia*.

1620 Francis Bacon, philosopher, scientist, and Lord Chancellor of England, publishes his most celebrated work, *Novum Organum*.

EUROPE
1618–48 Thirty Years' War. Battle casualties few but many deaths caused by diseases (e.g., typhus, plague, scurvy, and dysentery).

BELGIUM
1620 Van Helmont (1577–1644), a founder of biochemistry, teaches that a chemical substance survives in its compounds (*Conservation of Matter*).

NETHERLANDS
1620 Cornelius Drebbel is said to have improved the microscope and built the first submarine.

HISTORY OF HOSPITALS

The Crusaders rode into the Holy Land around the turn of the century, leaving in their wake a chain of military hospitals to tend to the injured as well as those struck by the unfamiliar diseases of a strange land. Back home in Europe, Christian institutions continued to foster and hold the medical fort. Benedictine monks, credited with establishing hundreds of monastic infirmaries, were the outstanding pillars of selfless and untiring medical care. Though secular hospitals had been emerging in Europe from the mid-medieval period, the big imperative came during the English Reformation. Henry VIII's dissolution of monasteries in the 1530s created in an abrupt gap in health care; the answer

Top: St. Johns Hospital in Bruges dates back to the 12th century.
Above: Vienna General Hospital in 1784.

was state-sponsored hospitals. The nature of the hospital system was acquiring another dimension. Geographically, too, the frontiers expanded. About this time, the New World was bestowed with its first medical outposts by Spanish, French, and British colonizers.

Voluntary hospitals, supported by endowments from wealthy philanthropists, cropped up steadily in Europe. Apart from the clutch of institutions set up in London, 18 other English cities acquired new hospitals in the mid-18th century. The modern hospital, comprehensively manned by a gamut of doctors and supporting staff—a concept that had first manifested in the medieval Islamic world—was now taking firm shape. Specialization, too, began to emerge. The city of Vienna, in Austria, was one of the foci of this transformation, with the founding of the huge Vienna General Hospital (also a teaching and research center) and some of the world's earliest specialized clinics in dermatology; ear, nose, and throat; and ophthalmology.

From the 19th century onward, the public health care system grew at a rapid pace in both Europe and the United States. For many decades, this remained a nonprofit service provided by the government and private organizations. In the latter half of the 20th century, entrepreneurial

1620 Raymund Minderer's *Medicina militaris* published.

BRITAIN
1621 Robert Burton (1516–1639) gives a major description of depression in his *Anatomy of Melancholy*.
1622 *London Weekly News.*

ITALY
1622 Gasparo Aselli (1581–1626) describes the lacteal vessels (the lymph channels of the intestines).

BRITAIN
1624 Thomas Sydenham, "The English Hippocrates," born:

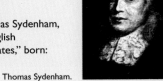

Thomas Sydenham.

Will launch clinical diagnosis and accurate descriptions of diseases.

ITALY
1626 Santorio Santorio (1561–1636) records use of clinical thermometer and pulse clock.

DUTCH EAST INDIES
1627 Cholera first studied by a Dutchman, J de Bondt (Bontius). Describes disease in 1642.

BRITAIN
1628 Harvey publishes *De Motu Cordis*, which describes the circulation of blood throughout the body.
1630 Thuillier Père affirms that St. Anthony's Fire (ergotism) is due to corn smut.

ITALY
1632 Severino: First book of surgical pathology.

players entered the field. The for-profit hospital was born. Now, commercial medical centers claim to offer services and facilities superior to those available in traditional institutions. However, they are costlier and mostly out of reach for the majority of the population. The profusion of hospitals in a competitive environment brought into being accreditation systems run by independent bodies, through which hospitals are objectively evaluated for the quality of services they render. Most of these, such as the Trent Accreditation Scheme (UK) and the Community Health Accreditation Program (USA), have been developed in the West, and are subscribed to by institutions from all around the world.

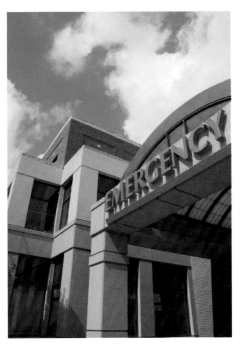

With tremendous advances in medical science and technology in the last few decades, the tools and expertise to manage disease and health disorders have substantially improved. This has meant an increase in life spans, and thus a rise in elderly populations. Paradoxically, this translates to having to care for more people, for a longer time, and thus the need for more health care capacity. Coupled with this are burgeoning populations across the developing world, often economically weak and without access to quality medical care; and the spread of new diseases, caused both by lifestyle, societal, and environmental factors, as well as globalization. The 21st-century hospital system is challenged to keep apace.

The emergency entrance for a present-day hospital.

HOSPITALS

HOSPITALS TIMELINE

c. 4000 BCE Deities and temples associated with healing in Greece, Rome, Egypt.

c. 500–300 BCE Emperors Ashoka in India and Pandukabhaya in Sri Lanka establish hospitals.

c. 100 BCE Roman military hospitals.

c. 1–500 CE Christian hospitals founded by St. Basil, St. Chrysostom, St. Fabiola, St. Augustine, and St. Sampson in the Roman empire.

Academy of Gundishapur gains prominence in Sassanid Persia as center for medical education.

c. 500 CE–1000 Muslim-run hospitals in Mesopotamia, Egypt, Tunisia, Spain, offer diverse treatment for all.

c. 1000–1500 Christian missionaries at the forefront of providing medical care.

Knights Hospitaller build hospital at Jerusalem for Christian pilgrims (c. 1100);

Hospital of the Holy Ghost, Montpellier, France (1145). Important medical schools at Salerno and Naples, Italy.

c. 1500–1750 First hospitals in North America. Hospital de Jesus Nazareno at Mexico City (1524); Hôtel-Dieu du Précieux Sang at Québec, Canada (1639); at Manhattan Island, present-day USA (1663).

1530s Monasteries and their hospitals closed down in England by Henry VIII.

c. 1700–50 Voluntary hospitals in England. By Huguenots (1718); Westminster Hospital (1719); Guy's Hospital (1724); London Hospital (1740); Royal Infirmary of Edinburgh (1729).

St. Chrysostom.

1948 Establishment of National Health Service, public-funded health care in England.

1951 Joint Commission on Accreditation of Hospitals set up in USA to evaluate quality of hospital services.

1965 Establishment of Medicare and Medicaid public-funded health care in the U.S.

1968 Hospital Corporation of America founded. It goes on to become the world's largest private provider of health services.

1993 Trent Accreditation Scheme, to assess hospital standards, set up in the UK.

1997 Chris Hani Baragwanath Hospital in Johannesburg, South Africa, acknowledged the largest hospital in the world. More than 2,000 people check in every day.

2000 onward Increasing costs of medical care in the West prompts patients to seek cheaper, high-quality hospitalization in developing countries like Cuba, Philippines, Jordan. India, one of the major recipient countries, expects an annual growth rate of 30 percent, reaching annual revenues of $2 billion by 2015.

Hospitals of the future emerge. They are completely wireless, paperless, and will, eventually, be filmless. Neck-worn, voice-activated communication devices are used by the staff. Biometric thumbprint technology employed to open cabinets. Computer screens in rooms enable instant access to test results and reports.

The Royal London Hospital.

BRITAIN
1633 Stephen Bradwell publishes first book on first aid.
1636 Francis Glisson is Regius Professor at Cambridge; will write on rickets in 1650.

USA
1636 Assembly of Virginia and in **1638** Assembly of Maryland pass acts regulating surgeons' fees.

FRANCE
1637 Descartes shows that visual accommodation depends upon change in form of lens.

NETHERLANDS
1638 Drebbel said to have improved thermometer.

PORTUGAL
1638 Padre Acugna, a Portuguese monk, introduces *oil of copaiva*.
1639 First printing press in North America (Cambridge, Massachusetts).

FRANCE
1639 First Paris Pharmacopeia.

USA
1639 Virginia Assembly passes law regulating medical practice.

SPAIN
1640 Malaria arrives in Spain. Juan del Vigo introduces cinchona, a substance from Peruvian bark associated with quinine. It proves useful in treating malaria.

ITALY
1640 Severino produces local anesthesia by means of snow and ice.

GERMANY
1642 Wirsung discovers pancreatic duct (named after him).

NETHERLANDS
1642 Jacob Bontius (1592–1631), in *De medicina Indorum,* describes beriberi and cholera.

BRITAIN
1643 Typhus affects both the armies in the English Civil War.
1644 Matthew Hopkins, the witch finder, brings many unfortunates to trial.

FRANCE
1644 Descartes (1596–1650) publishes treatise on *dioptrics* (assisting vision with refraction, as with a telescope lens). He describes reflex action.

NETHERLANDS
1646 Diemerbroek publishes monograph on plague.

USA
1647 Giles Firmin lectures on anatomy in Massachusetts.
1646 Syphilis appears in Boston, Mass. **1647** Yellow fever appears in Barbados and spreads through American ports. **1659** Diphtheria at Roxbury, Massachusetts.

GERMANY
1648 Glauber prepares fuming hydrochloric acid.

BELGIUM
1648 *Ortus medicinae* written by Van Helmont, founder of biochemistry.

ITALYS
1648 Athanasius Kircher (1601–80) describes ear trumpet.
1648 Francesco Redi disproves theory of spontaneous generation.

BRITAIN
1649–1734 Sir John Floyer writes *The Physician's Pulse-watch, c.* 1707, and the first book devoted to geriatrics in 1724.

USA
1649 Act regulating the practice of medicine in Massachusetts.

BRITAIN
1650 Glisson (1597–1677) describes rickets in *De rachitide.* Sylvius shows association of tubercles in the lung with pulmonary phthisis (later shown to be pulmonary tuberculosis).
1651 Nathaniel Highmore (who practiced medicine at Sherborne) discovers the maxillary sinus (in jaw).
1651 Harvey's treatise on generation of animals published.
1652 Thomas Culpeper's *Herbal* published.
1653 Francis Glisson (1597–1677) describes anatomy of liver.

Marcello Malpighi.

MARCELLO MALPIGHI
1628–1694

Malpighi, who taught at Bologna and Pisa, was the founder of biological microscopy. He developed techniques for the preparation of tissues to be studied under the lens. He was able to confirm the existence of the air vesicles in the lungs and the air capillaries between the arteries and veins that Harvey had surmised. He described much about the structure of the skin, spleen, and kidneys.

ANTONY VAN LEEUWENHOEK
1632–1723

A linen merchant from Delft, Holland, who enjoyed making magnifying lenses in his spare time, Antony van Leeuwenhoek initially used the lenses to help him count threads in linen weaves. A self-taught expert, he did not read Latin and therefore had some difficulty in keeping up with scientific advances. Nonetheless, Leeuwenhoek was able to make a lens that would magnify 270 times. It was he who invented the "solar microscope," discovered the male spermatozoa, and first recognized red blood corpuscles—which Malpighi had seen but thought were fat globules. Leeuwenhoek's work paved the way for the development of the germ theory.

Antony van Leeuwenhoek.

JOHN AND WILLIAM HUNTER
1728–1793 AND 1718–1783

A former army surgeon, John Hunter is regarded by many as the founder of surgical pathology. As well as some courageous and expert experimental surgery, he collected a vast number of specimens for the Royal College of Surgeons in London. Many claim that he raised surgery from a technique to a science.

His brother, William, was also famous as an obstetrician and an anatomist who founded a successful school of anatomy in London.

John Hunter.

Lady Mary Wortley Montagu in Turkish dress.

SMALLPOX VACCINATION

On her travels in Turkey as wife to the British ambassador there, Lady Mary Wortley Montagu had witnessed a form of inoculation (called variolation) against smallpox. Pus or scabs from victims of the active disease were scratched into the skin of healthy people.

In April 1718, she had her small son variolated and went on to advocate the idea in Britain, having her daughter treated in London in 1721. This took place amid fierce debate, as physicians, apothecaries, surgeons, politicians, royalty, and the Church argued ferociously about the safety and ethics of the procedure.

In 1721, during an outbreak in Boston in the USA, variolation was carried out on a large scale and greatly reduced the numbers of deaths from the disease. Back in Great Britain, Princess Caroline had two of her daughters variolated in 1722.

There were some untimely deaths and outbreaks from using too virulent strains, resulting in mounting opposition. However, Edward Jenner introduced vaccination at the end of the century. Noting the resistance to the disease of individuals who had already contracted cowpox, he used the cowpox virus instead of active smallpox. ("Vaccination" comes from the Latin word for "cow.") This proved a much safer preventive measure. Inevitably, however, it was still a controversial subject, and there were emotive reactions to the idea of introducing cow matter into human beings—but the method was soon proved effective. By 1801, more than 100,000 had been vaccinated in England, and vaccination was being implemented worldwide.

1654 Otto von Guericke of Magdeburg's (1602–86) well pump inspires Boyle to get his assistant to devise air pump for his vacuum experiments. Boyle proves air essential to animal life.

DENMARK
1652 Thomas Bartholin describes lymphatic system.

GERMANY
1653 Johann Schultes's (Scultetus, 1595–1645) *Armamentarium chirurgicum* shows graphic representation of amputation of the breast.

ITALY
1654–1720 Giovanni Maria Lancisi discusses possibility that malaria might be caused by bites of mosquito.

FRANCE
1656 Lazar houses abolished.
1657–69 Pandemic malarial fever.

BRITAIN
1656 In Oxford, Boyle injects a dog with opium.

Christopher Wren (1632–1723), another of the Oxford group, also injects a dog with "Wine

Culpeper House advertisement, 1930.

This was a century of pioneers who promoted greater understanding of the human body and treatments. Semmelweiss stressed the importance of hygiene, introducing disciplines that greatly reduced deaths after surgery and following hospital childbirth. Chemist Louis Pasteur and bacteriologist Robert Koch proved diseases were spread by microorganisms, while Joseph Lister introduced antisepsis. Several dentists and surgeons are credited with the first use of modern anesthetics, while Florence Nightingale revolutionized nursing and hospital practice.

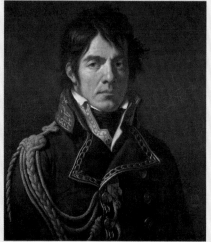

Dominique-Jean Larrey.

DOMINIQUE-JEAN LARREY
1766–1842

The demands of war have always meant advances in invention and discovery and improvements in surgical procedures. Dominique-Jean Larrey, chief doctor and military surgeon to Napoleon's Grande Armée, was the first to introduce field units to give first aid and provide immediate surgery for the battle-wounded. He invented the ambulance system with his *ambulances volantes* to carry injured soldiers to the dressing stations.

Dedicated and caring, during the Russian campaign in 1812 he is said to have performed 200 amputations during 24 hours—and experimented with using refrigeration as a form of anesthetic. His attention to the wounded from both sides of the battle was a precursor of the principles of the Red Cross.

LOUIS PASTEUR
1822–1895

Louis Pasteur was a chemist and microbiologist whose discoveries contributed greatly to 19th-century understanding and treatment of disease. Through his investigations of a disease in silkworms, he recognized the manner in which infectious diseases spread through microorganisms and how to prevent this. In effect, he proved the existence of germs and established bacteriology as a science.

His discovery that heat could kill microbes led to pasteurization of milk. Then, following his work on anthrax he produced an anti-rabies vaccine. Experiments on rabbits and dogs convinced Pasteur he could prevent this hitherto fatal disease developing in humans—if caught in time. The prevailing treatment was to apply red-hot irons to the wound, yet, despite this painful ordeal, victims were still susceptible to rabies, a particularly

Louis Pasteur.

gruesome fatal disease. So when a young lad was brought to Pasteur after being badly bitten by a rabid dog, he was persuaded to undertake his first human experiment. He saved the boy's life—and many more since.

FLORENCE NIGHTINGALE

Prior to the implementation of Florence Nightingale's revolutionary ideas on nursing, in the 19th century the nurse's role had often been regarded as lowly and degrading. In some Dickens' novels, for example, they were depicted as low-class thieves and drunkards.

Having persuaded her family to let her receive some rudimentary training, Florence Nightingale's reputation as a determined, dedicated reformer became known, and, in due course, she took her skills and new ideas into the barrack hospital at Scutari in Turkey, where the wounded from the Crimean War were being housed in dire conditions—with desperate shortages of water, soap, linen, bedding, and bandages.

Her great organizational skills, her determination to improve conditions, and ability to teach other nurses how to best treat patients established Florence Nightingale as a pioneer in modern nursing, along with other reformers such as Mary Seacole. She went on to establish the Nightingale School of Nursing in London.

and Ale into the mass of Blood by a Veine, in good quantities, till I have made him extremely drunk ..."

1656 Rolfink shows that cataract is clouding of the lens.

1656 Wharton (1614–73) studies glands. His *Adenographia* is published.

BELGIUM
1657 Jan à Gehema urges that field chest of drugs be furnished to armies by the state.

ITALY
1658 Athanasius Kircher (1601–80) attributes plague to a *"contagium animatum,"* suggesting that a microorganism is responsible for infectious disease.

NETHERLANDS
1658 Swammerdam describes red blood corpuscles.

SWITZERLAND
1658 Wepfer demonstrates lesion of the brain in apoplexy.

ITALY
1659 Marcello Malpighi (1628–94) outlines lymphadenoma or Hodgkin's disease and in **1660** he discovers capilliary anastomosis.

Marcello Malpighi.

GERMANY
1660 Schneider shows nasal secretion does not come from pituitary body (Galen).

BRITAIN
1660s Boyle and Richard Lower (1631–91) transfuse blood from one dog to another. At a meeting of the Royal Society in 1667, Lower transfuses blood from a sheep into a "poor and debauched man ... crackd a little in his head." He survives. In 1667, Lower transfuses blood from dog to dog.

1660 Thomas Willis (1621–75) describes and names puerperal fever.

1661 Robert Boyle (1627–91) defines chemical elements and isolates acetone.

1661 Scarlatina appears in England.

DENMARK
1661 Stensen discovers duct of parotid gland (the

JOSEPH LISTER
1827–1912

Joseph Lister.

An English surgeon, Joseph Lister, pioneered the modern use of antiseptics in surgery—the prevention of infection during surgery by the use of chemicals.

When Joseph Lister began his career in medicine, there was still much ignorance over how germs spread and the importance of hygiene. Often surgeons worked in clothing stiff with blood from previous operations and operated on wooden tables where blood and pus remained from earlier surgery. Moreover, their operations sometimes took place on the battlefield or in private homes—not necessarily in a purpose-built site.

Lister had always been interested in the problems of inflammation, and concerned about the gangrene and putrefaction that so often occurred after an operation or injury. All the attention and work of the surgeons and other medical personnel was in vain when a wound turned septic.

The prevailing theories were that there was spontaneous generation of germs, or that the oxygen in the air could harm a wound, but as soon as Lister became aware of Pasteur's work on bacteria, and his understanding of germs being in the air, Lister was convinced there must be a means of preventing these germs entering a wound, of somehow destroying the bacteria before any harm was done.

After one initial failure, his first experiments, using phenol (carbolic acid) to clean up the operating instruments and work surfaces, proved very successful. He wrote up the results in the *Lancet* in 1867, so setting the scene for experiments with various ways of combating germs in theater, including in due course the implementation of asepsis—scrupulous cleanliness of the operating theater, the instruments used, and the people working there.

Lister also developed the use of sulphochromic catgut for sealing wounds. This could be rendered antiseptic and left in situ.

The understanding and use of Lister's hygienic methods meant that deaths following surgery dropped from over 40 percent to less than 1.

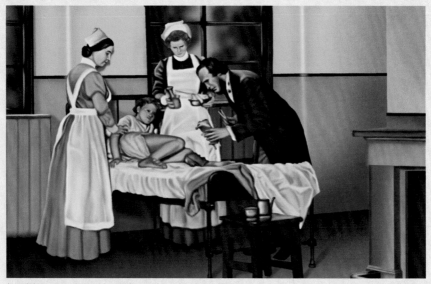

Joseph Lister introduces the use of antiseptic in hospitals in Britain.

duct opens into mouth from gland in front of ear).

ITALY

1661 Marcello Malpighi (1628–94) publishes first account of capillary system (*De pulmonibus*) and describes histology of lungs.
1662 Lorenzo Bellini discovers excretory ducts of kidneys.

NETHERLANDS

1662 De Graaf shows ova arise in the ovary.

De Graaf.

FRANCE

1662 Descartes publishes first treatise on physiology (*De homine*).

BRITAIN

1662 Charles II charters the Royal Society. John Graunt (1620–74) founds medical statistics.

NETHERLANDS

1663 Sylvius describes digestion as a fermentation.
1664 Swammerdam discovers valves of lymphatics, and De Graaf examines pancreatic juice, realizing its importance in digestion of food.

BRITAIN

1664 *Cerebri anatome* published by Thomas Willis (1621–75). A classification of cerebral nerves, it is illustrated by Sir Christopher Wren.

Thomas Willis.

1665 Great Plague of London.
1665 Robert Hooke (1635–1703) describes plant cells, and includes microscopic drawings in his *Micrographia*.
1665 First volume of *Philosophical Transactions* (Royal Society) of London.

FRANCE

1665 First number of *Journal des sçavans*.

ITALY

1666 Marcello Malpighi's treatise on the viscera published.

USA

1666 Coroners appointed for each county of Maryland.

EUROPE

1666–75 Smallpox in Europe.

FRANCE

1667 Jean Baptiste Denis of Paris transfuses blood from lamb to man.

BRITAIN

1667 Hooke shows true function of lungs by artificial respiration. Walter Needham shows fetus is nourished by placenta.

USA

1668 Yellow fever appears in New York.

BRITAIN

1668 Mauriceau's obstetric treatise published.
1668–72 Epidemic dysentery in England (described by Sydenham and Morton).
1669 Richard Lower's *Tractatus de corde* shows that the change from dark to bright red blood is associated with the uptake of some substance from the air passing through the lungs. This was all the more remarkable in that the substance, oxygen, had not yet been discovered.

Robert Hooke's improved microscope.

Robert Hooke's drawing of a flea, the kind that carried plague.

ANESTHETICS

The control of pain has been fundamental to the progress of surgery from fairly primitive operations to the intricacies of modern microsurgery. Prior to the development of anesthetics, surgical procedures were limited by the degree of pain a patient could endure and the great risk of death from shock. Surgery had to be very fast. While the senses could be dulled by using drugs that included alcohol and plant extracts (such as mandrake root), surgeons would still aim to complete an amputation in less than a minute.

It was Sir Humphry Davy who, in 1799, discovered the effectiveness of nitrous oxide (laughing gas) as an anesthetic. Then, in 1838, Michael Faraday revealed that ether reduced sensitivity to pain. Sadly for those many patients who suffered in the meantime, these two discoveries were largely ignored by established medical circles for several years.

Humphry Davy.

It was an American dentist, Horace Wells, who, in 1844, used nitrous oxide on himself and then invited a friend to extract a tooth from his jaw while he was "under the influence." He went on to use the gas on patients, with mixed results. His partner, William Morton, however, conducted experiments with ether and rendered himself unconscious as a result. At Massachusetts General Hospital in October, assisted by Morton, surgeon John Warren painlessly removed a neck tumor from a patient who had breathed in ether.

Horace Wells.

Morton tried to keep the nature of the gas he had used a secret, but in December 1846, in London, Robert Liston successfully amputated a patient's leg while using ether as an anesthetic. Before long, ether was being implemented during surgery in Europe and in the USA.

James Simpson.

In 1847, James Simpson began experimenting with various gases, even holding dinner parties where he and his friends explored their effects. This dangerous enterprise led to the discovery of chloroform as an anesthetic. Simpson went on to use this to relieve women during the pain of childbirth. Despite much opposition, anesthesia during labor became widely accepted— especially after Queen Victoria, in 1853, had it administered by her doctor, John Snow, to ease her pain during the birth of Prince Leopold. John Snow went on to study anesthesia and how to administer this safely.

Michael Faraday.

By 1884, cocaine had been used, and, by the turn of the century, procaine and barbiturates were being explored.

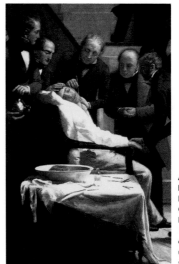

A new era begins. Massachusetts General Hospital, 1846: The first operation using ether as an anesthetic.

PENICILLIN

Alexander Fleming in his laboratory.

In 1928, British bacteriologist Sir Alexander Fleming discovered penicillin by accident at St. Mary's hospital in London. He had been researching antibacterial substances that would be non-toxic to human tissues and had just begun to study influenza. By chance, a green mold developed on a neglected culture plate of staphylococcus. This unplanned contamination proved fortuitous when the observant Fleming realized that there was a circle completely free of bacteria around the area of the mold. He went on to experiment further and found that a liquid mold culture (he named this penicillin) prevented the growth of staphylococci—even when diluted 800 times! It was discovered that the mold could produce at least four penicillin, but only one has been used extensively.

An invaluable antibiotic, non-toxic to human cells, penicillin was finally isolated in 1940 and has since been responsible for saving thousands of lives. It proved particularly effective in reducing deaths through disease or infection among the Allied casualties in World War II and in the control of venereal diseases. Unfortunately, microorganisms are highly adaptable, and strains are now developing that are resistant to penicillin and other antibiotics.

1670 Physic Garden at Edinburgh (now Royal Botanic).

ITALY
1670 Malpighi describes Malpighian bodies in spleen and kidneys and in **1673** describes development of chick embryo.

Illustration of chick development by Malpighi.

NETHERLANDS
1672 De Graaff describes the Graafian follicles in the ovary.
1673 Leeuwenhoek (1632-1723) makes microscope and describes red blood cells, discovers the following: **1674** spermatozoa; **1675** protozoa; **1679** striped muscle; **1680** yeast plant; **1683** describes bacteria; **1689** discovers rods in retina and finer anatomy of cornea.

BRITAIN
1674 Mayow (1640–79) finds *igneoaërial spirit* (oxygen) essential for combustion and respiration.
1674 Robert Hooke designs a theater for the Royal College of Surgeons.
1674–75 Willis discovers sweet taste of diabetic urine.
1675 Sydenham (1624–1689) differentiates scarlatina from measles.
1676 Richard Wiseman describes TB of joints.

USA
1674 Printing press at Boston, Massachusetts.
1677 Smallpox in Boston.

ITALY
1675 Malpighi's *Anatome plantarum*.

SWITZERLAND
1677 Peyer describes lymphoid tissues in small intestine, still known as Peyer's patches.

EUROPE
1677–81 Pandemic malarial fever in Europe.

FRANCE
1678–1761 Pierre Fauchard is known as the "Father of Dentistry." His book *The Surgeon*

T he functioning of the mind at the physiological, as well as the intellectual and emotional levels, has perhaps been the least understood aspect of the human body. The study of the mind, and the treatment of related ailments, lies in the sphere of two fields: psychology and psychiatry.

Bedlam was a principal London tourist sight. There is an old tale that "gate receipts" totalled about £400 for the year 1776. True or not, visiting the hospital for the mentally ill was a popular pursuit.

PSYCHOLOGY

P sychology takes into its ambit all the mental processes that influence perception and manifest as personality and behavior. Psychology involves both research and application. Whereas the former is an academic discipline, the latter, focused on analyzing, improving, and treating mental function and disorders, is clinical. Certified psychologists hold doctoral degrees from teaching institutes.

The seeds of Western psychology lie in the philosophies of the ancients such as Aristotle and Socrates. However, psychology emerged as an independent, scientific discipline only in the early modern era with the establishment of the world's first dedicated laboratory in Leipzig, by Wilhelm Wundt (1832–1920).

From the thousands of students who attended Wundt's lectures, many went on to acquire degrees and become professionals. Building on Wundt's experimental methodologies, his student, Edward B. Titchener, propounded psychology's first major school of thought. Structuralism, as it was called, sought to study human thought processes by breaking them down into much smaller parts.

Meanwhile, psychology had taken firm roots in America. G. Stanley Hall (1844–1944), a former student of Wundt and William James, had set up the first psychology lab on the continent at Johns Hopkins University. James, acknowledged as the father of American psychology, conceived the Functionalist theory,

Dentist, A Treatise on Teeth describes basic oral anatomy and pathology, ways to remove decay and restore teeth, periodontal disease (pyorrhea), orthodontics, replacement of missing teeth, and tooth transplantation.
1679 Nicolas de Blegny publishes the first medical periodical (*Nouvelles découvertes*).

BRITAIN
1679 James Yonge describes flap amputation.

USA
1681 Printing press at Williamsburg, Virginia.

ITALY
1680–81 Borelli, professor of mathematics at Pisa, studies mechanics and "physical laws" of the body; publishes *De motu animalium*.
1682–1771 Examination of the dead body is developed by the Italian pathologist Giovanni Battista Morgagni.

SWITZERLAND
1682 Brunner describes duodenal glands (discovered in 1679 by his father-in-law, Wepfer).

FRANCE
1683 Duverney's first treatise on otology (the science of treating the ear).

BRITAIN
1683 Sydenham's (1624–89) treatise on gout.

FRANCE
1684 Bernier classifies races of humankind by color of the skin.

PRUSSIA
1685 Prussian ordinance regulating medical fees.

USA
1685 Printing press at Philadelphia.
1685 Bidloo's *Anatomia*.
1685 Vieussens' *Nevrographia* on brain, spinal cord, and nerves. Best illustrated 17th-century work on subject.

BRITAIN
1687 Isaac Newton's *Philosophial Naturalis Principia Mathematica*: important scientific work.

1689 Walter Harris (1647–1732), physician to William and Mary, publishes treatise on diseases of children: *De morbis acutis infantum*.

BRITAIN
1690 Locke's *Essay on Human Understanding* published.
1690 Sir John Floyer counts the pulse by using the watch.
1691 Clopton Havers publishes *Osteologia nova* (Haversian canals).

GERMANY
1690 Justine Siegemundin publishes treatise on midwifery.

USA
1691 Yellow fever in Boston.
1691 Autopsy of Governor Slaughter in New York.
1692 Salem witchcraft trials.

The Salem witch trials.

EUROPE
1692 Jan Cocnan Ammann (1663–1730) teaches deaf-mutes. Methods published in two books, 1692 and 1700.

BRITAIN
1693–94 England's Queen Mary II, aged 32, dies of smallpox in a devastating plague that sweeps across Europe.

POLAND
1693 Acoluthus of Breslau resects the lower jaw.

As watch mechanisms became more accurate, so did pulse-taking, which joined urine examination as a form of clinical diagnosis.

psychology's second major school of thought. Like Structuralism, Functionalism confined the study of the human mind to the conscious realm. However, it departed from Structuralist theory in that it regarded the nature of mental processes as continuous rather than the sum of small parts. To James is also credited Pragmatism, which called for focusing on the practical use, as opposed to the truth, of an idea.

SIGMUND FREUD

Of all the pioneering luminaries of psychology, no one has had more of an impact than Sigmund Freud (1856–1939), the founder of psychoanalysis. Freud was an Austrian physician who became interested in the mental disorder termed "hysteria." Through his treatment of a woman named Bertha Pappenheim, he came to the conclusion that the underlying causes of mental disorder could be traced to adverse childhood experiences, caused by a disturbance in the play of natural pleasure-seeking instincts. These experiences, which continued to fester in the unconscious mind, could be brought to the fore and mitigated through psychoanalysis. Psychoanalytic therapy involved helping the patients recognize and talk about their distressing experiences. Bertha, who had been helped by this treatment, called it "the talking cure." Freud's deductions were elucidated in his theory of psychosexual development.

Freud's fascination with the unconscious mind was shared by his close associate Carl Jung. However, Jung later broke away from Freud due to disagreements on the role of sexuality in psychological development. Jung's interests lay in analyzing the symbolism in dreams as a means to unraveling the mysteries of the mind. He formulated his own theory called analytical psychology.

The work of Ivan Pavlov (1849–1936), a Russian physiologist, opened another major front in the study of psychology. Pavlov, in his studies on the digestive physiology of dogs, observed that the animals began salivating in anticipation of being given food. From this he inferred that behavior was not a product of the unconscious or conscious mind. Instead, it was a conditioned reflex, and should be considered in an observable and scientific context. Pavlov's ideas found many subscribers and were further developed, particularly by John B. Watson and B.F. Skinner, as behaviorism.

New thought on the conscious mind emerged in the second half of the 20th century. It came from Carl Rogers (1902–87), who stressed that personal experience was the determining factor for "truth as it is in the process of becoming in me." He believed in the power of free will and self-determination in shaping one's life. This school of thought, called humanistic psychology, was augmented by Abraham Maslow's (1908–70) hierarchy of needs theory, famously depicted by the five-tier pyramid, in which physiological necessities like food and sleep form the bottom tier, and self actualization, represented by creativity, spontaneity, etc., find their place at the apex.

Contemporary psychology has come to be viewed from different perspectives, such as biological, cross-cultural, evolutionary, and cognitive—centered on memory, problem-solving, language, and decision-making. The cognitive perspective has expanded enormously in recent times. Theories of various schools are utilized for each perspective, whenever considered useful. Specialized psychology has also become associated with areas such as forensics, industry, children, and neurology, and the future will see the emergence of many more specialities.

Sigmund Freud (left) and his associate Carl Jung (far left) in the early years of the 20th century.

USA
1693 Printing press in New York.

GERMANY
1694 Camerarius gives experimental proof of sexuality in plants.

BRITAIN
1695 Nehemiah Grew discovers magnesium sulphate in Epsom Waters (Epsom salts).

USA
1699 Infectious diseases act in Massachusetts.

BRITAIN
1700–10 Sir John Floyer invents a special pulse watch that runs for exactly one minute.

FRANCE
1700 History and memoirs of the French Academy of Sciences published.

ITALY
1700 Ramazzini (1633–1714) publishes treatise on occupational diseases *De morbis artificum diatriba.*

BRITAIN
1701 Robert Houstoun taps ovarian cyst.

Prior to anesthetics, amputees required considerable restraint. Sometimes those who assisted were given the limb as a token.

GERMANY
1702 Stahl (1660–1734) states phlogiston theory, concerning combustion and the belief in an invisible "fire element."

BRITAIN
1703 House of Lords authorizes apothecaries to prescribe as well as dispense drugs.

NETHERLANDS
1703 Leeuwenhoek (1632–1723) discovers parthenogenesis of plant lice.

USA
1703–1850 Devastating epidemics of yellow fever in tropical and subtropical zones.

GERMANY
1704 Dr. Eysenbarth practices as a mountebank in Germany.

ITALY
1704 Valsalva (1666–1723) publishes *De aure humana tractatus* and describes *Valsalva's* maneuver.

BRITAIN
1705 Robert Elliot, first professor of anatomy at Edinburgh.

FRANCE
1705 Brisseau and Maître Jan show that cataract is the clouded lens.
1706 First laboratory of marine zoology at Marseilles.

EUROPE
1707 Influenza pandemic in Europe.
1707 Dionis's *Cours d'opérations de chirurgie* published.

SWITZERLAND
1708–77 Albrecht von Haller, brilliant writer, botanist, and physiologist who studies the nervous system.

ITALY
1710 Santorini's muscle in larynx discovered.
1712 Torti of Modena uses cinchona bark in pernicious malarial fever.

The cinchona tree.

FRANCE
1713 Dominique Anel catheterizes lachrymal (tear) ducts.

BRITAIN
1714 Daniel Turner (1667–1742): *Treatise of*

PSYCHIATRY

Psychiatry studies the mind from a medical perspective. Being a branch of medicine, its practitioners are required to be qualified physicians before they specialize in psychiatry. Psychiatrists diagnose mental disorders in physiological terms, and prescribe treatment through medication. As an additional qualification, some psychiatrists also undertake training in psychoanalysis.

Early hypotheses that mental disorders were caused by physiological defects go back to ancient Greece and Rome. Hippocrates was one who proposed this view in the fifth century BCE. However, for many centuries, Western civilization generally ascribed mental disorders to malevolent supernatural influences. It was in the Muslim world, during the medieval period, that attempts were made to analyze illnesses of this kind in a clinical context and address them in a more compassionate and institutionalized way. Between the eighth and ninth centuries, hospitals for the mentally ill were introduced in Baghdad, Fez, and Cairo. Patients were treated not through exorcism or isolated confinement, but by drugs, baths, and other kinds of therapy. Physicians such as Muhammad ibn Zakariya Razi, Najabuddin Muhammad, and Ibn Sina were at the forefront of this approach.

It was only in the 18th century that European physicians began to accept that mental disorders could be addressed through medical means. Amongst those who led the way was William Battie (1703–76), president of the Royal College of Physicians. Battie's *A Treatise on Madness*, was one of the first tomes on the subject. The term "psychiatry" was coined by Johann Christian Reil (1759–1813), a medical professor in Berlin University. In the 19th century, asylums became the learning and practicing grounds for scientific psychiatric work. Their role began to change from that of custodial to one where humane treatment was delivered. Germany, with close to two dozen asylum-affiliated universities, was the center of the boom. What was ironic was that whereas, on one hand, mental illness

Johann Christian Reil.

Karl Ludwig Kahlbaum.

had come to be regarded as curable, and with this enlightened new view "madhouses" had been considerably relieved of their inmates, on the other hand, there was a massive surge of admissions to the new institutions, for reasons not yet totally clear. The number of asylums rose sharply. Both in Europe and the USA, they came to be packed with tens of thousands of individuals. The progress of the preceding decades threatened to come apart as, stretched to their seams, they faced prospects of reverting back to mere detention centers.

Meanwhile, clinical research into mental disorders, which was to take psychiatric science to the next level as a medical discipline, was continuing. The German psychiatrists Karl Ludwig Kahlbaum (1828–1909) and Ewald Hecker (1840–99) did pioneering work in categorizing and describing mood disorders. Another German, Emil Kraepelin (1856–1926), made further strides in this direction. His detailed studies of depression, dementia, and particularly schizophrenia, are regarded as landmarks in the development of psychiatry. Emphatic that the rudiments of mental illness were biological and genetic, the pathological evidence of which should be searched for in the brain, he nudged the course of psychiatry further into the physiological realm. With Sigmund Freud postulating his own theories at this time, it was an exciting period in the exploration of the mind. Bumping into each other, both psychology and psychiatry made

diseases incident to the skin. Regarded as founder of British dermatology.

A pharmacy in 1722.

With anatomy now accepted, there was often a shortage of bodies to dissect, and body snatching could prove profitable.

FRANCE
1714 Dominique Anel invents fine point syringe.

GERMANY
1714 Gabriel David Fahrenheit constructs 212-degree mercury thermometer.
1716 Surgeon General appointed in German Army at salary of 900 marks per year.

USA
1716 New York City issues ordinance for midwives.

GERMANY
1718 Lorenz Heister's (1683–1758) work on surgery published. Heister was founder of German scientific surgery.

ITALY
1719 Morgagni (1682–1771) describes syphilis of cerebral arteries.

BRITAIN
1718 Lady Mary Wortley Montagu has son inoculated with smallpox.
1720 A new theory of consumptions by Benjamin Marten forecasts the existence of the tubercle bacillus.
1721 Zabdiel Boylston inoculates for smallpox in Boston.

FRANCE
1720–21 Plague in Marseilles.
1721 Palfyn exhibits obstetric forceps to French Academy of Surgery.
1721 Floyer's *Psychrolusia* published.
1724 Guyot of Versailles attempts catheterization of the Eustachian tubes in ears.

A mastectomy operation was performed on this woman by Lorenz Heister in 1720. She survived.

BRITAIN
1723 Yellow fever reaches London.
1723 William Cheselden (1688–1752) describes supra pubic (abdominal wall) surgery for removal of bladder stone.
1724 John Maubray gives private instruction in obstetrics in England.
1724 Sir John Floyer writes first book devoted to geriatrics.

FRANCE/BRITAIN
1725 A.de Moivre (born in France in 1667, died in Britain in 1754) publishes memoir, *Annuities Upon Lives.*

PRUSSIA
1725 Prussian edict regulating practice of medicine.

BRITAIN
1725 John Freind's (1675–1728) *History of Physick* published. First English historian of medicine.
1726 Stephen Hales (1677–1761) makes first measurement of blood pressure.
1726 Chair of midwifery in the University of Edinburgh. Joseph Gibson first Professor of Midwifery in any university.
1727 Cheselden performs lateral operation for bladder stones.
1728 John Hunter, scientist, experimenter, and surgeon, born.

some of their major advances in the decades surrounding the turn of the century.

The latter half of the 20th century saw many complementary as well as conflicting developments. The two internationally accepted standards for diagnosing and classifying psychiatric disease were published. These are the section on mental disorders in WHO's *International Classification of Diseases and Related Health Problems* (1949), and the *American Psychiatric Association's Diagnostic and Statistical Manual of Mental Disorders* (1952). An anti-psychiatry movement emerged in the 1960s. It was fueled by growing skepticism regarding diagnosis of mental disease that had resulted in thousands being consigned to asylums, which, in turn, were overcrowded to the point of providing insensitive, often inhumane, care. Certain methods of treatment, for example electroconvulsive therapy, were opposed. Even administration of drugs was disapproved of. The science of psychiatry came under another cloud in 1972, when David Rosenhan conducted an experiment wherein eight persons from random backgrounds, with no history of mental disorder, were presented at mental hospitals. All were diagnosed with different mental ailments, admitted and treated for varying periods, and discharged. The inference was that psychiatric diagnostic and treatment techniques were glaringly imperfect as they could not discern the sick from the healthy. Ultimately, lobbying groups were successful in forcing legislation for the establishment of community mental health centers, and patients were steadily released from state-run institutions into the care of the community.

Psychiatry distinguishes itself from psychology and psychoanalysis by asserting the physiological character of mental disease. Logically, then, its mode of treatment is pharmacological. Modern psycho-pharmacology can be said to have begun with the discovery of acetylcholine, the first neurotransmitter, by Henry Hallet Dale (1875–1976) and Otto Loewi (1873–1961) in the early part of the 20th century. With the identification and development of dozens of chemical agents and drugs in the last 60 years, psychiatry has shaken off its doubters and strengthened its claim as a true and effective science in the treatment of mental disorder. The synthesis of chlorpromazine in the early 1950s, as a highly effective anti-schizophrenia drug, was one of the big leaps forward. It was followed by lithium carbonate for mood disorders and a host of antidepressants and anti-psychotics. Far better understanding of the nervous system, where chemical processes crucial to psychiatric symptoms occur, has been achieved through neuroscience and imaging. And like other branches of medicine, psychiatric research is scouring the deepest depths of the human organism for solutions. Genes associated with diseases such as schizophrenia and bipolar disorder have already been identified.

The formidable gates to the Yarra Bend Asylum in New South Wales, Australia, an institution devoted to the treatment of the mentally ill, c. 1850.

1728 Cheselden makes an operation for artificial pupil.

EUROPE
1729 Influenza pandemic in Europe; another in 1732

FRANCE
1728 Fauchard (1671–1761) publishes *Le chirurgien dentiste*.
1730 Daviel improves cataract operation.

BRITAIN
1730 First tracheotomy (incision of windpipe) for diphtheria by George Martine.
1730 James Douglas describes the peritoneum.

FRANCE
1730 Réamur (1683–1757) introduces 80-degree thermometer.

USA
1730–31 Thomas Cadwalader teaches anatomy in Philadelphia.

FRANCE
1731 Friedrich Hoffmann (1660–1742) describes chlorosis (the "Virgin's Disease").
1732 Winslow's anatomy published.

NETHERLANDS
1732 Boerhaave's *Elementa chemiae* published.

BRITAIN
1733 George Cheyne describes Cheyne-Stokes respiration.
1733 Stephen Hales's (1677–1761) *Haemastaticks* describes measurement of blood pressure.
1735 English laws against witchcraft repealed.
1735–85 John Brown. He believes that all disease was due to increased excitability (sthenic) or decreased excitability (asthenic). Favorite remedies are laudanum and whisky. The Brunonian system for treating disease involves administrating either sedatives or stimulants.

USA
1735 Scarlatina appears in the United States.

SWEDEN
1735 Linnaeus's (1707–78) *Systema naturae* published.

Linnaeus.

SWITZERLAND
1736 Haller (1708–77) points out function of bile in digestion of fats. Haller was a very important physiologist.

FRANCE
1736 JL Petit (1674–1760) first to open mastoid and perform a cholecystectomy (an operation on the gall bladder).

GERMANY
1738 Haller becomes first professor of anatomy, botany, and surgery at the newly established University of Göttingen.

GERMANY/NETHERLANDS
1738 Johann Nathaniel Lieberkühn (1711–46) invents reflector microscope.

FRANCE
1739 Sauveur-François Morand makes first excision of hip joint.

GERMANY
1740 Friedrich Hoffmann (1660–1742) describes rubella.

BRITAIN
1740 Thomas Dover invents *Dover's Powder*. He was a buccaneer.
1741–99 William Withering. He uses digitalis extracted from foxgloves to cure dropsy. Now known to be a useful drug in the treatment of heart failure. Is said to have learned about its use from a Shropshire peasant woman.
1741 Archibald Cleland, an army surgeon, catheterizes Eustachian tube.

FRANCE
1741 Nicolas André calls the study of bones orthopedics.

SWEDEN
1742 Celsius invents 100-degree thermometer.
1745 Linnaeus (1707–78) describes *aphasia*.

Bleeding with leeches was common for centuries.

EUROPE
1742 Pandemic influenza in Europe.

THE QUACK

Since people who are ill, incapacitated, or in pain are always eager to try a new remedy—and are more often than not willing to part with money in order to do so—throughout history there have always been those eager to exploit the susceptibilities of these unfortunates and their relatives. Sellers of medicines would appear at fairs and, especially in the United States, toured in covered wagons to proffer their wares.

A tooth-puller provides public entertainment.

Fear of a dread disease encouraged the onlookers to buy drugs to cure syphilis, tuberculosis, infertility, and the like.

Not all touring quacks were complete charlatans, and the occasional one may have helped to improve the lives of his or her customers, if only by the placebo effect. Bottles of various tonics were offered, and, while some may indeed have been genuine herbal cures, most were of no real medicinal value. There was often a good deal of showmanship and trickery involved, with wildly exaggerated claims made for the products—many of which contained alcohol as a solvent and so certainly had an effect of some kind on the user!

New discoveries, such as electricity and radium, were supposedly incorporated into some of the nostrums or implements, and the gullible were lured into parting with their cash for cures and means of rejuvenation, for aphrodisiacs, to grow more hair, or to prevent its turning gray!

Licensing, legislation against unauthorized or unqualified practitioners, controls on unsubstantiated claims for products, and the registration of new drugs and products has limited the impact of quackery today, but there are still many cases of exploitation, in one form or another—and probably always will be!

STILL A MEDICAL MERRY-GO-ROUND

While anatomy and surgical skills were becoming more refined in the "professional" and science-based world of medicine in the 1700s, there were still many practices from the medieval age perpetuated in the medicine readily available to ordinary people. Every fairground or market was likely to include tooth-pullers selling their skills and quacks selling their wares. The choice of eyeglasses bought was based on "trial and error" rather than prescription, and charlatans extorted vast sums of money from a gullible public. Joanna Stephens gathered a princely £5,000 for a supposed means of dissolving kidney stones.

Meanwhile, the deformed provided subjects for many a peepshow—as did the mentally ill. London's Bethlehem Hospital (Bedlam) was open to sightseers so that they could view the insane.

Witches were still seen as a threat, as the Salem witch trials in the USA proved, so "wise women" healers sometimes went in fear of their lives.

BRITAIN
1743 Stephen Hales (1677–1761) publishes treatise on ventilation.
1744 Alexander Monro (1697–1767) publishes handbook of comparative anatomy.
1745 Barbers separated from Barber surgeons in England.

GERMANY
1745 C.G. Kratzenstein uses electrotherapy.

FRANCE
1745 Antoine Deparcieux introduces ideas of "mean expectation of life." In due course mortality and morbidity rates become accepted statistics for insurance purposes.

SWITZERLAND
1747 Haller's (1708–77) *Primae lineae physiologiae* published. First textbook in physiology.

FRANCE
1749 Buffon's (1707–88) *Natural History* published.
1749 Senac's treatise on the heart published.

SWITZERLAND
1749 Meyer orders phthisical patients (suffering a wasting disease of the lungs) to mountains at Appenzell.

BRITAIN
1750 A Sea Bathing Infirmary at Margate becomes the first British hospital for the treatment of TB, founded by John Coakley Lettsom, a well-known London physician.
1750 By now, male doctors regularly attend women in labor.
1752 William Smellie (1697–1763) invents obstetric forceps with a simple lock. *Treatise on Midwifery*.
1752 Sir John Pringle's (1707–82) *Observations on diseases of the army*. It is at Pringle's suggestion at the Battle of Dellinger (1743) that arrangements are made with the French commander that military hospitals on both sides should be considered as sanctuary. Pringle is physician to Earl of Stair in command of the British army.
1753 James Lind's (1716–94) book *A Treatise on the Scurvy* published. It shows that citrus juices can cure the disease.

FRANCE
1752 Réaumur (1683–1757) experiments on digestion in birds.
1753 Jacques Daviel originates modern method for extraction of cataract.

GERMANY
1754 First woman with a medical doctorate graduates at the University of Halle.
1755–1843 Life of Samuel Hahnemann, who advocates treating patients with drugs that produce the same symptoms as the diseases, but later adds that the smaller the dose, the more effective the drug. He is the founder of homeopathy.

Samuel Hahnemann.

SOUTH AFRICA
1755 Smallpox outbreak in Cape Town—it soon spreads inland.
1755 Zinn's atlas of the eye published.

BRITAIN
1756 Percivall Pott *A treatise on ruptures*. Classical surgical work on hernia.
1756 Russel describes "Aleppo boil."

GERMANY
1756 Philip Pfaff, dentist to Frederick the Great, describes casting plaster models from impressions in wax to make false teeth. The craftsmen (usually woodworkers), who fashion the prostheses designed by Adam Brunner, are the forerunners of dental technicians.

SWITZERLAND
1757 Haller's *Elementa physiologiae corporis humani*. One of the most important works in the history of medicine.

BRITAIN
1757 Lind's (1716–94) treatise on naval hygiene published—an essay on how best to preserve the health of seamen in the Royal Navy.
1758 William Battie publishes *Treatise on Madness*.

NETHERLANDS
1758 De Haën employs thermometer in clinical work.

GENETICS

enetics is the science of biological heredity. It studies the transmission and appearance of characteristics in living organisms from parents to offspring. As with many disciplines of medicine, genetics' early surmises are attributed to the great minds of ancient Greece, such as Hippocrates and Aristotle, who both decided that inherited characteristics were passed on through the reproductive organs.

MENDELIAN INHERITANCE

Left: Stamp of Gregor Mendel who used the pea plant (above) as the basis of a path-breaking study on biological heredity.

It was not until the 19th century that the German–Czech Augustinian monk, Gregor Johann Mendel (1822–84), made the first important scientific discoveries concerning heredity. Mendel combined his formal training in statistics with an acute sense of observation in a study of pea plants. He found that though new plants inherited the characteristics of their parents, the expression of these characteristics were not as a blend of both parents, but as of either one of the two. He also calculated that the statistical probability of a particular inherited characteristic being expressed in the subsequent generation was 25 percent. At that time, the scientific world was overshadowed by Charles Darwin's seminal work *On the Origin of Species*, and Mendel did not get his just recognition. About 20 years later, Hugo de Vries (1848–1935), in his book *Intracellular Pangenesis*, posited that hereditary traits were carried as bodily particles (he called

them "pangenes"), and transmitted via the reproductive process. The word "gene," derived from "pangene" by Wilhelm Johannsen (1857–1927), conveyed his departure from the Pangenesis theory. Johannsen's thesis was based on his own work on plant seeds. In the beginning of the 20th century, Mendel's work was "rediscovered" by de Vries and others, and its significance recognized as the law of Mendelian inheritance. At the International Conference on Plant Hybridization in London (1906), William Bateson (1861–1926), a strong backer of Mendel's theory, popularized the term "genetics" for the study of inheritance.

Hugo de Vries.

BRITAIN
1759 John Bard operates for extra-uterine pregnancy.

USA
1760 Act to regulate practice of medicine in New York City.
1760 William Shippen Jr. lectures on anatomy in Philadephia.

ITALY
1761 Morgagni's (1682–1771) *De sedibus.*

AUSTRIA
1761 Auenbrugger's *Inventum novum* published (not appreciated until translated by Corvisant, 1808). He finds that by tapping gently on the chest, fluid in the chest cavity as well as other signs of disease could be detected. This notion of "percussion" is developed after watching his innkeeper father tapping beer casks.

Leopold Auenbrugger.

1762 Von Plenciz's theory of *contagium animatum. Opera medico-physica* shows how Leeuwehoek's *animalculae* relate to contagious diseases.

SWEDEN
1763 Botanist and medic, Carl von Linné, or Linnaeus, publishes his classification of disease, *Genera morborum.*

FRANCE
1764 Antoine Louis, a surgeon of repute, claims to have introduced digital compression for hemorrhage.

SWEDEN
1764 Von Rosenstein of Uppsala's book on children's diseases and their treatment: Influences development of modern pediatrics.

FRANCE
1766 Desault's bandage for fractures introduced.
1766 Cavendish discovers hydrogen.

AUSTRIA
1767 Frank's statistics show importance of public health measures. After his treatise in **1779** he becomes known as the "Father of Public Hygiene."

Johann Peter Frank.

EUROPE
1767 Influenza pandemic in Europe.

BRITAIN
1767 Charles White resects shoulder joint and in **1768** resects head of humerus.
1768 Whytt describes tuberculous meningitis. Observations on the dropsy in the brain.
1768 Lind's important treatise on tropical medicine: *An essay on diseases incidental to Europeans in hot climates.*
1769 Pott's treatise *On fractures and dislocations* published. His pioneer work stresses need for early setting of fracture. Describes fracture of lower tibia, fibula (ankle). Also known as Pott's Fracture.

GERMANY
1768 Wolff's classic on embryology of chick's intestines.

USA
1770 Pennsylvania quarantine act.

FRANCE
1770 Abbé de l'Épée invents sign language for deaf-mutes.
1771–1802 Bichat shows how individual tissue can be diseased. (Morgagino had dealt with whole body organs.) *Anatomie générale, apliquée à la physiologie et à médicine*—an important book.

EAST INDIES
1770–71 Smallpox sweeps through East Indies, possibly killing as many as three million people.

BRITAIN
1771 John Hunter's treatise on teeth published: *On the diseases of the teeth.* He lectures on theory and practice of surgery.
1771 Priestley and Scheele isolate a gas that Joseph Priestley calls "phlogisticated dephlogisticated air," later termed "oxygen" by Lavoisier. Priestley also discovers nitrous oxide and makes observations on different kinds of air (**1772**) and ammonia (**1774**).
1772 Rutherford discovers nitrogen.

THE FRUIT FLY

Chromosomes—sub-nuclear bodies found in all living cells except red blood cells and platelets—had been visually identified in the 19th century. Chromosomes occur in pairs, and each human cell has 46 chromosomes—23 pairs. One of these pairs determines sex: Nettie Maria Stevens (1861–1912) and Edmund Beecher Wilson (1856–1939) are credited with pinpointing the distinction between the male and the female (denoted XY and XX, respectively) chromosome pair. In 1906, the American Thomas Hunt Morgan (1866–1945) postulated that the information that controls patterns of inheritance resides in chromosomes. Morgan brought the fruit fly (*Drosophila melanogaster*)—possibly the most completely studied cellular organism in biology—into the net of genetics. His extensive investigation of this insect in the famous "fly room" at Columbia University substantiated much of the Mendelian patterns of inheritance. In 1933, Jean Brachet (1909–98) identified the presence of the DNA (deoxyribonucleic acid) molecule in a chromosome, and RNA (ribonucleic acid) in the cytoplasm, the part of the cell outside the nucleus but within the cell membrane. Soon thereafter, in 1941, Edward Lawrie Tatum (1909–75) and George Wells Beadle (1903–89) determined that genes, which are subunits of DNA, were actually instructional codes transmitted via RNA to amino acids in the cytoplasm, which, in turn, based on these instructions, went on to form specific proteins and glyco-proteins. By now, it was beyond question that the material of heredity lay in the chromosome, and the era of classical genetics came to an end. Further answers lay in the structure and workings of DNA.

Nettie Maria Stevens.

Above: *Drosophila melanogaster*, or the fruit fly.
Left: Thomas Hunt Morgan.

ITALY
1772 Anatomist Antonio Scarpa discovers ear labyrinth.

USA
1772 New Jersey act regulates medical practice.
1773 First insane asylum in U.S. at Williamsburg, Virginia.

SWEDEN
1774 Scheele discovers chlorine. **1776** Scheele and Bergmann discover uric acid in bladder stones.

BRITAIN
1773 Charles White urges cleanliness in midwifery to prevent puerperal fever and pioneers asepsis.
1774 William Hunter's *The Anatomy of the human gravid utuerus exhibited in figures*: Fine anatomical atlas with life-size plates of human uterus.
1774 Jesty, a Dorset farmer, vaccinates wife and two sons with cowpox direct from an infected udder.
1775 Pott describes occupational cancer—sweeps' boys develop cancer of scrotum through exposure to soot.
1776 Cruikshank discovers severed nerves will grow together.

WORLD
1776–1805 Scarlatina pandemic in both hemispheres.

AUSTRIA
1776 Plenck's classification of skin diseases published, *Doctrina de morbus cutaneis*. Divides 115 skin diseases into 14 classes.

BRITAIN
1776 Jasser operates successfully on mastoid.
1777 John Howard's investigation of prisons and hospitals published.
1777 Huddart—first reliable record of color blindness, written to Joseph Priestley.
1779 Pott describes deformity and paralysis from tuberculous spinal caries: Pott's disease of the spine.

FRANCE
1777 Lavoisier describes exchange of gases in respiration.

GERMANY
1778 Von Siebold performs symphysiotomy (cutting through pubic bones to help delivery).

INDONESIA
1779 Bylon of Java describes dengue fever.

FRANCE
1779 Mesmer's memoir on animal magnetism published. The term "mesmerism" is derived from his name and becomes basis for treatment by suggestion.
1779 Housz discovers that plants give off carbon dioxide.

USA
1780 Benjamin Franklin invents bifocal lenses.

BRITAIN
1781 Henry Cavendish (born 1731 in France, died in Britain) determines composition of water; in **1784** he discovers hydrogen.

GERMANY
1781 Kant's *Critique of Pure Reason* published.

FRANCE
1783–85 Chemist, Lavoisier decomposes water, proves that combustion needs only oxygen, and overthrows theory of phlogiston (an imaginary fire element).

Antoine Lavoisier.

AUSTRIA
1783 Austria separates surgeons from barbers.

ITALY
1784 Cotugno discovers cerebro-spinal fluid.

BRITAIN
1785 Withering's treatise on the foxglove.
1785 John Hunter discovers collateral circulation and introduces proximal ligation (tying up a bleeding artery) in aneurysm (a swelling of the artery). This closing off of arteries saves many limbs from amputation.
1785 Physician to British Fleet, Sir Gilbert Blane publishes *Observations on diseases incident to seamen*. A supporter of Lind, he effectively improves conditions in the Navy.
1785 Withering publishes *An account of the*

TRACING GENETIC DISORDERS

A vital step in this direction was the ascertainment of the double-helix nature of DNA folding by James D. Watson (b.1928) and Francis Crick (1916–2004). Scientists now focused their attention on cracking the DNA gene code, and the 1970s saw the sequencing of individual genes in simple bacteria as well as in humans. Once the basis of inheritance had been firmly established, the natural logic was that diseases that ran in families must also follow the rules of genetics. This idea was pursued by Victor A. McKusick (1921–2008) at the Johns Hopkins Hospital, Baltimore, where he studied rare familial disorders such as Marfan's syndrome. Newfound understanding of genetics impacted several fields in medicine, principally hereditary metabolic disorders, developmental anomalies, and cancer. Alfred G. Knudson Jr.'s (b.1922) "two-hit" hypothesis (1978) was an effort to explain the differences in inherited and sporadically acquired, apparently identical eye tumor (retinoblastoma). He suggested that in inherited retinoblastomas, one genetic change is inherited and therefore present

The double helix DNA strand.

in all cells. The second genetic aberration (mutation) occurs only in the retinal cell that turns cancerous. Inherited tumors would occur at an earlier age, would be multiple or bilateral, and there would be greater risk of developing other tumors. The "two-hit" hypothesis has well stood the test of time, and the genetics of cancer has today developed to a stage where it has been conclusively shown that all cancers have a genetic basis, either inherited or mutations that have occurred in life, or a combination of both. The stage was now set for innovative thinking, techniques, and strategies all trying to understand the effect of the genetic code and its aberrations.

ANALYSIS AND TESTING

By the 1990s, complete genomes of simple organisms such as yeast and roundworms had been deciphered. At the beginning of that decade, the Human Genome Project, the most staggeringly ambitious endeavor in the field of genetics, was launched. Its goal was to map the entire human genome.

In the meantime, new discoveries in the field of protein synthesis have led to far-reaching consequences. Since some proteins are produced by specific combinations of genetic code, scientists have been able to follow trails from protein to the genetic origin of defects such as sickle cell disease and thalassemia. Genetic inheritance has also become the basis of successful organ transplants, for it is well known now that live transplants from closely related individuals—who bear the closest gene similarity to the patient—are less likely to be rejected by the patient's body.

Early genetic analysis included the karyotyping test that was used for detecting abnormalities by charting an individual's chromosomal component. This was adequate for highlighting large chromosomal defects, but it could not reveal smaller genetic anomalies, and it is now regarded as a relatively unsophisticated test. New, more advanced methods—such as in-situ hybridization, polymerase chain reaction, and DNA micro-array techniques—enable scientists to pinpoint a specific genetic abnormality quickly and accurately, instead of only being able to point to a range of possible abnormalities.

DNA fingerprinting or profiling, originally developed in the 1980s but now increasingly refined, can not only identify an individual by traces of one's unique DNA, but can also show whether or not two persons are related, and to what degree. With today's tests able to analyze tiny amounts of genetic material, DNA can be used to settle paternity or maternity disputes, as well as to identify crime suspects.

foxglove about his use of digitalis to cure dropsy.

Foxglove—source of digitalis; its effects were explored by William Withering.

1786 John Hunter publishes *A Treatise on the Venereal Disease*. Hunter inoculates himself with pus from a patient with gonorrhea, who also has syphilis: This Hunter does not know. When Hunter develops a syphlitic chancre (sore), he thinks it confirms his theory that both diseases are caused by the same pathogen—a confusion not cleared up until 50 years later!

1786 Lettsom describes drug habit and alcoholism.

ITALY
1787 Paolo Mascagni publishes atlas of the lymphatics.

EUROPE
1788 Influenza pandemic.

BRITAIN
1789 John Hunter describes intussusception, a form of bowel obstruction.

FRANCE
1789–99 French Revolution. Chemist Lavoisier guillotined **1794**.

USA
1790 Medical journal published in New York.

1791–99 Baynham of Virginia operates for extra-uterine pregnancy.

POLAND/GERMANY
1791 Soemmering publishes first volume of his anatomy.

GERMANY
1792–1821 Frank's *De curandis hominum morbis epitome* published in 7 volumes.

USA
1792 Cotton gin (Eli Whitney).
1793 Carey describes yellow fever epidemic in Philadelphia.

BRITAIN
1793 Bell differentiates between gonorrhea and syphilis.
1793 Baillie's *Morbid Anatomy* published, covering some of the most important parts of the human body.
1794 John Hunter publishes *Treatise on the blood inflammation and gunshot wounds*.

FRANCE
1793–1815 Treatment of wounded in the Napoleonic wars leads to advances in surgery. A great military surgeon, present at all Napoleon's battles, Dominique-Jean Larrey performs over 200 amputations in 24 hours during Russian campaign. He develops "flying ambulances"— wagons to carry stretchers during battle and a transport system to bring speedier attention to wounded. His care for patients on both sides will eventually form basis of the Red Cross.

GERMANY
1794 Gumpertz publishes Greek text of Asclepiades.
1794 John Hunter describes transplantation of animal tissues.

ITALY
1794 Antonio Scarpa's *Tabulae nevrologicae* illustrates his important work on nerves of the heart.

USA
1796 Yellow fever in Boston.

BRITAIN
1796 Jenner vaccinates James Phipps with material from a cowpox sore.

Jenner performing a vaccination.

THE HUMAN GENOME PROJECT

Preliminary work leading up to the Human Genome Project started in 1984. By 1989, the USA Department of Energy and the National Health Institute had set up the necessary organizational infrastructure to facilitate one of the most path-breaking initiatives in the history of medical science, i.e. to identify and sequence the human DNA's 20–25,000 genes, made up of three billion chemical base pairs. The project got off the blocks in 1990, involving researchers at universities and institutions across the USA, UK, France, Germany, Japan, and China. DNA was provided by volunteers whose identity was kept confidential. At the end of its 13-year course, not only did the project accomplish more than its core goals, but it had many other significant spin-offs. Legislation on ethical and practical issues, such as the Genetic Privacy Act and extension of the Americans with Disabilities Act, were promulgated. In 1997, UNESCO adopted the Universal Declaration on the Human Genome and Human Rights. New technologies, as they developed, were made commercially available. Parallel projects, like the Microbial Genome Project (1994), were set up.

Maps of the human chromosomes began to be regularly produced from 1995 onward. The first chromosome was completely sequenced in 1999. In 2000, a rough draft of the human genome, comprising 90 percent of the sequencing, was ready. In 2003, 99 percent of the genome had been sequenced, with less than 400 gaps, and an accuracy rate of 99.99 percent for every 10,000 chemical base pair. The Human Genome Project was complete, two years ahead of schedule. Moreover, at a total cost of $2.7 billion, it had cost less than the original estimate of $3 billion. Along the way, it had mapped the genomes of a few other organisms, including the mouse and the rat.

With such a wide-ranging, accurate scope, data on the human genome has been likened to "all the pages of a manual needed to make the human body." Scientists are now engaged in the quest of reading and understanding this manual, a mammoth task in itself. It is estimated that drugs based on this research are still 10 to 15 years away, but the inevitable benefits of highly individualized and effective medical care resulting from the undertaking will be unprecedented.

The Human Genome Project set up to identify and sequence
all the genes in human DNA.

1797 Wollaston discovers uric acid in gouty joints. Writes *On gouty and urinary conditions*.
1797 Currie publishes reports on hydrotherapy in typhoid fever.
1797 Rollo advocates meat diet in diabetes.

USA
1797 *Medical Repository* (New York) published.
1797–99 Yellow fever in Philadelphia.

BRITAIN
1798 Malthus's *Essay on Population*.
1798 John Haslam describes general paralysis of the insane. *Observations on insanity*—now known to be due to syphilis.
1798 Dalton describes color blindness.
1798 Jenner's *Inquiry* published.
1798–1808 Willan's treatise on skin diseases published. *On cutaneous diseases*.
1799 De Carro introduces Jennerian vaccination.

USA
1799 Congress passes quarantine act.
1800 Waterhouse introduces Jennerian vaccination in New England.

BRITAIN
1800s Industrial Revolution: Many work in difficult conditions in factories and mines.
1800 Sir Humphry Davy discovers anesthetic effect of nitrous oxide ("laughing gas") and suggests its use during surgical operations—not effected until 1804.
1801 Thomas Young describes astigmatism.
1802 Heberden's *Commentaries:* Rolliston said it had the distinction of being the last important treatise written in Latin.

FRANCE
1800 Founder of modern histology and tissue pathology, Bichat publishes *Traité des membranes*.
1800 Cuvier's *Comparative Anatomy* published.
19th century Bloodletting still a popular treatment. Forty million leeches imported into France in one year.

EUROPE
1800s Silver amalgam, a refinement of filling materials in dentistry, is first discovered by Europeans.

BRITAIN/USA
Early 19th century Many water supplies

polluted. Sewage finds its way from cesspools into wells and waterways. Garbage pollutes the streets or is in open dumps.

Drinking water carried many diseases, such as cholera.

FRANCE
1801 Pinel publishes psychiatric treatise. He is credited with reforming the treatment of the insane from prison-like conditions to hospital-type care.
1801 Bichat's *Anatomie générale* published. He revolutionizes descriptive anatomy.

BRITAIN
1803 Percival publishes code of medical ethics. UK and USA medical professions adopt much of this in their ethical works.

ITALY
1804 Scarpa describes arteriosclerosis (hardening of arteries).

GERMANY
1806 Sertürner isolates morphine.
1807 Compulsory vaccination introduced in Bavaria and Hesse.

BRITAIN
1809 Allan Burns describes various cardiac conditions.

Medical surgery has been in existence since prehistoric times. The earliest procedures were performed on the skull (Russia, *c.* 12,000 BCE) and on the teeth (Indian subcontinent, *c.* 7,000 BCE). Though procedures improved through the centuries, the results were so uncertain that they were almost always used as a last resort of treatment. Success rates were poor; instruments, like quills, knives, drills, saws, hooks, forceps, and pinchers were often crude and imprecise; and knowledge of physiology and anatomy was insufficient. Breakthroughs in the 19th and 20th centuries provided the means to effectively tackle surgery's three big problems: pain, bleeding, and infection. From the latter half of the 20th century, driven by rapid and revolutionary advances in technology, modern surgery has become a highly sophisticated and precise science, equipped to address a vast variety of conditions with minimal risk and discomfort to the patient.

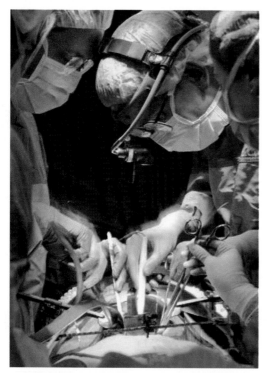

Above: Modern surgery encompasses the learning of centuries and has made astounding progress in recent years—but disease is still ever-present.
Right: Heart surgery in progress.

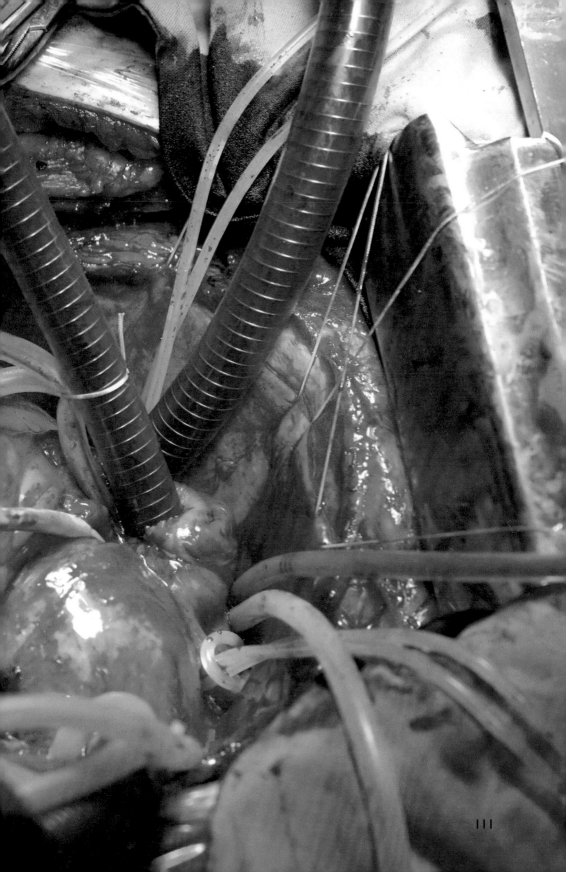

MICRO AND KEYHOLE SURGERY

Microsurgery utilizes an operating microscope to magnify operation fields and assist in delicate surgical procedures such as plastic surgery, middle ear surgery, brain surgery, and ophthalmic surgery. Microsurgery is critical in reconnecting blood vessels and nerve ends of dismembered limbs and in vascular surgery.

Keyhole or laparoscopic surgery, on the other hand, refers to any surgical technique that uses very small incisions to gain access to the target organ. In the abdomen, for example, access is usually gained by small incisions of about 0.2 inches (5 mm) in length. Several such incisions, referred to as ports, are required for insufflations of the abdomen with gas (usually carbon dioxide), insertion of the endoscope (a long slender viewing instrument), and placing a device for visualization of the operative field.

Laparoscopic surgery has been especially useful in areas where conventional surgery requires large incisions and prolonged immobilization. Apart from the abdomen and the chest, it is employed for the urinary tract and joints. Today, major tumor and organ resections are also being done. Reduced need of painkillers, early postoperative mobilization, and avoidance of complications due to anesthesia are some of the benefits.

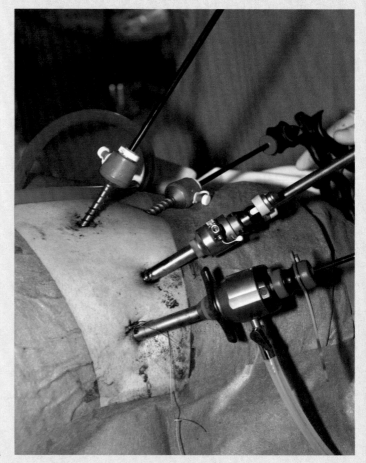

A laparoscopic surgery involving minimal invasive techniques.

USA

1809 McDowell of Kentucky performs ovariotomy (removal of ovary) with help of his nephew. Mrs. Crawford arrives for her operation resting her large tumor (at first believed to be a pregnancy) on the horn of her horse's saddle.

FRANCE

1810–19 Gall and Spurzheim publish extraordinary treatise on the nervous system. They teach that the shape and irregularities of the skull are projections of the underlying brain and indicate mental characteristics. Gives rise to popular pseudo-science of phrenology.

1812 Napoleon's surgeon, Baron Larrey, first uses local anesthesia. During the retreat from Moscow, he amputates limbs painlessly after freezing them.

Dominique-Jean Larrey could amputate a leg in 15 seconds.

BRITAIN

1811 Sir Charles Bell describes motor functions of spinal nerve roots: *Idea of a new anatomy of the brain.*

1812 Davy knighted. Among his discoveries are sodium, potassium, boron, and acetylene. He investigates many chemical reactions and invents miner's safety lamp.

1812 Miranda Stewart Barry, dressed as a man, attends Edinburgh University as James Barry and qualifies as a doctor in 1812, aged 15. After serving with the Duke of Wellington and becoming assistant surgeon at the Battle of Waterloo in 1815, she becomes Inspector General in 1858. Only after her death is it discovered that James Barry was a woman.

USA

1812 Rush writes first American book on psychiatry, *Medical inquiries and observations upon the diseases of the mind.*

FRANCE

1815–19 Laënnec invents stethoscope.

BELGIUM

1815 Battle of Waterloo.

1815 Apothecaries Act.

1817–30 Pandemic of cholera: Frst of many this century, it spreads from India and China through Europe and USA.

BRITAIN

1817 John King's book on extra-uterine pregnancy.

1817 Parkinson describes Parkinson's disease: *An essay on the shaking palsy.*

USA

1817 Plantson invents dental plate.

FRANCE

1818–19 Pelletier and Caventou isolate strychnine and quinine.

NETHERLANDS

1818 Reimer introduces frozen sections.

ITALY

1818 Amici: First achromatic microscope.

BRITAIN

1819 Bostock describes hay fever.

USA

1820 First U.S. Pharmacopeia.

1820–21 Philadelphia: College of Apothecaries opens; College of Pharmacy founded, first in USA.

1821–25 William Beaumont treats a war patient evidently dying of a close shotgun blast. He survives with permanent exterior opening to his stomach. Beaumont makes studies of gastric juices on this patient.

FRANCE

1820 Coindet uses iodine in goiter.

1822–40 Magendie, pioneer in physiology and pharmacology, demonstrates Bell's law of spinal nerve roots. He studies spinal canal and nervous system and analyzes actions of drugs.

François Magendie.

1824 Flourens publishes work on cerebral physiology.

BRITAIN

1824 Prout investigates acidity of gastric juice.

NON-INVASIVE SURGERY

Today's surgical procedures do not need incisions, use of body passages, or violation of the skin. Instead, lasers or ultrasound waves are used to burn or crush tissue, for example to treat hemorrhoids, enlarged prostates or prostate cancer, fibroids of the uterus, superficial skin blemishes, and ophthalmic problems. The surgery is performed in a sterile environment with all the precautions of a conventional procedure. Another common application of ultrasound is to pulverize kidney stones. In this case, the patient sits in a water-filled tub, and a lithotripter machine is used to generate shock waves through the water, shattering the stones into tiny pieces that can be passed in urine.

NATURAL ORIFICE TRANSLUMINAL SURGERY (NOTES)

NOTES is the current frontier in minimally invasive surgery wherein access is obtained through natural orifices. The transvaginal approach has been successful in obtaining abdominal access to cholecystectomy in women, and the transgastric approach has been used for cholecystectomy as well as appendisectomies. Another approach is through the urinary bladder. NOTES eliminates abdominal incisions and has the potential advantages of cutting down of antibiotic and anesthesia requirements and duration of hospitalization. Other benefits include minimizing the possibility of abdominal wound infections and herniations, better postoperative pulmonary and diaphragmatic function, and allowing scarless abdominal surgery. NOTES could be the next major paradigm shift in surgery, just as laparoscopy was during the 1980s and 1990s.

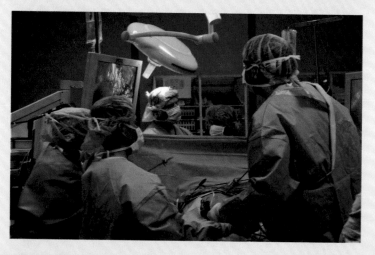

A laparoscopic cholecystectomy being performed on a Vietnamese patient aboard *Mercy* during the Pacific Partnership mission in the Socialist Republic of Vietnam, 2008.

RADIO FREQUENCY ABLATION (RFA)

RFA, or radio-frequency ablation, involves the insertion into the body of probes through which high-frequency radio waves are transmitted. These raise the temperature of internal tissues and can be used to burn away a tumor, an improperly functioning nerve discharge, or a malformed vessel. The procedure is particularly used to deal with liver tumors and liver resections, as well as tumors of the kidney, breast, and lung. It is also popular in the treatment of cardiac arrhythmias and varicose veins.

FRANCE

1825 Bouillaud describes and localizes aphasia (loss of speech due to brain damage).

1825–1893 Charcot, important neurologist and a great French clinician, researches epilepsy and other neurological diseases. One of his pupils is Sigmund Freud. He works at Salpêtrière hospital in Paris, giving theatrical presentations of patients to demonstrate his cases.

1826 Laënnec gives classical description of bronchitis and other thoracic diseases.

1826 Dupuytren describes congenital dislocation of hip joint. Very important in anatomy and pathology. He also performs daring feats of surgery and devises ingenious instruments.

1827 Seglas invents endoscope.

BRITAIN

1827 Richard Bright describes disease of the kidney, since known as "Bright's disease."

1827 Lord Lister born.

1828 Blundell reports first human-to-human blood transfusion that patient survives.

Joseph Lister.

ITALY

1827 Cuthbert invents reflecting microscope.

ESTONIA

1827–31 Von Baer discovers mammalian ovum.

USA

1828–1917 Dr. Andrew Taylor Still: Father of osteopathy.

GERMANY

1828 Wöhler synthesizes urea; forerunner of organic chemistry.

FRANCE

1829 Braille introduces printing for the blind.

BRITAIN

1830 Lister perfects achromatic microscope.

ITALY

1830 Priessnitz, a Silesian peasant, is run over by a wagon and given up as a hopeless case. Using wet compresses and drinking vast amounts of water, he recovers and institutes his "water cure for disease."

USA

1831–1915 Greene Vardiman Black, leading reformer of dentistry, devises a foot engine enabling dentists to keep hands free while powering drill. Black suggests dental caries and periodontal diseases are infections brought about by bacteria. In 1960s, scientific evidence finally confirms this.

USA/FRANCE/GERMANY

1831 Guthrie (U.S.), Soubeiran (France), and Von Liebig (Germany) discover chloroform independently.

1832 In Germany, Liebig discovers chloral: A widely used sedative.

BRITAIN

1832 Hodgkin, Quaker and philanthropist, describes a malignant disease of lymph glands, now known as Hodgkin's disease.

FRANCE

1832 Robiquet isolates Codein.

WORLD

1832 Cholera spreads out to circle the globe, from Asia to Europe and then the USA, where there are 3 outbreaks during century.

BRITAIN

1832 Anatomy Act passed.

1832 British Medical Association founded.

1833 Marshall Hall investigates reflex action.

USA

1833 William Beaumont publishes experiments on digestion.

FRANCE

1834 Dumas obtains and names pure chloroform.

1835 Pierre Charles Alexandre Louis founds medical statistics.

1835 Cruveilhier (1791–1874) describes disseminated sclerosis (now known as multiple sclerosis).

IRELAND

1835 Robert James Graves' classical account of exophthalmic goiter now known as Graves disease.

BRITAIN

1835 Malcolmson describes beri-beri.

ROBOTICS IN SURGERY

The era "surgery from anywhere" commenced with the advent of robotic surgery. A surgeon can remotely guide robots in surgical procedures without being actually present at the venue where the surgery is performed. This enables access to rare expertise, without the patient having to travel to the place where the surgeon practices. As yet not a completely accepted technique, the possibilities for robotic surgery are limitless, allowing the real-time sharing of surgical know-how in all corners of the globe. Robotic surgery promises to be to surgeons what telemedicine is to a physician and a pathologist.

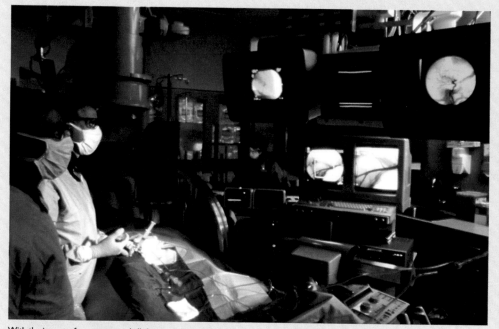

With the impact of computers and all the new technology, certain areas of surgery are now being done by "remote control."

INTERVENTIONAL RADIOLOGY

This sub-branch of radiology (the branch of medicine dealing with X-rays and other imaging radiation) uses catheters, balloons, and stents— narrow tubes inserted into blood vessels or other body passages—in order to remove obstructions, widen narrowed ducts, and help treat tumors by stopping blood supply to them. Interventional radiologists stent a variety of ducts, especially the bile duct, as well as all vessels in the body except coronary arteries, which are treated by interventional cardiologists. Blocking or occluding selective blood vessels results in a less bloody surgery, and at times, the occlusion of blood supply is in itself the treatment of a tumor.

1836 Richard Bright describes acute yellow atrophy of liver. Investigates mechanism of urinary secretion.

BRITAIN
1836 Marsh's test for arsenic introduced: Famous in many murder trials.

GERMANY
1836 Schwann discovers pepsin in stomach; in **1837** discovers yeast cell. Regarded by many as founder of germ theory of putrification and permentation; in **1841** he shows bile essential for digestion. Important work on nerves and muscles.

USA
1837 Gerhard shows that typhus and typhoid are separate diseases.

BRITAIN
1837 Introduction of registration of deaths introduced in England and Wales.

GERMANY
1837 Schönlein's *Peliosis Rheumatica* describes skin condition of purpura, now known by his name.
1838 Schleiden describes plant cells.

FRANCE
1838 Epileptic children in Paris are removed from Hospital of the Incurably Ill and given some education.

AUSTRIA
1839 Skoda's treatise on percussion and auscultation lays groundwork for diagnosis today.

USA
1839–40 The Baltimore College of Dental Surgery: First dental school in the world.

FRANCE
1840s Brown-Séquard, a founder of endocrinology, demonstrates function of suprarenal gland. He repeats Galen's experiment of cutting spinal cord; is first to work out physiology of spinal card and demonstrate "crossing" of its sensory fibers. Tries to develop testicular juices as rejuvenating agents for men.

BRITAIN
1840s England pioneers principles and practices of public health, passing the Public Health Acts that bring about cleaner water and mains drainage.
1840 Basedow describes syndromes of exophthalmic goitre—eye protrusion, neck swelling, palpitations—known in UK as Graves' disease.
1841 Pharmaceutical Society of Great Britain founded following a meeting at the Crown and Anchor Tavern in the Strand, London.
1842 Chadwick's report demonstrates link between environmental conditions and public health.
1843 Simpson, Huguier, and Kiwisch introduce uterine sound.

USA
1842 Long operates with ether anesthesia.
1843 Holmes's *Contagiousness of puerperal fever*—a medical classic.

BRITAIN
1844 Hutchinson invents spirometer to measure air capacity of lungs.

IRELAND
1845 Francis Rynd invents an instrument to give hypodermic infusions.

GERMANY
1845–58 Virchow discovers much about human cell, thrombosis, phlebitis, embolism. Establishes diagnosis of leukemia (in **1845** Virchow and Bennett describe leukemia). Creates modern pathology.

USA
1846 Sims invents a vaginal speculum.

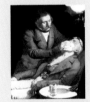

Morton using ether on a patient.

1846 William Thomas Morton uses ether to put patient to sleep during dental operation. Demonstrates this at Mass General Hospital.

FRANCE
1846 François Magendie, pioneer in physiology

REGENERATIVE MEDICINE

STEM CELL THERAPY

The stem cell is defined as a precursor cell, or a cell whose daughter cell may divide and differentiate into other cell types, such as blood cells, tissues, and organs. Stem cells are classified as embryonic or adult. Embryonic stem cells, as the name suggests, are derived from the embryo. Adult stem cells nestle in specific organs. Their task is to maintain, repair, and renew the differentiated cells of that organ. Stem cell differentiation is controlled by chemical factors, which, in some cases, can be manipulated. Using this property, stem cells today are being transplanted and used in a variety of unique ways to repair damaged heart and nerve tissue and replenish ablated bone marrow, insulin-producing islet cells of Langerhans in the pancreas, and cells in the eye and skin. Though stem cell research has a long way to go, it promises to alter treatment systems in a major way.

ORGAN TRANSPLANT

Tissue and organ replacement is steadily becoming a mode of addressing problems of bodily deteriorations amongst aging and sick populations. Approximately 500,000 Americans undergo such transplants annually. Although organ transplants began in 1954 with the first kidney transplant, only in the 1980s did the method gain impetus with cornea, heart, single and double lung, bone marrow, and liver transplants.

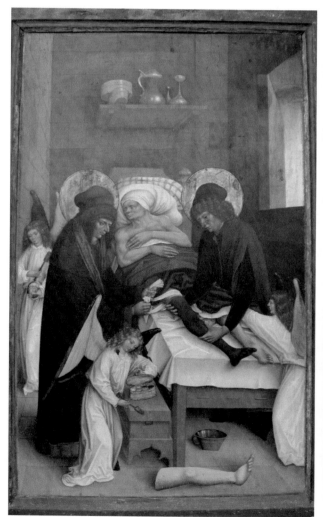

A 16th-century painting of the 3rd-century saints Cosmas and Damian miraculously transplanting the leg of a Moor onto the body of the Roman deacon Justinian, who had lost his leg due to gangrene.

and pharmacology, studies spinal nerves.

1846–54 Bernard describes digestive function of pancreas; in **1848** discovers glycogenic function of the liver in sugar metabolism; in **1849** produces diabetes by puncture of the fourth ventricle; and in **1851** describes vasomotor function of sympathetic nervous system. In **1854** he discovers function of vasodilator nerves of brain.

AUSTRIA
1847 Semmelweis shows septicemia to be cause of puerperal fever.

BRITAIN
1847 Simpson gives chloroform to a "Highland boy who spoke only Gaelic." Later uses chloroform for relief of pain during childbirth.

USA
1847 First school for mentally retarded founded in Massachusetts.

GERMANY
1848 Du Bois-Reymond's treatise on animal electricity.

BRITAIN
1848 Public Health Act creates general and local boards of health.

GERMANY
1848 Helmholtz locates source of animal heat in muscles.

NORWAY
1849 Danielssen and Boeck publish studies on leprosy, providing impetus for a national, government-sponsored research center.

USA
1849 The first English woman to graduate as a doctor: Elizabeth Blackwell at Geneva Medical School of New York.

BRITAIN
1849 Addison describes pernicious anemia and a disease of the adrenals—Addison's anemia and Addison's disease.

USA
1850 William Detmold opens abscess of the brain.

GERMANY
1850 Waller states "law of degeneration" of spinal nerves.
1850 Helmholtz measures the velocity of the nerve current.
1851 Helmholtz invents ophthalmoscope, vital diagnostic instrument for examination of eye interior.
1851 Ludwig investigates nerves of salivary secretion.

FRANCE
1851 Pravaz introduces hypodermic syringe.
1852 Mathijsen introduces Plaster-of-Paris bandages.

USA
1852 American Pharmaceutical Association founded.

SWITZERLAND
1852 Kölliker's treatise on histology (organic tissues), *Handbuch der Gwewbelenhre*.

RUSSIA
1852 Pirogoff employs frozen sections in his *Anatome topigraphica*.

BELGIUM
1852 International Congress of Hygiene.

BRITAIN
1853 Queen Victoria accepts chloroform during the birth of her seventh child, Prince Leopold. She publicly announces how very grateful she is for the relief this gave her, thus allowing anesthesia to become more acceptable.
1853 Burnham: First successful abdominal hysterectomy.
1854 1,400 cases of cholera in London; 618 deaths. John Snow ends the epidemic by demonstrating that only those who drank from the Broad Street water pump contracted the disease. This pump is closed down and the outbreak ceases.

John Snow.

USA
1854 Goodyear rubber dental plate.

BIONIC PROSTHESIS

Regenerative medicine has not been able to address functionally and structurally complex organs such as the eye, ear, and hand. However, acute knowledge gained by studying the characteristics and functions of the human body has been applied to the design of non-organic devices. For example, material science and electronics have combined to produce the bionic hand, bionic eye, and bionic ear. The bionic hand, developed as a result of 20 years of engineering effort, made history when it was provided to a child in 2000. Since then, stronger and bigger models have been manufactured for adults. The device comprises battery-operated motors that assist in its mechanical functions. The bionic ear resulted from the pioneering research of Professor Graeme Clark in the late 1960s. The bionic eye is currently awaiting clinical trials. Research has a long way to go to have a significant positive impact.

Above: The ancient Egyptians of the Third Intermediate Period developed this wood and leather prosthetic toe to facilitate an amputee's ability to walk.
Below: A United States Army soldier plays foosball with two prosthetic arms.

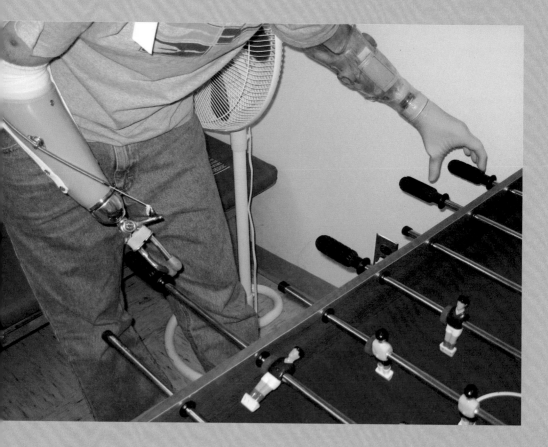

GERMANY
1854 Rudolf Virchow (1821-1902) describes neuroglia (connective tissues in nerve centers and retina).

1855 Singing teacher, Garcia, invents laryngoscope for examination of vocal chords.

FRANCE
1857 Bouchet performs intubation of larynx for croup.

GERMANY
1857 Graefe introduces operation for a squint-eye.

1858 Niemann isolates cocaine.

1858 Virchow publishes *Die Cellular Pathologie*: Foundation of cellular pathology.

FRANCE
1858 Marey's discoveries help doctors, with some degree of accuracy, to assess absolute pressure of blood in a human artery.

BRITAIN
1858 Medical Act states that doctors in Britain must be registered and complete a minimum standard of education before being included on a register of qualified medical practitioners.

GERMANY
1859 Kolbe synthesizes salicylic acid: Acetylsalicylic acid is aspirin.

1859 Kirchhoff and Bunsen develop recording spectroscope.

FRANCE
1860 Menière describes aural vertigo, a form of severe giddiness known as Menière's disease.

GERMANY
1860 Von Tröltsch devises first modern mastoid operation.

NETHERLANDS
1860 Donders, who studied many eye defects, introduces spectacles for astigmatism and in **1862** publishes studies on astigmatism and presbyopia.

AUSTRIA
1861 Semmelweis publishes book on childhood fever.

USA
1861–65 American Civil War. Many outbreaks of communicable diseases.

FRANCE
1861 Broca reports that speech control is located in left frontal lobe of brain.

1861 Pasteur discovers anaerobic bacteria and in **1863** that bacteria are destroyed by heat; he invents pasteurization.

GERMANY
1861 Schultze defines protoplasm and cell.

1862 Felix Hoppe Seyler discovers hemoglobin.

1862 Bruns performs first operation with laryngoscope. Lewin also does this in the same year.

1863 Preparation of barbituric acid (barbiturates) by Baeyer.

FRANCE
1862 Artery clamps invented.

1863 Pasteur investigates silkworm disease, which was affecting economy of France.

1865 Villemin demonstrates that TB is due to a specific agent, which he calls a germ.

BRITAIN
1863 Harrington invents clockwork dental drill.

1864 Edmund Alexando Parkes's important *Manual of Practical Hygiene* published.

1865 First real test of Lister's antiseptic procedures performed in treatment of compound fracture.

1865 Elizabeth Garrett Anderson obtains Diploma of Society of Apothecaries, London.

AUSTRIA
1865 Gregor Mendel publishes experiments on plant hybrids, which form basis of science of genetics. These were overlooked and neglected until 1900. His theory of inheritance shows that genes carry sets of instructions from parents to offspring.

Gregor Mendel.

GERMANY
1866 Voit (1831–1908) establishes first hygienic laboratory in Munich.

1867 Kussmaul introduces intubation of stomach.

1869 Esmarch introduces india rubber bandage devised to provide bloodless field for limb surgery.

During no other period in history has progress in medicine acquired such momentum as in the 21st century. Continuously improving electronic and computerized technologies are providing ever more high-accuracy tools to doctors for diagnosis and imagery.

For example, sonography, which uses the fact that body tissues are opaque to ultrasound, is now well established. This has been enhanced with Doppler tools that use low-intensity ultrasound to determine the strength of blood flow within the tissue. Miniaturized ultrasound probes permit examination of areas that are otherwise difficult to assess, such as the wall of the esophagus (gullet) or the mediastinum, an area behind the sternum, and they also guide needle biopsies in these otherwise inaccessible body sites.

Magnetic resonance imaging (MRI) analyzes tissue depending upon the tissue's water content and has now been extended to MR spectrometry, where the amino acid content within tissue is assessed, giving an estimate of tissue metabolism that can be correlated with a disease. And, a series of experimental radio-pharmaceuticals may, in the future, refine diagnosis by estimating relative metabolic activity in tissue. One technique born out of this is the PET scan (see below).

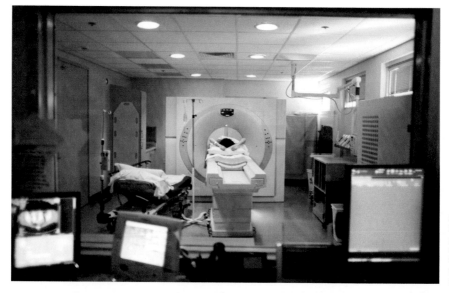

A CAT scan in progress, seen from the monitor room.

VIRTUAL ENDOSCOPY

This new radiological technique assesses lumens (tubular body cavities) such as the intestinal tract, trachea, blood vessels, and coronary arteries. Direct inspection by optical devices is replaced by simulated exploration using 3-D medical images created by CT (computed tomography) or MRI scanners. Virtual endoscopy can be applied in situations where an optical endoscope cannot be used, for example, when it is too dangerous or in case of obstructions. Virtual endoscopy provides viewing control and options that are not possible with real endoscopy: direction, angle and scale of view, immediate translocation to new views, lighting, and measurement. Visual feedback positioning systems and navigation guides can orient the virtual endoscopist relative to the actual anatomy. Virtual endoscopy has extended the realm of lumen visualization to the heart, spinal canal, inner ear (cochlea, semi circular canals, etc.), biliary and pancreatic ducts, and large blood vessels. It has the potential to replace coronary angiograms, which is the current technique for outlining coronary artery obstructions.

POSITRON EMISSION TOMOGRAPHY (PET-CT) SCAN

Measuring important body functions such as blood flow, oxygen use, and sugar (glucose) metabolism, a PET scan maps metabolically active tissue. CT imaging uses special X-ray equipment, and in some cases a contrast material, to produce multiple images or pictures of the body's insides. The combined PET-CT scans provide images that pinpoint the location of abnormal metabolic activity within the body. Together, they have been shown to provide more accurate diagnoses than the two scans performed separately. This technique has proved to be a boon in identifying cancer and cancer recurrence.

THE PILLCAM

Visualization of the entire small intestine (approximately 20 ft / 6 m) is not possible with endoscopy. In some situations where all measures, such as multiple colonoscopies, upper endoscopies, small bowel X-rays, arteriography, and, ultimately, intra-operative endoscopy, have failed, the Pillcam (video capsule endoscopy) may provide an answer. This device is a capsule containing a light source and a camera that can take photographs at the rate of two frames per second. When swallowed, it transmits visuals of the small intestine to a recorder worn by the patient. The battery is good for 50,000 color images in an eight-hour journey. This technique has been especially useful in detecting sites of intestinal bleeds, small tumors, and Crohn's disease. The Pillcam does not replace standard techniques such as endoscopies and colonoscopies.

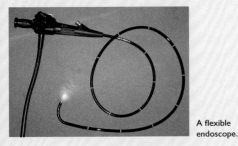

A flexible endoscope.

CZECHOSLOVAKIA
1867 Rokitansky performs nearly 60,000 autopsies in 50 years.

FRANCE
1867 Claude Bernard, founder of experimental physiology, establishes principle of homeostasis, that red blood corpuscles carry oxygen, discovers much about the functions of internal organs and digestion, and links pancreas to diabetes.

RUSSIA
1867 Ivan Petrovich Pavlov—famous for his dogs! He contributes to understanding of conditioned reflexes. His work is misused for brainwashing techniques.

GERMANY
1867 Helmholtz (1821–94) publishes treatise on physiological optics.
1868 Wunderlich's *Das Verhalten Eigen wasme in Krankeiten*: Classical work on temperature in disease—founded use of clinical thermometer.
1869 Virchow (1821–1902) urges medical inspection of schools.
1870 Fritsch and Hitzig investigate localization of functions of brain.
1870 Gustav Simon reports successful planned removal of kidney.
1871 Weigert stains bacteria with carmine.

Advertisement forbidding burials of cholera victims.

BRITAIN
1872 Artery clamps developed by Wells.
1872 Infant Life Protection Act passed in England.

GERMANY
1873 Schwartze and Eysell revise mastoid operation.
1874 Ehrlich introduces dried blood smears and improves stain methods.

GERMANY/AUSTRIA
1873 Billroth excises the larynx.
1873 Revaccination compulsory.

BRITAIN
1873–74 Sir William Gull describes myxedoema (thyroid deficiency) and anorexia nervosa.
1874 Tait carries out first hysterectomy.

MODERN DIAGNOSTIC TECHNIQUES

IMMUNOHISTOCHEMISTRY AND IN-SITU HYBRIDIZATION

Cancer cells often are dissimilar to the parent tissue. They have to be recognized in their altered morphological appearance. Immunohistochemistry identifies cells by monoclonal antibodies that attach to highly specific receptors on cells. Monoclonal antibodies are produced by the hybridoma technique of Milstein, Köhler, and Jerne. They innovatively fused cells that had been sensitized to antigens with cells that produce antibodies (plasma cells). These plasma cells were malignant in nature and therefore multiplied and produced antibodies endlessly. The technique can reveal much about a cell—where it belongs, how fast it is dividing, whether it produces any hormone, and if it is stimulating new blood vessel growth (angiogenesis). Best of all, this technique is optimized for directly working on tissue obtained by biopsy.

Similarly, another technique, in-situ hybridization, can identify genetic abnormalities in cells in a thin slice of tissue. By this method, cells harboring genetic mutation can be visualized, whereas in techniques that depend upon extracting DNA from the cell for study, the tissue structure is lost and visual correlation not possible.

THE GENE CHIP

The Affymetrix Corporation pioneered the gene chip in 1994. This can enable the detection in the body of genetic codes that predispose an individual to metabolic disease or cancer. The device consists of a cluster of DNA codes that are mutations for known diseases. The patient's DNA is layered over the chip and, after a series of steps, the result is read by an automated scanner and processed by computers. A vast range of diseases can be screened. The technique is making a huge impact in cancer research and the quest for its treatment. For example, in some breast cancer cases, the test simultaneously screens 21 genes. Relating the findings with other data specific to the patient, a recurrence score is arrived at, which determines the usefulness

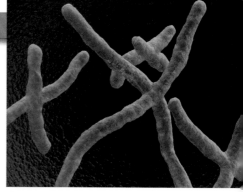

Chromosomes.

of chemotherapy to that patient. This is the first in a category of tests known as in vitro diagnostic multivariate index assay (IVDMIA). A similar test is now under validation for colon cancer.

THE FUTURE

The completion of the Human Genome Project has afforded a deep insight into the genetic structure of humans and, to some extent, its influence on bodily function and immunity. Increasingly, it is being revealed that chronic diseases such as hyperlipidemias, diabetes mellitus, coronary heart disease, hypertension, allergies, and cancer have a genetic basis that is variably impacted by environmental and infective factors. Worldwide genetic assessment of patients is giving clues to the disparity of disease around the globe. Rapid refinement in techniques and technologies to study genetics has contributed to a huge movement in defining the molecular basis of disease. Well established technologies like polymerase chain reaction (PCR) for DNA amplification, including real-time PCR, are bringing fresh information every day. These technologies will be germane in refining treatment tailored to individual genetic composition. Slowly, but surely, the laboratory will tell individuals what is the best treatment for them. Every individual in the future may be able to carry his or her genomic map on a flash drive, readily available for modulate treatment to a given disease.

1875 Public Health Act—will remain charter of English public health for next 60 years.

1875 Sir Thomas Barlow describes infantile scurvy, Barlow's disease.

FRANCE

1873 Cuignet introduces retinoscopy.

1874 *Loi Roussel* enacted for the protection of infants.

GERMANY/AUSTRIA

1875 Meat inspection compulsory.

USA

1875 Mitchell introduces rest cure for treatment of nervous diseases.

ITALY

1876 Lombroso's doctrine of "criminal type," *L'uomo delinquente.*

BRITAIN

1877 Sir Patrick Manson shows mosquitoes transmit *Wucheria bancrofti* as cause of filarial elephantiasis in humans. First proof that infective diseases transmitted by insect vector.

1879 First *successful* cholecsytectomy (cutting out of a gall bladder).

GERMANY

1877 Cohnheim makes successful inoculation of tuberculosis in rabbit's eye.

1878 Von Volkmann successfully removes a cancer of the rectum, and Freund excises a cancerous uterus.

1879 Czerny describes vaginal route for total hysterectomy.

Discoveries: 1879 Neisser—gonococcus (which causes gonorrhea). **1880** Eberth—typhoid bacillus. **1882** Koch—tubercle bacillus **1883** Klebs—diphtheria bacillus. **1883** Koch—cholera bacillus. **1884** Nicolaier—tetanus bacillus.**1887** Weichselbaum—meningococcus **1889** Von Behring—antitoxins.

Robert Koch.

Introductions: 1876 Koch—growing anthrax bacilli on artificial media and in **1881**—plate cultures **1882** Flemming investigates cell division. **1886** Von Soxhlet—sterilizes milk

X-ray of Koch's wife's hand.

for infants. **1890** Koch tuberculin. **1895** Wilhelm Röntgen takes first X-ray d of his wife's hand.

FRANCE

1880 Laveran first sees parasite of malaria fever.

1880 Pasteur isolates streptococcus, staphylococcus, and pneumococcus.

BRITAIN

1880 Balfour's *Treatise on comparative embryology.* Classical summary of previous knowledge.

1880 Sir William Richard Gowers, one of founders of modern neurology: *Diagnosis of Diseases of the Spinal Chord.*

SWEDEN

1881 Medin discovers epidemic nature of poliomyelitis.

GERMANY

1881 Billroth resects (cuts away) the pylorus (opening of stomach into duodenum) for cancer.

1882 Sänger describes "classic Caesarean section."

1886 Ernst Von Bergmann introduces steam sterilization of instruments and dressings.

FRANCE

1883 Pasteur vaccinates against anthrax and in **1885–86** develops first effective vaccine against rabies: *Méthode pour prévenir la rage.*

1888 Roux and Yersin investigate toxins of diphtheria.

USA

1884 Koller uses cocaine in eye surgery.

1885 Halsted first experiments on local infiltration anesthesia and in **1890** introduces rubber gloves for surgery at Johns Hopkins.

BRITAIN

1883 Pioneer pathologist Theobald Smith operates successfully for extra-uterine (ectopic) pregnancy and in**1898** differentiates between bovine and human tubercle bacilli.

1885 Bennett and Sir Rickman Godlee credited with first successful removal of a brain tumor.

1886 An amendment to the Medical Act makes midwifery training part of doctors' training.

1887 Gowers and Horsley operate on spinal cord. Sir Victor Horsley is a pioneer brain surgeon who removes spinal cord tumors.

1888 Nuttall discovers bactericidal powers of blood serum.

1889 Infectious Diseases (Notification) Act in England and Wales.

THE INTERNATIONAL RED CROSS AND RED CRESCENT MOVEMENT

Distressed by the human suffering at the 1859 Battle of Solferino, in Italy, Swiss businessman Henry Dunant not only lent a hand in caring for the wounded of both sides, but also created a humanitarian movement that grew to become the largest volunteer force in the world. Its emblem, the red cross on the white background, adopted in 1863, is the reverse of the Swiss flag colors. Dunant and four other like-minded individuals were the moving spirits behind the 1864 Geneva Convention, the founding document for international humanitarian law, first signed by 12 states. The overarching guiding principle was impartial care for all.

Henry Dunant.

During World War I, the Red Cross dispatched two million parcels to prisoners. During World War II, it persuaded all parties to apply the protective provisions of the 1929 Geneva Convention to civilians, regardless of the side they belonged to (though it was unable to bring people imprisoned in Nazi concentration camps under this cover). Today, 150 years after its inception, 187 national societies and more than 100 million volunteers, including highly qualified medical professionals, are affiliated to the International Red Cross and Red Crescent Movement. Apart from wartime assistance, its vastly enhanced scope includes helping vulnerable people and communities affected by natural disasters, disease, malnutrition, and other health issues. The Red Cross is active in fields ranging from first aid to AIDS, including polio, measles, tuberculosis, and other diseases.

Above: Red Cross workers provided assistance to residents affected by Hurricane Gustav, Texas, 2008.
Right: U.S. Medical Corps ambulance.

USA/EUROPE
1890s Pharmaceutical industry advertisements appear. Beechams' Pills spread from Britain to USA.

JAPAN/GERMANY
1890 Von Behring and Kitasato discover diphtheria and tetanus antitoxins and provide basis for serotherapy.

GERMANY
1890 Behring treats diphtheria with antitoxin.
1891 Institute for Infectious Diseases in Berlin opens.
1891 Quincke popularizes lumbar puncture.
1893 A chemist markets aspirin, using it to treat rheumatism.

USA
1892 Welch and Nuttall discover gas gangrene bacillus.

RUSSIA
1892 Ivanovski's work on tobacco mosaic disease develops knowledge of viruses.

DENMARK
1893 Finsen, founder of phototherapy, demonstrates therapeutic value of the actinec ray and ultraviolet light.

BRITAIN
1894 Sir William Arbuthnot Lane introduces pinning of fractures, but metals used were often rejected by the body.

JAPAN • FRANCE
1894 Kitasato and Yersin discover plague bacillus.

GERMANY
1894 Schleich develops infiltration anesthesia.
1895 Kirstein devises direct vision laryngoscopy.

AUSTRIA
1895 Freud (with Breur) publishes *Studien über*

Hysterie on the revelation of the "unconscious mind."

FRANCE
1896 Becquerel discovers radioactivity in uranium.

Sigmund Freud.

BRITAIN
1896 Dibdin introduces biological purification of sewage.
1897–98 Ross discovers parasite responsible for malaria and role of mosquito in bird malaria.

JAPAN
1897 Shiga discovers dysentery bacillus.

USA
1897 Medical student, Walter B. Cannon, uses solution of radio-opaque bismuth as a diagnostic meal to outline stomach.
1897–98 Cannon discovers barium suspensions, which show up alimentary canal on X-ray plate.

JAPAN
1898 Pierre and Marie Curie discover radium.

GERMANY
1898 Killian uses direct bronchoscopy.

Marie Curie.

GERMANY
1898–99 Dreser introduces drugs heroin and aspirin into medicine.

USA
1899 Reed, Lazear, and others establish transmission of yellow fever by mosquito, *Aëdes aegyptic* in *The etiology of yellow fever*. Lazear dies from yellow fever after accidental mosquito bite.

AUSTRIA
1899 Gärtner uses tonometer for measuring blood pressure by means of finger ring.
1900 Freud publishes *The interpretation of dreams*, which has a wide influence beyond medicine.

BRITAIN
1900 Manson's experiments prove mosquito vector of malaria: Volunteer is his son!

GERMANY
1900 Wertheim introduces radical operation for uterine cancer.

127

WOMEN: THEIR ROLE AS DOCTORS

Women have always been carers of the sick. In ancient civilizations such as ancient Egypt and Babylonia, they sometimes became skillful practitioners, especially in midwifery, but also in the dressing of wounds and nursing the sick.

In the later medieval period, nuns were strongly committed to caring for the sick, while ladies of the manor developed great knowledge of herbs and other treatments. At the same time, wise women who understood herbal remedies became a part of every community.

It was only when science and formal training developed that women were allowed fewer opportunities in the medical field—except perhaps in Italy, where their medical education was permitted and some women held prestigious university chairs.

Portait of Elizabeth Blackwell by Joseph Stanley Kozlowski, 1905.

EIGHTEENTH AND NINETEENTH CENTURIES

In the 18th-century Western world, it was generally believed that any intellectual activity diverted women's energies from their reproductive system and was bad for them. Any attempt to pursue an academic profession was regarded with great suspicion and prejudice.

By the 19th century, women had been thoroughly subjugated as far as the medical profession was concerned, with, as ever, the notable exceptions of midwifery and nursing. Women had always continued to be involved in obstetrics, as midwifery was considered a female domain, and so given scant credence as a proper science, while nursing, of course, had always been a female occupation. By 1860, Florence Nightingale had, following her great reforms in the care of the wounded and sick soldiers during the Crimean War, opened her training school for nurses at St. Thomas's Hospital in London and had established nursing as a far more respectable and better organized profession (see page 79).

However, while women could continue to demonstrate their value in certain medical areas, the idea of their becoming doctors was seen by most of the 19th-century establishment as ridiculous. Despite this opposition, some determined women began to prove their worth. Eventually, the first female doctors fought their way through repeated rejection and obstacles to achieve the necessary qualifications and grudging acceptance.

JAMES BARRY (1797–1865)
It is believed that the Inspector General of the British Army in 1858, James Barry, who had a highly successful career in surgery for some fifty years was, in fact, a woman in disguise. Her real sex was discovered only during the autopsy that followed her death.

Her height and stature, clean-shaven face, and high-pitched squeaky voice might have puzzled her colleagues, but it seems that her skilled marksmanship and an aggressive attitude sufficed to ward off any suspicion.

To avoid embarrassment, the war department and medical association arranged for James Barry to be buried as a man!

HARRIOT HUNT (1805–75)
In America there was just as much opposition to women training as doctors as in Europe.

BRITAIN
1901 Dutton and Forde identify parasite of Gambian fever: Helps understanding of sleeping sickness that in **1903** Bruce and Nabarro show is transmitted by tsetse fly.

1901 In Scotland, hospital beds set aside for first ever prenatal care.

GERMANY
1901 Koch states bubonic plague may have been due to rats and in **1905** investigates African fever.

AUSTRIA
1901 Three major blood cell groups A, B, and O described by Landsteiner: His work leads to safer transfusion.

USA
1902 International Sanitary Bureau established (later Pan-American Health Organization).

GERMANY
1902 Formula patented for barbituric acid—used to make sleeping pills.

BRITAIN
1903 Smith perfects new operation for eye cataracts.

USA
1903 Dentists propose porcelain for fillings or crowns.

NETHERLANDS
1903 Einthoven invents string galvanometer, first practical ECG (electrocardiograph).

1903 Rocci invents sphygmomanometer to measure blood pressure.

GERMANY
1904 Sauerbruch designs negative pressure chamber for chest surgery.

USA
1904 Atwater invents respiration calorimeter.

BRITAIN
1904 Bayliss and Starling discover chemicals stimulate secretions: Theory of hormonal control of these develops.

FRANCE
1905 Psychologist Alfred Binet develops a way of testing the brain on its ability to reason.

BELGIUM
1905 Bordet and Gengou discover bacillus of whooping cough.

USA
1906 Food and Drugs Act.

1906 "Typhoid Mary," most famous typhoid carrier, discovered.

AUSTRALIA
1906 Bancroft demonstrates dengue transmitted by mosquito bites: *Aëdes aegypti.*

CANADA
1906 Surgeons perform kidney operations on animals to prove human transplants possible.

USA
1907 Immigrants given health check to ensure not carrying any contagious disease; unhealthy ones may be sent back home.

GERMANY
1907 Wassermann introduces sero diagnostic test for syphilis.

FRANCE
1907 Calmette devises conjunctival test for TB.

1907 Doctors announce discovery of a serum which cures dysentery.

BRITAIN
1908 Sleeping Sickness Bureau founded.

TUNISIA
1909 Nicolle shows body lice spread typhus.

USA
1910 Law against white slave traffic.

BRITAIN
1910 Marine and others suggest that goiter (enlargement of thyroid) may be prevented by taking iodine.

CZECHOSLOVAKIA
1910 Jansky demonstrates four basic blood groups A, B, AB, and O.

In Boston, Harriot Hunt was rejected by her fellow students after the dean there had granted her admission to Harvard Medical School, so she was forced to leave. However, she was still determined to find an entry into the medical field somehow and managed to obtain an MD degree at Syracuse as a homeopathic physician.

While not able to qualify as a fully fledged doctor, in due course she became a professor of midwifery and of diseases of women and children at Rochester College, USA.

ELIZABETH BLACKWELL (1821–1910)
Elizabeth Blackwell had enormous difficulty in breaking through the wall of prejudice and resistance to women as physicians, but eventually her determination and sheer hard work enabled her to achieve her ambitions. She became the first woman to be entered onto the British Medical Register as a qualified doctor.

Elizabeth Blackwell was born in England but brought up in the USA. She supported

Dr. Elizabeth Blackwell was the first non-cross-dressing woman to attain an MD in the USA and become a doctor in 1849. She was accepted on the UK Medical Register in 1859.

herself by teaching while she studied science in order to qualify for her entrance into college.

The Geneva College of Medicine in New York eventually admitted her. The dean agreed to accept her only if his students voted unanimously in her favor, but he was very surprised when they did. It is believed this may have been as an act of capriciousness, a "prank" to aggravate the dean. It is unlikely in the climate of the time that the male students en masse were seriously trying to break down the conventions of the day!

Elizabeth Blackwell proved an excellent student who gained top marks throughout the course and attained her degree in 1849.

There was still much opposition to a woman actually working in the profession, but, in June 1849, Elizabeth Blackwell began studying obstetrics in Paris. She eventually went on to open a clinic for poor women and children in New York, and, in 1874, she was appointed the Professor of Gynecology at London School of Medicine for Women.

In 1860, the rules changed! Only those who had studied in British universities were allowed to register as doctors in Great Britain. In effect, this excluded female doctors in the UK as no British university then allowed women to study medicine.

ELIZABETH GARRETT ANDERSON (1836–1917)
An intelligent and well-educated young lady from a wealthy established family, Elizabeth Garrett was strongly committed to the fight for women's rights. She became involved in the Society for the Emploment of Women and the *English Women's Journal* in the 1860s. It was a meeting with Elizabeth Blackwell (who wrote an article about the struggle ahead for women wishing to become physicians for the *English Women's Journal* in 1860) that inspired Elizabeth Garrett to try to become a doctor.

She worked as a student nurse at the Middlesex Hospital until it was discovered that she had been unofficially attending lectures given to medical students. Regarded as an "impostor," she was ordered to leave.

Undeterred, she carried on studying privately with professors at both St. Andrews

Dr. Elizabeth Garrett Anderson—a caricature.

FRANCE

1910 Gattefossé applies lavender oil to a burn, which heals quickly with little scarring; he studies therapeutic actions of plant oils.

Lavender.

USA

1910 X-ray machine guides a surgeon to remove a nail from the lung of a boy.

1910 Ricketts demonstrates woodtick as vector of Rocky Mountain Spotted Fever, which he differentiates from typhus.

1910 Flexner produces poliomyelitis experimentally.

1911 Rous transmits malignant tumor, as a filterable virus.

1911 First prenatal clinic opens in Boston.

SWEDEN

1911 Gullstrand receives Nobel Prize for optical research.

GERMANY

1911 Ehrlich tests Salvarson in treatment of syphilis: Regarded as birth of chemotherapy.

SWITZERLAND

1911 Bleuler proposes the term "schizophrenia."

GERMANY

1912 Sudhoff opposes theory of American origin of syphilis: Believes it existed in Europe pre-Columbus.

FRANCE

1912 Odin claims he has isolated and cultivated a cancer microbe.

1912 Professor Dastre pioneers cornea graft to restore lost eyesight.

AUSTRALIA

1912 First prenatal clinic opens in Sydney.

BRITAIN

1912 Bass and Johns cultivate malarial plasmodium in a test tube.

USA

1912 Cushing describes *The pituitary body and its disorders.*

1912 Public Health Services set up.

1912 Children's Bureau established (Washington, DC).

POLAND

1912 Funk proposes name "vitamine" (vitamin) for substances that prevent deficiency diseases.

FRANCE

1913 De Sandfort devises ambrine (paraffin-resin solution) treatment for burns.

GERMANY/AFRICA

1913 Schweitzer starts his great work in Africa, building hospitals and fighting leprosy.

BRITAIN

1913 International Medical Congress.

JAPAN

1913 Noguchi demonstrates *Spirochaete pallida* in brains of syphilitic patients. Dies of yellow fever in Ghana when investigating disease.

USA

1913 Supreme Court denies "rights" of individuals when inimical to public welfare.

BRITAIN

1914–18 Modern plastic surgery develops with Gillies pioneering use of pedicle flaps of skin from one part of body to another.

1915 Dakin introduces new antiseptics.

1915 British introduce tetanus antitoxin for all wounded soldiers.

FRANCE

1914–18 Carrel and Dakin devise treatment of infected wounds.

USA

1915 Fitzgerald describes zone therapy.

JAPAN

1916 Futaki and others discover spirillum in rat-bite fever.

ITALY

1916 Vanghetti introduces cineplasty—using muscle above stump to activate artificial limbs.

and Edinburgh universities and eventually became the first woman licentiate of the Society of Apothecaries in 1870—and hence an official physician.

Elizabeth Garrett went on to run a dispensary for women and children in Marylebone, London, and, after working with suffragettes, studied in Paris, where she finally became a Doctor of Medicine in 1870, the first British woman to achieve an MD degree.

She married and became Elizabeth Garrett Anderson and, in time, the mother of two girls. But she continued her work for women's causes, becoming dean of the London School of Medicine for Women in 1883—a post she held for twenty years.

The courage and determination of these first two female doctors paved the way for others to follow and for colleges to permit them to pursue their studies, despite fierce opposition and, literally, mud-slinging. Male students hurled insults and mud at women who had to force their way through an angry mob to attend an anatomy examination in Edinburgh in 1870.

THE EFFECT OF THE GREAT WAR

As in many other erstwhile male-dominated provinces, women's work at home and abroad during World War I proved their value in the medical field, changed attitudes, and greatly helped to promote their acceptance as doctors. This is vividly demonstrated by the growth in the number of women qualifying as physicians in the UK after the war:

Year qualifying	Women	Men
1917	78	539
1918	68	341
1919	99	175
1920	210	374
1921	602	325

The U.S. Navy nurse corps, 1908.

By 1985, some 5,476 women were acting as general practitioners in Britain, while there were 20,714 male doctors. This figure of approximately 26 percent rose to 33 percent by 1998, approximately the same percentage of female doctors out of all physicians in the U.S. In the U.S. today, there are slightly more female medical students than male students, but for various reasons women still lag behind in the number of practitioners.

Founded in 1848, the New England Female Medical College holds the unique distinction of being the first institution in the world to formally educate female physicians and award the MD degree. It was subsequently renamed Boston University School of Medicine (BUSM) in 1873, and is one of the graduate schools of Boston University.

BELGIUM
1917 Willems early mobilization of joint wounds changes orthopedic practice.

USA
1917–18 American Commission investigates trench fever.

WORLD
1918–19 Influenza pandemic kills up to 30 million people.

BRITAIN
1919 British Ministry of Health established.

1920s Marie Stopes opens first birth control clinic, offering free consultations and contraceptives. Examinations carried out by a midwife, and, if necessary, patients are referred to the clinic's female doctor.

Birth control clinic, 1920s.

BELGIUM
1920 First Congress of Medical History (Antwerp).

CANADA
1921 Insulin treatment for diabetes developed by Banting and Best.

FRANCE
1921 Development of a vaccine against tuberculosis from living, non-virulent bovine bacilli by Calmette and Guérin.

1921 Nylen uses a monocular microscope during an operation on the ear for deafness.

1922 McCollum (and others) identify vitamin D. It promotes proper bone growth and helps combat rickets.

1924 Albert Calmette introduces BCG preventive vaccination of children against tuberculosis.

BRITAIN
1925 First successful insulin treatment is performed in Europe at Guys Hospital, London.

FRANCE
1926 Pasteur Institute announces discovery of an anti-tetanus serum.

USA
1928 The iron lung, developed in 1927 by U.S. physicist Philip Drinker, is used for the first time in the USA.

HUNGARY
1928 Biochemist Szent-Györgyi manages to isolate vitamin C.

Human kidney transplants begin in the 1950s.

BRITAIN
1928 Sir Alexander Fleming discovers penicillin, the first antibiotic.

1928 Hindle introduces first vaccine for immunization against yellow fever.

1928 Elastoplast sticking plaster dressings first manufactured.

GERMANY
1928 Ascheim and Zondek introduce first usable pregnancy test.

NETHERLANDS
1930 Chemist Debye uses X-rays to investigate structure of molecules.

USA
1932 Scientists announce development of first vaccine against yellow fever.

GERMANY
1932 Evipan, a barbiturate anesthetic, introduced by Weese and Scharpff.

1932 First electron microscope constructed by Ruska and Knoll.

1932 Anti-malarial drug atebrin (mepacrine) synthesized by Mietzsch, Mauss, and Walter Kirkuth.

USA
1933 Anti-beriberi vitamin identified by Robert Williams and colleagues.

1934 Mixter and Barr demonstrate role of intervertebral disc herniation in sciatica.

GERMANY
1935 Domagh finds that pronotosil, a dye stuff derived from sulphanilamide, protects mice against fatal doses of streptococci.

PORTUGAL
1935 First pre-frontal leucotomy introduced by Moniz; used to treat certain psychoses.

WOMEN: THEIR ROLE AS DOCTORS

WOMEN IN MEDICINE : MILESTONES

1849 USA Elizabeth Blackwell gains her MD (Doctor of Medicine) from Geneva Medical College, NY.

1850 USA Philadelphian Women's College of Medicine established.

1859 UK Elizabeth Blackwell admitted to the UK Medical Register with an American MD (Doctor of Medicine) degree, but foreign medical degrees are subsequently disallowed.

1865 Switzerland Universities accept female students.

1865 UK Elizabeth Garrett obtains Licentiate of the Society of Apothecaries (who then close the loophole).

1869 France Women are accepted to study medicine.

1869 Germany Women are accepted to study medicine.

1870 USA University of Michigan is first American state school to accept women medical students.

1870 Sweden Women are accepted to study medicine.

1871 Netherlands Universities accept female medical students.

1872 Russia St. Petersburg accepts women wanting to study to become doctors.

1874 UK Founding of the London School of Medicine for Women by Sophia Jez-Blake. Although women achieve the necessary results in examinations and equal their male counterparts, they are awarded only Certificates of Proficiency, not MD degrees.

Dr. Sophia Louisa Jez-Blake.

1876 USA The American Medical Association accepts women members.

1876 Ireland The Dublin College of Physicians licenses women with existing continental degrees.

1877 UK Royal Free Hospital, UK, admits female medical students to clinical training.

1892 UK British Medical Association admits female doctors.

1914 UK Outbreak of First World War: UK War Office initially rejects offers of service by female doctors. Their services are, however, welcomed by other Allied Powers.

Dr. Gerti T. Corli.

1941 India Indian Medical Service invites medical women to apply for temporary commissions.

1947 USA/ Czechoslovakia Dr. Gerti T Corli—first woman to win Nobel Prize in medicine/ physiology.

1977 USA Dr. Rosalyn Yalow— second woman to win Nobel Prize in medicine.

Dr. Rosalyn Yalow.

1990 UK Proportion of women entering UK medical schools reaches 52 percent.

1895 UK Louisa Aldrich-Blake first woman to become Master of Surgery (London).

1996 USA Women constitute more than 40 percent of medical students in the U.S.

Louisa Aldrich-Blake.

2010 USA In the U.S., 30.5 percent of doctors are women.

USA
1936 Anti-beriberi vitamin produced synthetically.

USSR
1937 Artificial heart by Vladimir P. Demikhov.

USA
1938 New York is first state to pass a law requiring medical tests for U.S. marriage licenses.

BRITAIN
1938 Dodds and others introduce first synthetic estrogen (stilbestrol).

AUSTRIA
1940 Landsteiner and Wiener find an additional agglutination factor in blood, the Rh antigen, following experiments using a Rhesus monkey.

BRITAIN
1940 The experiments of Florey and Chain effect a method for production of stable, solid penicillin for therapeutic use.

WORLD
1942 World Health Organization (WHO) set up as an agency of the United Nations.

NETHERLANDS
1942–43 First kidney dialysis machine is developed in secret for the Dutch resistance by Willem Kolff.

1944 Surgeon Alfred Blalock performs first successful heart operation on a newborn baby.

USA
1944 First eye bank is opened by Manhattan and New York hospitals.
1944 Waksman discovers streptomycin, a useful antibiotic effective against brucellosis and tuberculosis.
1945 A vaccine against virus A and B influenza is used on the U.S. Army for the first time.
1945 World's first fluoridated water supply is available in Michigan.
1945 Benadryl is developed to treat common allergies such as hay fever and asthma.
1950 First human kidney transplant, performed by Lawler.
1946 Dr. Benjamin Spock publishes *Baby and Child Care*, which tells parents to hug their children and follow their instincts, rather than imposing set routines and rigorous discipline.

1947 Gerty T Cori is first woman to win the Nobel Prize in medicine, along with her husband Carl F. Cori, for their discovery of the process in the catalytic metabolism of glycogen.

BRITAIN
1948 National Health Service starts.

USA
1948 The Kinsey Report.
1950 Howard Green grows human skin for grafting from a 1 square millimeter (0.0016 sq in) amount taken from a newborn baby. This grows to an area of 60 square centimeters (9.3 sq in) in 20 days.

FRANCE/USA
1950 Küss in Paris and Murray in Boston, with their colleagues, transplant first kidneys from deceased to living patients.

USA
1952 An artificial heart is first used in an operation at Pennsylvania Hospital.
1953 Virologist, Dr. Salk, successfully tests a vaccine against polio.

BRITAIN
1953 Structure of DNA discovered by Crick and Watson.

DNA double helix structure.

WORLD
1955 World Health Organization declares that, with DDT and world support, malaria may be eradicated. (By the 1960s toxicity of DDT is better understood and DDT spraying becomes less common.)
1955 WHO says that atomic waste poses serious health risk.

USA
1955 Pincus and others invent contraceptive pill.
1956 First successful kidney transplant is carried out between identical twins by Merrill and others.

Sperm and ova: Birth control and fertilization become important issues.

From the second half of the 20th century, the world of sports has found itself increasingly mired in controversy regarding the use of performance-enhancing drugs, also called "doping." As the practice became widespread, ethical and health concerns—almost all such substances have side effects, ranging from mood swings to heart and liver problems—prompted governments and sports organizations to ban their use. Testing methods were developed, and athletes are now severely penalized if found to be using listed substances and practices.

Performance-enhancing substances have been employed from far back in history. Athletes of ancient Greece and the gladiators of ancient Rome ingested plant-based stimulants, such as certain species of mushrooms, to increase their prowess. In battle, the fierce Berserker fighters of 9th- and 10th-century Scandinavia psyched themselves up for armed conflict with similar potions.

MODERN BEGINNINGS

In the 19th century, relaxants and stimulants trickled into modern sport. Long-distance walking up for armed conflict in Britain and America were where they first made their mark. Opium, alcohol, caffeine, and even nitroglycerine were used to increase endurance. In 1886, Welsh cyclist Arthur Linton overdosed on trimethyl alcohol and became the first recorded drug-induced fatality in sport. Strychnine, a plant extract, with the property to stimulate the central nervous system, was another stimulant used in small quantities. Though it helped Thomas Hicks win the 1904 Olympic marathon, being highly poisonous, it also almost took his life.

Above: Arthur Linton.
Right: Hicks winning the marathon in 1904, after taking strychnine to boost his performance. It nearly cost him his life.

AMPHETAMINES AND STEROIDS

The two world wars gave impetus to the production of new synthetic drugs. Supplied to soldiers to boost their physical states, they also found their way into sports. The first major testing ground of a class of stimulants called amphetamines (also known as "speed") was the 1936 Berlin Olympics. Amphetamines reduced fatigue and maintained alertness and aggression. About this time, the most notoriously well-known drugs currently used in modern sport were experimented with. These were anabolic steroids (AAS), derivatives of the male sex hormone, testosterone. Adolf Butenandt, a German chemist, was a pioneer in their development. AAS have powerful muscle- and bone-building effects, which are of therapeutic value for frailty caused due to illness. They also promote aggressive behavior. They were tested on German soldiers and prisoners, including, it is believed, Hitler himself.

Adolf Butenandt.

SCANDINAVIA

1956 Fijoe and Levan state there are 46 normal human chromosomes. This leads to discovery of Down syndrome.

BRITAIN

1957 Smoking and cancer directly associated.

SWEDEN

1958 Internal cardiac pacemaker invented. Ake Senning carries out first successful implant.

A titanium pacemaker.

1958 Thalidomide shown to cause birth defects.

NEW ZEALAND

1960 Enders and others develop attenuated measles virus vaccine.

1963 Doctors give the world's first successful blood transfusion to an unborn baby.

1963 Measles vaccine introduced.

BRITAIN

1963 Successful human kidney transplant at Leeds.

USA

1966 Artificial blood developed by Clark and Gollan.

SOUTH AFRICA

1967 First heart transplant performed by Christiaan Barnard at Cape Town. The patient dies 18 days later.

Open heart surgery. Cristiaan Barnard.

BRITAIN

1967 St. Christopher's Hospice in London pioneers hospice care for the terminally ill.

1968 Epidural anesthesia relieves pain of childbirth.

1968 Britain's first successful heart transplant operation in London. The first triple heart, lungs, and liver transplant.

1969 Human eggs are fertilized in a test tube for the first time at Cambridge University.

WORLD

1969 WHO admits plan to eradicate malaria has failed.

USSR

1970 Balloon surgery develops.

Mini balloon can be inflated in an artery.

BRITAIN

1970 First pacemaker driven by a battery.

1970s CAT scanner developed.

1970s–80s Dental decay in adolescents and young adults halved with use of fluoride.

SOUTH AFRICA

1971 First combined heart and lung transplant.

SWITZERLAND

1972 Borel discovers that a material (cyclosporin-A) from a Norwegian mushroom can be used to suppress immune system and allow transplants to take (to avoid rejection of transplanted organs).

USA

1972 Syphilis Scandal: It is revealed that the Public Health Service has been studying syphilis in black men in Macon County, Alabama, for 40 years without treating them.

AUSTRALIA

1976 Shannon develops a bionic artificial arm with a strong hand grip.

USA

1976 First artificial functioning gene created.

1977 Rosalyn Yalow is second woman to receive Nobel Prize for medicine.

BRITAIN

1978 World's first "test-tube" baby born.

JAPAN

1979 Artificial blood made by Riochi Naito.

COACHES AND GOVERNMENTS GET INTO THE ACT

During the next 50 years, the use of anabolic steroids mushroomed across a wide spectrum of sports. Strength sports, where muscle bulk mattered most, were the first to tap their impressive benefits. In the USA, methandrostenolone was developed by John Ziegler, physician to the American weight lifting team. It was put on the market by Ciba, under the brand name Dianabol. During the Cold War era, East Germany ran a state-sponsored program of steroid administration to its athletes, the existence and scale of which was discovered only after the "Iron Curtain" lifted in the 1990s. During this secretive program, the country of under 20 million came up with some amazing results: in the three Olympics from 1968 to 1976, East Germany's gold medal tally leapfrogged from nine to 20 to 40. Often, steroid pills were supplied as a matter of course, in the routine manner of vitamins, as part of the daily diet, and very often, the athletes were unaware of what they were being given by their coaches. This was the case in the Eastern Bloc as well as in the West.

ALARM BELLS

Cyclist Tommy Simpson.

Whereas sportsmen and women were pushing the physical envelope and frequently setting new records, the concept of "purity" of sports performance and the ethics of artificial means to gain unfair advantage over those who chose to stay "clean" were becoming issues that had to be addressed. Also, the adverse effects of drug use were emerging. At the 1952 Oslo Winter Olympics, speed skaters became sick on amphetamines, and some years later, the same drugs claimed the lives of cyclists Knut Jensen of Denmark and Tommy Simpson of Britain. Though as early as 1928 the International Amateur Athletic Federation had banned drugs, the movement gathered momentum in the 1960s, when FIFA (Fédération Internationale de Football Association), UCI (Union Cycliste International), and then the IOC (International Olympic Committee) imposed similar bans. Pharmacological tests were devised for drug detection. In 1968, the IOC produced a list of prohibited substances, and testing began at the Mexico City Olympics.

THE NET CLOSES IN

Established in 1982, Don Catlin's UCLA Olympic Analytical Laboratory played a key role in drug testing. Its scientists came up with tests for EPO and steroids, including new-generation "designer" steroids like norbolethone and THG (tetrahydrogestrinone). WADA (World Anti-Doping Association) was set up in 1999 in order to unite the fight against the drug menace. Funded by the Olympic Movement and national governments, WADA's concerted efforts closed the gap between new drugs and credible testing through accredited anti-doping laboratories worldwide. WADA compiles and maintains the comprehensive list of banned drugs and methods. These are across several categories and are applicable in three contexts: Substances and Methods Prohibited at All Times (In- and Out-of-Competition), Substances and Methods Prohibited In-Competition, Substances Prohibited in Particular Sports.

Don Catlin.

SOME INFAMOUS DRUG ASSOCIATIONS

Amphetamines (stimulants)
Therapeutic use (now discouraged): Weight loss
Admitted use: Fausto Coppi (cycling), 1940s–50s

Stanazolol (anabolic steroid)
Therapeutic use: Anemia, hereditary angioedema
Positive test: Ben Johnson (track), 1988

Marion Jones.

Nandrolone (anabolic steroid)
Therapeutic use: Anemia, osteoporosis
Positive test: Petr Korda (tennis), 1998

THG (anabolic steroid)
Therapeutic use: None
Admitted use: Marion Jones (track),
1999–2001

Erythropoietin (hormone)
Therapeutic use: Anemia,
myelodysplasia
Positive test: David Millar (cycling), 2004

HGH (Human Growth Hormone)
Therapeutic use: To replace naturally occurring growth hormone in
the body
Admitted use: Jason Grimsley (baseball), 1998–2006

Kristin Otto: Sadly, her career is marred by revelations of widespread performance enhancement drugs use by East German athletes. Her former teammate Birgit Meineke, now a general surgeon, has commented publicly about the procedures utilized by the East Germans.

NEW TECHNIQUES AND DRUGS

As methods of detection were developed, the list of banned substances expanded. Anabolic steroids were included in 1975, and caffeine in 1983. Tests involved urine and blood analysis through methods such as **gas chromatography and mass spectrometry**. Yet new drugs and methods of enhancing sports performance were constantly emerging, and testing was always trying to catch up. More kinds of anabolic steroids were invented. In 1972, the Swedish doctor Björn Ekblom created "blood doping" (banned in 1986), whereby an athlete's blood is removed, and later infused back into the system to increase the carrying capacity of oxygen. Administration of additional quantities of EPO, or erythropoietin (banned in 1990), a naturally occurring hormone that produces similar effects, was a new technique. Human growth hormone (HGH), which increases the production of testosterone and muscle mass in the body, was discovered to be yet another ergogenic or external influence on enhanced performance, while the stimulant Modafinil was introduced in the 1990s.

GERMANY

1979 First human liver transplant.
1980s Magnetic resonance imaging (MRI) developed.

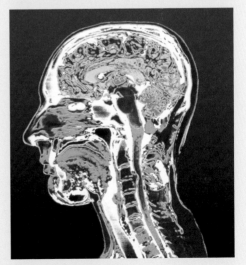

MRI scanning develops in 1980s.

Paul Bert.

The human body has been designed to function comfortably and optimally at oxygen and pressure levels that are normally present up to an altitude of about 8,000 ft. (2,438 m) above sea level. Above this height, as the air becomes thinner and atmospheric pressure reduces, the body is susceptible to physiological changes that can affect it adversely. The adverse effects can range from minor discomfiture to fatally severe.

INVESTIGATIONS BY BALLOONISTS

Altitude can be gained on land and in the air. On land, extreme altitudes are usually traversed by mountaineers and trekkers. The afflictions faced by them are broadly referred to as hypobaric hypoxia or AMS (acute mountain sickness), and observations of these unpleasant symptoms were first made more than 2,000 years ago. In the first century BCE, To Kan, a Chinese traveler, commented on facial pallor, headache, and nausea while crossing the Kilak Pass in high Asia. Over the centuries, altitude sickness was attributed to a variety of causes such as rarefied air and poisonous vapors from plants. It was not until the 18th century that serious attempts were made, mostly by balloonist-physicians, to understand high altitude-induced effects on the body's natural functioning. A significant such study on high-air composition was done by John Jeffries (1744–1819) in 1784. French physician Paul Bert's (1833–86) balloon forays resulted in *La Pression Barométrique*, a comprehensive work on physiological changes at high altitude.

HAPE AND HACE

A multitude of climbing expeditions in the 20th century resulted in a wealth of information on the subject. The Anglo-American Pike's Peak expedition of 1911 conducted a particularly thorough study on high-altitude physiological adaptation. Over the years, specific AMSs were identified and their treatments devised. These were often found to be caused by rapid ascents, without sufficient time given for acclimatization. The two extreme sicknesses

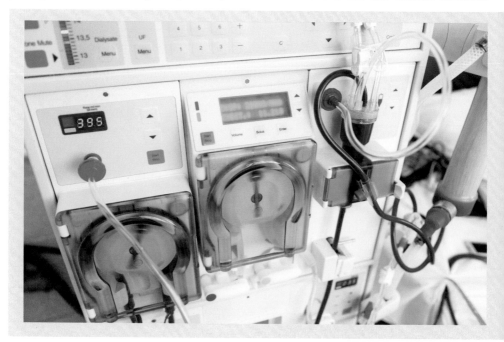

are HAPE (high altitude pulmonary edema), wherein fluid enters the lungs, and HACE (high altitude cerebral edema), in which there is a mild swelling of the brain. The symptoms noted by To Kan are common to both. Apart from these, HAPE is characterized by extreme fatigue, rattling breaths, tightness or fullness in the chest, blue-grey lips and fingernails. Typical symptoms of HACE are confusion and ataxia, or loss of coordination. The drugs found to be effective in these cases are acetazolamide, a respiratory stimulant that speeds up acclimatization, and dexamethasone, a steroid that mitigates the symptoms, rather than addressing the root physiological problem. The ultimate cure, of course, was proven to be descent to a lower altitude.

Igor Gamow, inventor of the Gamow bag, an inflatable pressure bag, big enough to hold a person, that is used to treat altitude sickness.

HOW MEDICAL SCIENCE HAS HARNESSED SPACE TECHNOLOGIES

In space: Taking images of the moon
Medical application: MRIs and CAT scans

In space: Electrical muscle stimulator to prevent atrophy
Medical application: Muscle toner for the paralyzed

In space: Foam cushioning for astronauts during liftoff
Medical application: Helps prevent bed sores

In space: Bodily fluids toxin removal system
Medical application: Dialysis machines

In space: Satellite communication
Medical application: Heart pacemakers use this to convey functional information

Left: Dialysis machines incorporate technology that was developed for applications in space.

WORLD
1980 WHO announces smallpox is completely eradicated. Later accidental infection at Birmingham of laboratory technician.

AUSTRALIA
1981 World's first test-tube twins born in Melbourne.

USA
1981 AIDS first recognized in New York and Los Angeles.
1982 First operation to implant an artificial heart in a human being in Utah.

AUSTRALIA
1983 Australian woman becomes first to give birth after receiving a donated egg.
1984 First baby born who began life as a frozen embryo.

USA
1984 AIDS virus discovered.
1986 Keyhole surgery develops.
1986 Burke and Yannas graft an artificial skin made from beef collagen and silicone plastic.
1987 Prozac is licensed by the U.S. Food and Drug Administration.
1988 Studies show osteopathic manipulation improves recovery time for lower back pain.

BRITAIN
1990 Scientists deny BSE poses a threat but in **1991** the first woman dies of Creutzfeld Jakob's disease, the human form of "mad cow disease."

BRITAIN
1991 Doctors develop a method of estimating when a patient infected with HIV may develop full-blown AIDS.

USA
1991 Eight people sealed inside giant Biosphere II greenhouse for a two-year experiment.
1992 Doctors say Legionnaire's disease can be caught via tap water as well as air-conditioning systems.
1992 A 35-year-old man is given a baboon liver transplant by surgeons at Pittsburgh but dies of a stroke three months later. The postmortem

AVIATION MEDICINE

Flying placed a specific set of demands on the human body, many of which were unfamiliar at first to medical science. The first physical functions that were identified as being especially important to this new activity were good eyesight and a stable vestibular system, the part of the inner ear that contributes to a sense of balance and an awareness of spatial orientation. Bearing in mind these physical criteria, in the early years aviation medicine focused simply on selecting suitable pilots. An early pioneer in this field was the American physician Theodore Lyster (1875–1933), who set up the Aviation Medicine Research Board (1917), in New York.

BETTER AIRCRAFT CREATE NEW DEMANDS
Aircraft performance improved rapidly from the First World War onward. As altitudes higher than those found on land were reached, ways had to be found to tackle environments of low oxygen and low barometric pressure. The need to study these conditions and develop suitable systems to ensure pilot health and efficacy led to the establishment of dedicated institutions and laboratories. In 1929, Louis H. Bauer (1888–1964) founded the Aero Medical Association—now the premier organization in the world for aerospace medicine. In the 1930s, Harry G. Armstrong discovered that, in the absence of adequate pressurization, the human body's fluids would vaporize at a height of 63,000 ft. (19,202m).

OXYGEN MASKS
Oxygen masks work on the hyperbaric principle, i.e., they supply oxygen into the body at positive pressure, therefore preventing hypoxia and gas embolism. The first such device, developed as early

SPACE MEDICINE

It is generally accepted that Earth's atmosphere ends and space begins about 60 miles (97 km) above the ground. Space is devoid of gravity and oxygen. Travelers in space are disconnected from the day-night cycle of Earth and are subject to harmful ionized radiation. Studying the effects of this environment on the human body and mind, and ways to combat its ill effects, are the realm of space medicine.

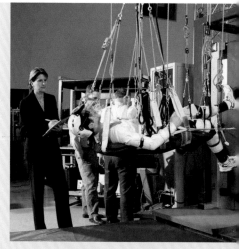

HUMANS REACH SPACE
Much of the early research in this field was done by the German physician Hubertus Strughold (1898–1987). Strughold later emigrated to the USA to lead the country's space medicine program. The USSR and the USA gathered useful data in the 1940s–50s by sending animals into space. In 1961, Soviet cosmonaut Yuri Gagarin became the first human to rocket out of Earth's atmosphere. As more humans traveled into space and stayed there for longer periods, medical knowledge increased. This was made possible by U.S. space shuttle missions and permanently orbiting space stations like *Salyut 1* and *Skylab* (1970s) and *Mir* (1986–99), where astronauts lived for months at a time. The Soviet cosmonautic medicine specialist Vladimir Polyakov spent more than 14 consecutive months on *Mir* conducting medical research. In 1998, John Glenn, who, in 1962 became the first American to orbit Earth, went up in the space shuttle *Discovery* at the age of 77 to facilitate a study on factors common to aging as well as time spent in space.

SICKNESSES IN SPACE
Findings over time showed that biological infections and changes in body vital signs were minimal in space, but motion sickness affected more than 50 percent of first-time crews. It was effectively treated

as 1894 by the Austrian physiologist Herman Von Schrötter (1870–1928), had enabled the meteorologist Artur Berson (1859–1942) to reach a record altitude of 30,000 ft (9,150 m). Oxygen mask mechanisms continued to improve through the decades.

COMBATING THE FORCES OF GRAVITY

"G" (gravity) forces created by fast radial acceleration and deceleration, especially while executing maneuvers in military aircraft, became a serious factor from World War II onward. One "g" is equal to the force of gravity in normal circumstances. Four to six "gs" can cause visual impairment and unconsciousness. Pilots flying modern high-performance aircraft can be subjected to as many as nine "gs." They can only achieve this when the "g" forces are countered by anti- "g" suits, special outfits that exert pressure on the lower half of the body, thereby preventing the accumulation of blood in these areas at the expense of the brain. The first pressurized suit was designed in 1934 by the American flyer Wiley Post (1898–1935), and the first anti- "g" suit was created by the Canadian medical researcher Wilbur Franks (1901–86), in 1942.

Wiley Post's pressure suit, 1935.

Above left: NASA's floating treadmill.
Above: Testing the fit of a spacesuit.

with drugs such as intramuscular promethazine, and in any case did not last more than 48 to 72 flight hours. The psychological effects of spending long durations in the closed environment of a space station with other people were not significant, perhaps because a criterion for choosing astronauts is their mental stability. The biological clock could be maintained by observing Earth time schedules. The chances of decompression illness, caused by sudden decrease in atmospheric pressure, were reduced by space suits. Similar to those used in aviation, they were inflated with 100 percent oxygen pressurized at one-third of atmospheric pressure.

REMEDIAL MEASURES

The deleterious effects of exposure to long-term radiation and the lack of gravity emerged as the two main concerns. It was found that astronauts on long-term missions received radiation doses many times that of a medical X-ray from solar flares, onboard nuclear equipment, and elements present in the earth's magnetic field. Shielding systems were developed to protect against this. The lack of an opposing force in the course of normal physical activity, due to a micro-gravity environment, promoted serious bone loss and muscle atrophy, including that of the heart. The oxygen-carrying capacity of blood decreased, as did the secretion of growth hormones. All this had to be countered by regular resistance and cardiovascular exercise while on board.

PARAMEDICAL SERVICE

Paramedical services refer to medical attention provided prior to hospitalization and advanced medical care. These services are provided by trained personnel, who are, however, not doctors. Paramedics come into play in case of emergencies like accidents or trauma, when the patient has to be administered life-saving treatment on the spot and transported safely to establishments staffed with doctors offering more comprehensive and specialized treatment.

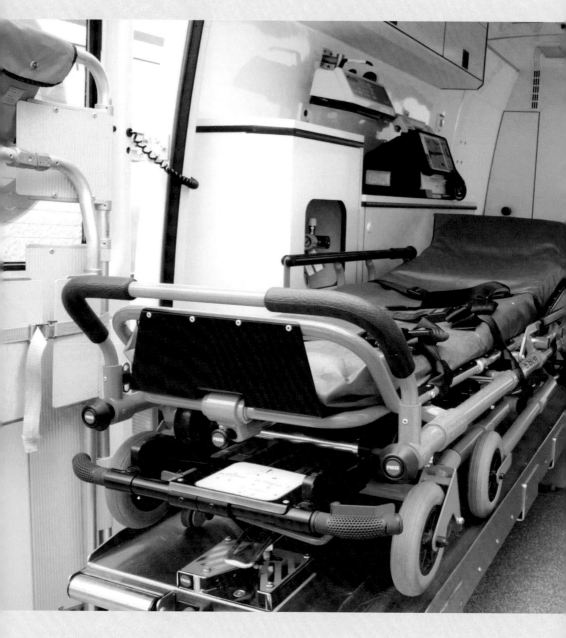

The interior of a well-equipped modern ambulance.

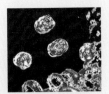

shows he had been infected with the AIDS virus.

SWITZERLAND

1992 Swiss vote against banning animals for medical and pharmaceutical experiments.

USA

1995 In tests, a handheld cancer "supergun" halts tumor growth in mice. It shoots microscopic gold "bullets" coated with genetic material into the body. These enter the cancers and stimulate the body's immune system to fight them.

BRITAIN

1995 Trials at Royal Marsden Hospital, London, show massage reduces anxiety and improves quality of life in cancer patients.

1995 Research suggests that hearts, lungs, and kidneys from specially bred pigs can be transplanted to humans.

1995 Scientists in Bradford isolate cells that regulate hair growth.

1996–97 Sheep cloned at the Roslin Institute in Edinburgh by Bulfield. Polly the Lamb is genetically altered to produce a protein for treating hemophilia.

1996 New treatment for cancer is tried: Two children are given cell transplants from umbilical cords of newborn siblings—similar to concept of bone marrow transplant.

WORLD

1996 WHO announces breakthrough in birth control for men: A weekly injection reduces sperm production to a negligible level.

1996 WHO sets up an obesity task force to combat a worldwide epidemic of obesity.

AUSTRALIA

1996 The world's first law permitting voluntary euthanasia comes into force in the Northern Territory, and a terminally ill cancer patient becomes first to die under this new legislation.

USA

1996 Scientists believe they may have identified cause of addiction to cigarette smoking.

THE FIRST AMBULANCE

Historically, these services evolved in a military context, where the wounded had to be extracted from the battlefield and carried back to the expert care of physicians. An initial precursor to the ambulance—the most essential and ubiquitous paramedic accompaniment—emerged in the late 18th century, when Napoleon's surgeon, Dominique-Jean Larrey (1766–1842) developed the *ambulance volante* (flying ambulance), a horse-drawn cart adapted into a retrieval vehicle for the injured from the front lines. Larrey's device was part of a full-fledged ambulance corps, which included surgeons, apothecaries, and bearers. The system of structured and timely medical care was put into effective use during the American Civil War (1861–65). Soon, the concept filtered into civilian life, where local bodies like the police set up their own emergency services. Following World War I, motorized ambulances became widespread.

Left: Dominique-Jean Larrey (1766–1842), Napoleon's military surgeon.
Below: Larrey's design for the *ambulance volante*.

St. John Ambulance

In 11th-century Jerusalem, St. John was a small hospice next to the Church of the Holy Sepulcher. It was run by monks for sick Christian pilgrims coming to the Holy Land. When the Crusades began, circumstances called for nursing, as well as defending the needy. The Order of the Knights Hospitaller of St. John was born. This was the beginning of what is today St. John Ambulance, a health care organization spread across 40 countries.

With the defeat of Christian states by Muslim armies, the Hospitallers reestablished themselves on the island of Rhodes in the Mediterranean Sea. Well connected and wealthy, the Knights also had a powerful presence in Europe. Ousted from Rhodes by Turkish forces in 1522, they relocated to Malta, where they reigned and continued their medical work, till defeated at the hands of Napoleon in 1798. The Knights broke up and settled across Europe, securing for themselves the protection of various rulers. The Order was revived in the 19th century. The Industrial Revolution was underway at that time, and there was a need for addressing poor health and disability caused by trying working conditions. The Hospitallers rose to the task. In England, St. John Ambulance units were set up across the country. Their stock increased not just because of their good work but also because of official recognition and strong support from the royalty. During the two World Wars, personnel of St. John Ambulance worked actively with the Red Cross.

Today, St. John Ambulance works in a variety of ways in different countries. It provides basic paramedical services, first-aid training, health-related equipment, ranging from mosquito nets for malaria prevention to money for cancer research, besides other charity.

The Knights Hospitaller.

BRITAIN

1997 A five-day-old baby, given a new liver, is Britain's youngest transplant patient.

1997 Government announces ban on sale of beef on the bone after new evidence that BSE ("mad cow disease") can be spread through bone marrow.

CHINA

1997 The influenza A (H5N1) virus (commonly known as "bird flu") first crosses from birds to humans.

BRITAIN

1998 A "bypass" is operated by a new kind of artificial "heart" and keeps a girl alive by allowing her heart to "rest" until she recovers from an otherwise fatal heart illness.

1998 A report in *New Scientist* states men who regularly give blood are less likely to suffer heart disease—seeming to support ancient medical practice of bloodletting. The only leech farm in Britain (near Swansea) sells 20,000 each year to specialist hospitals such as burn units.

1998 A report in *Nature* magazine suggests the HIV virus responsible for AIDS appeared in humans in Africa in the late 1940s. The virus was not identified until the 1980s, by which time AIDS is a worldwide epidemic.

THE PROFESSION DEVELOPS

By the 1960s and '70s, heart monitoring and fluid replacement systems had become standard ambulance equipment, and the skills of paramedic personnel had increased commensurately. In the U.S., firefighters found themselves entrusted with the dual task of functioning as paramedics. Relatively unnoticed up to now, paramedics were catapulted into public imagination through the television series *Emergency!* (In the UK, *Casualty*, a show based on a similar theme, was launched in the 1980s and has been running since then.) As paramedics began to emerge as professionals in their own right, various courses and qualification programs were established. These provided training varying from about 100 hours to over 1,400 hours at the local community, as well as university level. Substantial differences in skill sets led to a generally accepted demarcation between the lesser qualified EMT (emergency medical technician) and the more highly trained paramedic. Within these, too, there were sub-grades. Doctors began to relax tight supervision and direction of paramedic operations, trusting crews to independently follow generally established protocols.

TODAY'S PARAMEDICS

Various countries have evolved their own system of paramedical services, with personnel graded into categories ranging from the basic to the advanced. For example, in case of a cardiac emergency, depending on the skill of the paramedic, the treatment provided could range from cardiopulmonary resuscitation to restoring normal heart rate by administering an electric current through artificial pacemakers. Similarly, whereas a basic level paramedic's proficiency does not go beyond administering common medication like glucose, the advanced professional may have the competence to handle more than 50 drugs. In some countries, such as Germany, the emphasis is on providing as comprehensive as possible a treatment at the site itself. Sometimes, physicians are part of paramedic squads. Larrey's innovation has evolved into different forms, including vans, responder bicycles and motorcycles, boats, and helicopters. Fitted with sirens and beacons and a host of medical equipment, they function as very effective medical crisis transports.

Emergency response vehicles at the site of an accident.

OBESITY

The excessive accumulation of body fat to the extent that it adversely impacts one's health is called obesity, a condition that lies beyond the limits of being merely overweight. Obesity results from consuming more calories than your body uses, a calorific surplus arising from overeating, poor diet, lack of physical exercise, and genetic disposition. The extra calories are then stored in the body as fat. Obesity, or its approach, can be recognized by a thickening midriff, clothes becoming tighter, and higher than previous weighing-scale readings. Scientifically, a body mass index (BMI)—a scientific correlation of height and weight—of over 30 indicates obesity. Obesity can lead to Type 2 diabetes, hypertension, heart disease, stroke, cancer, and arthritis. It can also cause lack of self-esteem. Exercise and dietary adjustments can prevent and cure obesity, while other modes of treatment are appetite suppressants and fat-blocker drugs and bariatric (weight-reducing) surgery.

A tray of junk food, increasingly popular among the young today.

OBESITY TIMELINE

George Cheyne.

4th–5th century BCE Herodicus, Hippocrates, Polybus recognize obesity.

46–c. 122 CE Plutarch advises against growing corpulent.

131–201 CE Galen reduces the weight of a "huge fat fellow" with exercise, warm baths, and diet.

1547 Andrew Boorde, Henry VIII's physician, blames alcohol as the cause of obesity.

17th century Thomas Sydenham attributes corpulence to inefficiently functioning organs and an immoderate lifestyle. Tobias Venner is the first physician to use the word "obesity" in a medical context. George Cheyne notes, from his own condition, that obesity can bring on depression. He weighs 441 pounds (200 kg) and needs an attendant to follow behind him with a stool on which he can rest after every few steps.

1765 Joannes Baptista Morgagni proposes that the position of fat accumulation in the body is crucial.

1940s Metropolitan Life Insurance Co. publishes new height-weight tables.

1950s First bariatric surgeries.

1963 Weight Watchers International started by Jean Nidetch, an American housewife who lost weight with a home-designed diet.

1976–80 15 percent of U.S. adults are obese.

1982 Modern liposuction emerges.

1990s Phentermine and fenfluramine (Fen-Phen) become the most popular weight-reduction drugs. Found to cause heart disease, they are later withdrawn.

1994 More than 51,000 liposuction procedures are conducted in USA.

1996 Body mass index is the standard for measuring obesity.

2002 Obesity-associated cancers among women comprise half of all new cancers diagnosed.

2003–04 32 percent of U.S. adults are obese.

2007 300 million obese people worldwide.

2008 The U.S. Democratic Party Platform is the first national party platform ever to acknowledge the importance of addressing the obesity epidemic in the country.

Jean Nidetch, founder of Weight Watchers.

1998 Researchers at Guy's Hospital announce development of a vaccine that, painted onto teeth, appears to prevent decay for 6 months.

1998 Discovery of early dental implant. A young man from the 1st or 2nd century had a tooth made of wrought-iron hammered directly into his jaw.

FRANCE

1998 Dubernard and Owen carry out first arm transplant. Clint Hallam is given a new forearm and hand after a chainsaw accident.

USA

1998 World's first surviving octuplets born.

1998 Viagra, the new anti-impotence treatment, is approved by the U.S. Food and Drug Administration.

GERMANY

1999 Ebola: Suspected case in Berlin may be 1st in Europe. Scientists working on plant from West Africa that may help control virus.

USA

1999 Scientists develop technique for growing replacement bones. A woman is having her face rebuilt using bone grown on a mold attached to another part of her body.

1999 Scientists create a Living Computer, using neurones (nerve cells) from leeches.

1999 Arnowitz develops new skin-patch test for diabetes.

BRITAIN

1999 New immunization program against meningitis C announced.

1999 Doctors attempt to implant an artificial cornea into a man's cheek. The plastic lens will be removed later, together with the human cells grown around it, and used to replace the damaged cornea in one eye to restore his sight.

1999 Dolly the Sheep shows signs of accelerated genetic aging, raising new fears about cloning humans. The sheep, the first mammal cloned from an adult, appears perfectly normal but on a genetic level is at least 6 years older than she should be. DNA sequences that protect the ends of chromosomes are shorter in Dolly than in a normal sheep of her age.

LIFESTYLE DISEASES

DIABETES

The body's digestive process converts food into glucose for energy. Glucose, a sugar, is released into the bloodstream where a substance called insulin, manufactured by the pancreas, regulates its presence and distribution for storage into muscles, fat, and the liver. If the pancreas does not produce enough insulin, or the muscles, fat, and liver cells do not respond to insulin adequately, the result is a chronic condition of high blood sugar levels. This is called diabetes.

Apart from genetic predisposition, diabetes can be brought on by heart disease, high blood cholesterol levels, obesity, and a sedentary lifestyle. Symptoms include fatigue, increased thirst and frequency of urination, nausea, blurry vision, and weight loss despite an enhanced appetite. A positive diagnosis is arrived at by ascertaining glucose levels via blood tests and urine analysis.

There is no cure for diabetes. Immediate treatment may require hospitalization, while in the longer term diabetes can be controlled by regular monitoring of blood glucose, insulin injections, a planned food intake, regular exercise, and weight control. Diabetes' damaging effect on nerves and blood vessels, and therefore reduced sensation at the affected areas, can lead to foot problems, as minor injuries may not be noticed in time for early care.

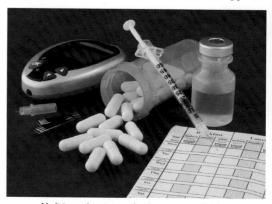

Medicine and equipment for the treatment of diabetes.

DIABETES TIMELINE

1552 BCE First known mention of diabetes by Egyptian physician Hesy-Ra, on the Ebers papyrus.

c. 120 CE First complete medical description of the disease by Greek physician Aretaeus of Cappodocia.

1776 English physician Matthew Dobson conclusively establishes that presence of "saccharine materials" in urine is an indication of diabetes.

1901 A relationship between the failure of the islets of Langerhans cells (discovered by German medical student Paul Langerhans in 1869) in the pancreas and the disease is proven by American pathologist Eugene Opie.

Eugene Opie.

1921–23 Frederick Banting discovers insulin. Its administration produces outstanding results; commercial production and availability begins.

1959 Type 1 (insulin dependent) and Type 2 (non-insulin dependent) diabetes categorized.

1966 First pancreas transplant.

1982 Humulin, the first biosynthetic human insulin, is developed for mass production by pharmaceutical giant Eli Lilly and Co.

1999 First successful islet of Langerhans transplant.

2006 Diabetes recognized as a global threat by the United Nations.

2008 Research indicates that people with resting heart rates over 80 beats per minute have higher chances of developing diabetes.

2011 Researchers in the USA announce a new, accurate, and simple method of identifying individuals who are pre-diabetic and who could take preventive measures to avoid developing diabetes. The hemoglobin A1c blood test averages blood glucose level over the past 8 to 12 weeks, needs only one test, does not require the patient to fast beforehand, and can be carried out in a physician's office.

AUSTRALIA

1999 Doctors in Sydney succeed in combining the genetical material of two donor mothers into one egg. The technique may give a chance of motherhood to older women whose eggs are imperfect. So far, 3 boys and 2 girls have been born using this technique.

1999 Scientists believe hair may provide a simple screening test for breast cancer, and to detect drug abuse.

BRITAIN

2000 Stephen Westaby installs the first permanent artificial heart.

USA

2000 Human Genome Project scientists sequence 90 percent of the human genome.

2000 National Institutes of Health officially recognize for the first time that stress reduction is important to alleviate mental and physical disease caused by modern lifestyles.

2000 *Time* magazine recognizes Siemens Biograph as one of the inventions of the year.

2000 Bill and Melinda Gates Foundation announces new global health grants of $28.5 million to eradicate guinea worm disease, caused by drinking infected water.

GERMANY

2000 Researchers decode all the genes of the meningitis bacterium, *Neisseria meningitis,* associated with epidemics of the disease, especially in developing countries.

NETHERLANDS

2000 First country in the world to legalize voluntary euthanasia.

AFRICA

2000 Out of 36 million HIV-positive people in the world, almost 25 million are in sub-Saharan Africa.

The universal symbol for AIDS awareness.

2001 Sixteen West African states renew their commitment to eradicating polio with a massive immunization campaign launched by WHO, UNICEF, and Rotary International.

USA

2001 16.9 million nuclear medicine procedures performed.

2001 St. Jude's Medical, Inc., announces the first implant of its new invention, the dual-chamber pacemaker, designed to better manage pacemaker patients suffering from atrial fibrillation, the most common cardiac arrhythmia.

2001 Researchers from the universities of Chicago and Michigan identify the first genetic abnormality: Mutations of gene Nod2 that increases susceptibility to Crohn's disease.

FRANCE

2001 Establishment of the Meningitis Vaccine Project with the objective to eliminate epidemic meningitis in sub-Saharan Africa.

USA/FRANCE

2001 First telesurgery, called the Lindbergh Operation, based on high-speed fiber optic services using surgical robotics, performed by a French doctor in USA on a French patient in France.

EGYPT

2001 The *Middle East Fertility Society Journal* reports that in an opinion poll among members of APART—an international association of assisted reproductive technology centers— three-quarters of the respondents expressed willingness to provide human cloning for patients in clinically indicated cases.

BRITAIN

2002 According to the *British Journal of Psychiatry,* thioridazine, a common drug used in the treatment of some psychoses, is now linked to sudden unexplained death.

USA

2003 Human genome sequencing complete. The accuracy is expected to be at least 99.9 percent.

2003 The first biotech pet, genetically modified zebrafish, available commercially.

2003 A new MRI scanner provides real-time updates during surgery and detects any part of a tumor that may have been overlooked.

CORONARY ARTERY DISEASE

Over time, deposits of plaque and cholesterol cause a narrowing and hardening of the inner walls of the arteries supplying blood to the heart. This can cause the heart to become starved of adequate blood and oxygen necessary for its efficient functioning. Coronary artery disease (CAD), as it is called, is the major cause for angina (chest pain), arrhythmia, and heart attacks.

Aging, family history, and gender—men are more predisposed than women—increase one's chances of getting CAD. With high blood pressure, a smoking habit, obesity, high cholesterol, diabetes, lack of physical exercise, and stress, the risks increase further. One may not feel any discomfort as the disease develops, but the classic symptoms, when they do appear, are angina, which usually passes within a few minutes, shortness of breath, fatigue, or heart attack, typically signaled by severe pain in the chest, as well as in the shoulder, arm, back, or jaw.

An arterial stent.

CAD can be detected through several tests. Electrocardiogram and echocardiogram—with or without physical exercise over short periods— employ electrical and sound waves, respectively, to decipher heart function. Angiograms involve the injection of a dye via a thin catheter, which is inserted into the arteries. The dye enables a visual profiling of potential trouble spots on X-ray images. Computerized tomography (CT) scans and magnetic resonance angiograms (MRA) are other computerized diagnostic technologies.

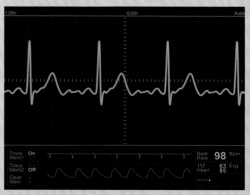

A heart monitor.

Lifestyle changes, where applicable, are imperative for any successful long-term treatment of CAD. These involve giving up smoking, adhering to a healthy diet, a regular exercise regimen, and avoiding stress. Some of the medication is the same as that prescribed for lowering blood pressure. Other drugs work by reducing cholesterol, opening up the arteries, and thinning the blood (aspirin). Surgical procedures involve creating a "bypass" around the affected artery. Stents and balloons, inserted by angioplasty, serve to keep the arteries open.

Stages of development of arteriosclerosis.

AUSTRALIA

2003 Influenza B-Brisbane, a new strain of flu, discovered by Queensland scientists.

VIETNAM

2003 Carlo Urbani sounds alarm to the possibility of a SARS (severe acute respiratory syndrome) epidemic, thus enabling a timely, effective response. Urbani himself dies of the disease a few weeks later.

USA

2004 Technology advances in CT and MRI imaging, and ultrasound, enable Johns Hopkins surgeons to prolong the lives of cancer patients by 30 to 50 percent.

TAIWAN

2004 First International Symposium on Tibetan medicine.

BRITAIN

2004 The first international standard for common genetic tests identifies Factor V Leiden, a genetic predisposition that induces defects in the body's natural anticoagulation system.

2004 The world's first stem cell bank in Hertfordshire. It is responsible for storing, characterizing, and supplying ethically approved, quality controlled stem cell lines from embryonic, fetal, and adult tissues.

USA

2005 The Shang Shung Institute in Massachusetts offers a four-year Traditional Tibetan Medicine Program, the only one of its kind anywhere in the West.

2005 New research at Oregon State University comes closer to explaining how vitamin C can prevent cancer and heart disease by getting rid of toxic byproducts of fat metabolism.

2005 Researchers at Harvard School of Public Health awarded a five-year $30 million grant to study the long-term effects on children of antiretroviral drug exposure.

ITALY

2005 Only one out of four Italians vote in the referendum to modify the country's law on assisted reproduction.

BRITAIN

2005 It is reported that pancreatic cancer patients have better prospects after surgery when their levels of protein calcyclin are low or undetectable in the cell nucleus.

CANADA

2005 More than $5 million are directed to support experiments investigating the use of adult stem cells to replace damaged cells in the heart, lungs, or blood vessels.

GERMANY

2006 A ban is pushed for on stem cell research in the European Union.

USA

2006 New surgery for morbid obesity through transoval endoscopic surgical technique at the American College of Gastroenterology.

2006 Alberto Ascherio's study at Harvard School of Public Health reveals that high vitamin D levels in the body may decrease risks of multiple sclerosis.

2006 Researchers at Mayo identify complex sleep apnea, wherein the patient stops breathing 20 to 30 times per hour each night. The Continuous Airway Pressure device, used in obstructive and central sleep apnea cases, is ineffective in its treatment.

ITALY

2006 The world's first unmanned robotic surgery.

ASIA

2006 Mangosteen, a tropical fruit grown in Southeast Asia, is now available as juice in commercial form for building up the immune system.

A mangosteen.

LIFESTYLE DISEASES

STRESS AND ANXIETY

Stress pertains to feelings of anger, frustration, or an unpleasant mental state, arising from specific situational circumstances or thoughts. Anxiety usually relates to fear or apprehension, often not ostensibly linked to any particular cause. Both states can occur together but not necessarily so. It is important to note that a small amount of stress is beneficial as it prevents inertia and motivates productivity.

Stress and anxiety can be brought on by non-medical as well as medical factors. Many of the former relate to the demands and dynamics of modern-day living. These include the pressures to perform in increasingly competitive business and social environments, long working hours, poor eating habits, domestic discordance, and not enough sleep.

Headaches are the most common symptom of stress.

Withdrawal effects of substances like caffeine, alcohol, nicotine, cocaine, and other recreational drugs can cause stress. So can the side effects of drugs taken for respiratory and thyroid disorders, and diet pills.

Loss of concentration, inability to sleep restfully, rapid breathing and heartbeat, propensity to irritability, headaches, and muscle tension are symptomatic of undue stress. Sometimes sweating, twitching or trembling, and a dry mouth accompany anxiety attacks.

The first step in treating these conditions is to identify the underlying causes. Very often, the best way is to talk to someone close or to a psychoanalyst. Cognitive-behavioral therapy (CBT) helps in reorientation of perspective. Changing to a healthier lifestyle by taking time out for leisure, exercise, and meditation, and correcting dietary habits are effective measures. Blood tests for thyroid dysfunction, and electrocardiograms, are sometimes used to determine possible clinical causes, which may be treated with types of antidepressants and a class of drugs called benzodiazepines.

HYPERTENSION

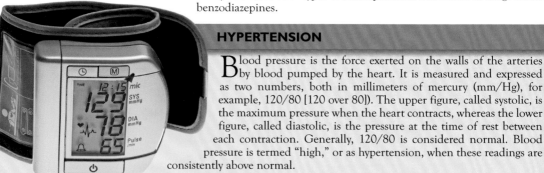

Blood pressure is the force exerted on the walls of the arteries by blood pumped by the heart. It is measured and expressed as two numbers, both in millimeters of mercury (mm/Hg), for example, 120/80 [120 over 80]). The upper figure, called systolic, is the maximum pressure when the heart contracts, whereas the lower figure, called diastolic, is the pressure at the time of rest between each contraction. Generally, 120/80 is considered normal. Blood pressure is termed "high," or as hypertension, when these readings are consistently above normal.

Often, there is no identifiable cause for hypertension. At other times, a variety of factors, independently or in combination with each other, are known to cause it. Some of these are excess intake of salt, anxiety and stress,

A sphygmomanometer used to measure blood pressure.

obesity, arteriosclerosis, kidney disease, and the side affects of certain drugs such as those used in appetite suppressants and birth control pills.

Symptoms can range from none at all to headaches, buzzing in the ear, chest pain, tiredness, and changes in vision. Hypertension can be controlled by medicines such as alpha and beta blockers, vasodilators, and angiotensin-converting enzyme (ACE) inhibitors, as well as by lifestyle changes, which call for regular physical exercise, low-fat and -salt diet, and weight reduction.

INDIA
2006 Brain Suite, a surgical technique used for abnormal bulging of a brain artery, is available for the first time in Asia.

SWITZERLAND
2007 Installation of the world's first BSD 500 hyperthermia cancer therapy system at Aarau. Hyperthermia is delivered here through microwave energy.

2007 The first extra-cranial stereotactic treatment (minimally invasive) done in Bern on a lung cancer patient. Three highly focused radiotherapy doses are delivered to destroy a tumor, which reportedly shrinks.

WORLD
2007 WHO Annual Report states that commercial flights, carrying more than 2 billion passengers a year, are an efficient mechanism for spreading disease rapidly across continents.

USA
2007 Special issue of *Science Times*, an associated publication of the *New York Times,* examines a cascade of research into the science of sleep.

2007 Triphala, a well-known Indian herbal supplement, is reported to have cancer-fighting properties.

AFRICA
2007 A WHO–UN publication on AIDS recommends male circumcision in Africa, as it can offer partial protection against AIDS.

ISRAEL
2007 Preliminary findings indicate that oral antisense oligonucleotide effectively and safely reduces neuro-muscular disease severity by 46 percent and improves muscle function and swallowing time in patients.

USA
2008 The first hybrid PET/MRI system for humans, installed by Siemens. PET evaluates metabolic aspects of disease, while MRI provides high-resolution anatomical information.

2008 A study at the University of Texas and National Institutes of Health shows the Chinese herb *tripterygium wilfordii Hook F* (TWHF) to be effective in the treatment of rheumatoid arthritis.

2008 Research at the University of Alabama shows that the investigational drug triphendial kills malignant cells in pancreatic and bile duct carcinoma.

2008 Pharma company Genentech, supported by the FDA, announces that cancer drug Tarceva (erlotinib) can lead to liver problems and fatalities.

2008 Advances in plastic surgery toward repairing facial injuries on soldiers in the war in Iraq is to be made available to civilian victims of city violence.

2008 Research indicates that palmitoleate, a newly identified hormone, can combat diabetes and conditions related to obesity.

2008 The EndoBarrier Gastrointestinal Liner, a new non-invasive devise inserted endoscopically into the small intestine through the mouth, could promote blood sugar control and weight loss.

2008 Scientists at Northwestern University report that people with chronic backaches have brains that are 11 percent smaller than non-sufferers, perhaps due to the stress of having to live with the condition.

2008 Researchers from MassGeneral Institute of Neurodegenerative Disease and Harvard School of Public Health claim that elevated levels of urate, a normal antioxidant in the blood, may slow progression of Parkinson's disease in men.

2008 *American Journal of Epidemiology* reports that drinking alcohol in the first three months of pregnancy results in an increased risk of producing infants with cleft lip and cleft palate deformity.

2008 OvaSure, a new blood test, is developed at Yale for early detection of ovarian cancer. It is yet to be validated.

2008 A link between the lack of protein MeCP2, associated with Rett Syndrome, and certain behavioral disorders is revealed.

2008 New research at the University of Michigan on how the protein HIV–1 Nef keeps immune cells from doing their normal work of detecting and killing infected cells.

2008 The protein Npas4, the first known "master switch" in brain cells, essential for proper brain function, is identified at the Children's Hospital, Boston. It regulates more than 200 genes that calm down over-excited cells, thereby restoring balance in neurological disorders.

In the medieval world, health and life insurance was provided by workers' guilds, which looked after members of the affected family in case of illness or death. In the late 17th century, the Englishman Hugh the Elder, scion of the illustrious Chamberlen family of medical practitioners, suggested the idea of medical insurance. In the 19th century, the Industrial Revolution transformed the economies of Europe and the U.S. Organized workforces felt the need for financial security in the event of loss of livelihood during their earning lives. The first formations to address this need were mutual benefit associations such as the Friendly Society and Saturday Fund in Great Britain, and La Société Française de Bienfaisance Mutuelle in San Francisco, USA. However, these organizations could offer very limited support due to non-compulsory, therefore relatively thin, participation.

THE FIRST PLANS

The London Guarantee and Accident Company Building, Chicago.

In the 1850s, the Franklin Health Assurance Company became one of the earliest of its kind in the U.S. to provide accident insurance for steamboat and railroad mishaps. The glimmerings of commercial insurance were evident. In 1911, Montgomery Ward & Co., the world's first mail-order business, went a step further from the voluntary model. It brought its employees under the first group insurance plan, negotiated with the London Guarantee and Accident Company, New York. As was the general order of the day, this was disability insurance, whereby the employee was covered for loss of income suffered because of medical leave. The coverage amounted to 50 percent of the weekly salary.

GOVERNMENTS STEP IN

Meanwhile, governments had begun to feel an obligation from another perspective to look after their citizens. This was the provision of medical treatment, as against cash coverage due to disability. Germany was the first to pass legislation on this subject in 1883. Great Britain followed in 1911 with the National Health Insurance Act, which ultimately led to the establishment of the United Kingdom's National Health Service in 1948.

2008 The *Archives of International Medicine* reports that a diet restricted in calories does not cause bone loss in young, overweight adults, provided adequate amounts of calcium and other nutrients are maintained.

2008 Dr. Gail Rebovic's oncoplastic surgery for breast cancer incorporates surgery and cosmetic reconstruction simultaneously. By minimizing the number of times patients have to go under the knife, it counters poor insurance reimbursements for plastic surgery.

2008 Identification of three phospatases enzymes by researchers at Baylor College of Medicine could be the beginning of a new treatment for prostate cancer.

2008 Researchers at NYC Cancer Institute and the Ronald O. Perelman Department of Dermatology identify mebandozole, a drug used globally to treat parasite infections, as a new agent for treating chemotherapy-resistant malignant melanoma.

2008 American Heart Association achieves its goal of reducing coronary heart disease and stroke risk by 25 percent since 2000. About half the reductions came from new treatments, and the other half from prevention campaigns.

SPAIN
2008 The European Study of Human Genetics announces the discovery of genetic mutations in eight new areas. This is expected to help in addressing intestinal disorders and shed new light on a range of autoimmune and inflammatory diseases.

BRITAIN
2008 Scientists in Newcastle test a new vaccine that could suppress effects of rheumatoid arthritis by using patients' own blood.

2008 National Heart and Lung Institute, Imperial College, says beta blockers used for angina, heart failure, and high blood pressure can raise blood sugar in diabetics and cause diabetes in high blood pressure patients.

USA/UK
2008 Inhaler drugs Atrovent (ipratropium) and Spiriva (tiotropium bromide), which open up airways for chronic lung disease patients, are reported to increase risks of heart attack, stroke, and cardiovascular death by 58 percent.

EUROPE
2008 Clinical trials demonstrate that, if intravenously administrated within a time window, the enzyme alteplase can minimize or prevent post-stroke disability.

ITALY
2008 The Moli-sani Project reports that one small square of dark chocolate consumed two or three times a week can reduce blood inflammation, and therefore the chances of cardiovascular disease.

Dark chocolate.

WORLD
2008 According to a WHO study undertaken over 2002–2006 in 81 countries, the incidence of multidrug resistant tuberculosis is highest in the world in Baku, Azerbaijan.

2008 Medical tourism is estimated to be at least a $10 billion industry. The biggest destinations are India, Mexico, and southeast Asia.

SWITZERLAND
2008 WHO urges governments to impose a total ban on all tobacco advertising, promotion, and sponsorship.

FRANCE
2008 On the basis of a study, drug company Sanofi-aventis approves the use of nasal spray Nasacort AQ (triamcinolone acetonide), for even two- to five-year-old children, in treating seasonal and perennial allergic rhinitis.

2008 The *European Heart Journal* reports that isoflavone, a chemical compound in chickpeas, legumes, and clovers, can improve artery function in stroke patients.

THE BLUE CROSS AND COMMERCIAL GROWTH IN THE U.S.

More hospitals began to offer pre-paid insurance services for groups. As medical science advanced and treatment became more effective, physicians and hospitals began to charge higher fees. In these circumstances, especially when America was hit by the Great Depression of the 1920s, the cost of decent medical care became unaffordable for most people. This led to the inception of the Blue Cross organization (now a nationwide federation of insurance-providing companies in America), which originated out of Baylor Hospital's (Dallas) 21-day-per-year pre-paid hospital expenses insurance for 1,500 school teachers. The government helped Blue Cross sustain these plans by giving organizations tax

breaks. Initially cautious of entering what they regarded as an enterprise of uncertain returns, private investors, encouraged by the success of the Blue Cross model, started venturing into long-term medical insurance more confidently. During World War II, the government imposed ceilings on employee wages, so companies, in order to woo labor from competitors, began offering insurance benefits incentives. In the following decades, the insurance industry grew at a fast pace. Compared to less than 10 percent of the population in 1940, nearly 70 percent had insurance in 1955. New plans with add-on coverages, such as for vision care, extended hospital stay, and prescription drugs, were now in the market.

Above left: The original logo of the Blue Cross Insurance Company.
Left: Baylor Hospital.

BRITAIN/NEPAL

2008 A closed-circuit oxygen device, invented over 50 years ago by British rocket scientist Tom Bourdillon, is jointly redeveloped by the High Altitude Laboratory at Namche (Nepal), Smith Medical, and University College, London, into a portable modern breathing circuit, which delivers a high concentrate of constant oxygen for a sustained period, irrespective of changing breathing patterns.

ISRAEL

2008 ReWalk, a robotic suit developed by Argo Medical Technologies, Ltd., helps people paralyzed from the waist down to stand, walk, and climb stairs.

INDIA

2008 Asia's first artificial heart implant at Narayana Hrudayalaya Hospital, Bangalore.

GERMANY

2008 "Bionic" microchips for the blind are successfully pioneered.

USA

2009 The ban on federal funding of embryonic stem cell research is lifted.

2009 The first signs of a potential AIDS vaccination is shown by a trial of 16,000 volunteers, suggesting a new vaccine is 31 percent effective at preventing infection.

2009 A study of more than 76,000 men determines that regular screening and early detection of prostate cancer does not lower the death rate from the cancer.

2009 A genetic clue to autism is discovered, when researchers working with the Autism Genetic Resource Exchange identify changes in a section of chromosome 5 as present in 15 percent of people with autism.

2009 Three separate genes linked to late-onset Alzheimer's disease are identified. One gene possibly affects the transmission of signals between nerve cells, the other two contribute to nerve-cell death.

CHINA

2009 Scientists succeed in breeding laboratory mice from stem cells that do not involve embryonic cells. Instead, adult skin cells were reprogrammed to develop into the mice.

INSURANCE

STATE-FUNDED SYSTEMS

Pre-paid health maintenance organizations (HMOs) emerged in the U.S. in the 1970s. They were distinct from conventional insurance providers in that the emphasis was on preventive care, and consultancy was restricted to their own panel of doctors. In the second half of the 20th century, public-funded health care was set up in dozens of countries. The aim was to provide free medical coverage to the vast sweep of national populations. In the USA, there are Medicare and Medicaid. Whereas the former is federally funded and serves the 65-year-plus age group, the latter, funded jointly by federal and state governments, is aimed at the low-income populace. Canada and Australia have their own programs. Besides their national schemes, countries of the European Economic Area (EEA) have introduced the European Health Insurance Card (EHIC), which entitles free or reduced-cost emergency treatment for individuals in member states. In the communist world, the erstwhile USSR's free health care system was inherited by Russia, while the Chinese state has been extending near universal coverage to its citizens. Certain African countries, such as Mali and Guinea, have adopted—with some degree of success—community-based mutual health insurance, a system built around autonomy, nonprofit motives, and responsible management. These programs are created by the population, health care providers, micro-finance institutions, or other social groups, with support from the state and development agencies.

Blue Cross sales booth.

MEXICO

2009–10 A new strain of influenza known as "swine flu" is first identified and spreads rapidly around the world causing a pandemic. A virus is developed in 2009.

USA

2010 Health care reform bill passed, giving health care coverage to about 95 percent of Americans.

2010 By now HAART, or highly active anti-retroviral drug combination therapy, has given a person with AIDS a life expectancy of 69 years, compared to a prognosis of only five years after diagnosis in 1996.

2010 Trials of screening heavy smokers for lung cancer with spiral CT scans decreased deaths from lung cancer by about 20 percent compared with annual chest X-rays.

2010 Biological indicators or biomarkers for Alzheimer's disease are identified. Eventually patients will be tested for these by brain imaging scans and spinal fluid sampling to detect very early signs of the disease.

AUSTRALIA/USA

2010 A multinational team identifies genetic mutations that give women a high risk of developing ovarian cancer.

2010 Australian and American researchers shrink tumors of cancers caused by genes known as microRNAs by applying a microRNA inhibitor.

AUSTRALIA

2010 New drugs that target BRAF gene mutations (present in about half of melanoma tumors in Australia) successfully shrink up to 80 percent of secondary melanomas.

SOUTH KOREA

2010 A new "superbug" bacterium that is resistant to antibiotics is found in two patients in Seoul.

BRITAIN

2010 A study showed that small doses of aspirin taken for several years can lower the risk of death from several cancers.

2010 Doctors at the Cancer Genome Project announce a new drug that treats tumors by targeting gene mutations.

2010 Researchers at the Juvenile Diabetes Research Foundation, Cambridge University, create an insulin pump connected to a sensor that continually measures blood-sugar levels in a diabetic patient and automatically delivers the correct amount of insulin.

HAITI

2010 In the wake of a disastrous earthquake earlier in the year, a cholera outbreak kills more than 1,000 people.

ITALY

2010 A 16th-century Latin book by surgeon Gaspare Tagliacozzi is discovered. In the book he explains one of the world's first known "nose jobs."

FRANCE

2010 Laurent Lantieri of the Henri-Mondor hospital, Paris, claims to have performed the world's first full-face transplant including eyelids, facial muscles, lips, and tear ducts.

USA

2011 Indianapolis researchers announce a new, accurate, and simple method of identifying individuals who are pre-diabetic and who could take preventive measures to avoid developing diabetes. The hemoglobin A1c blood test averages blood glucose level over the past 8 to 12 weeks, needs only one test, does not require the patient to fast beforehand, and can be carried out in a physician's office.

AFRICA

2011 An outbreak of polio in the Republic of Congo causes at least 179 deaths.

BRITAIN

2011 Surgeons at the Royal County Hospital, Guildford, use special glasses—similar to those used to view the movie *Avatar* in 3-D—to gain a 3-D image inside a body and conduct remote keyhole surgery.

CANADA

2011 A team from the University of Montréal's Department of Biochemistry show that PML molecules, present in benign cancer cells, work by arranging certain proteins in a network that suppresses other proteins that are needed for the cell to multiply itself over and over again. It therefore makes the cancer cell "senescent," whereas malignant cancer cells continue to replicate themselves.

ALFRED NOBEL

Swedish scientist and inventor Alfred Bernhard Nobel (1833–96) was the founder of the Nobel Prize.

A brilliant linguist, chemist, engineer, and entrepreneur, Alfred Nobel studied explosives and accrued a huge fortune from the manufacture of these, including dynamite, and from the exploitation of oil fields. In due course, he established factories and laboratories in 90 different sites in 20 countries. Nobel also invented synthetic rubber and fabrics and, by the time of his death, had 355 patents.

From a fund established under his will, the prestigious Nobel Prizes have been awarded annually since 1901, the fifth anniversary of Alfred Nobel's death.

1901

Physics GERMANY
Wilhelm Röntgen: Discovery of X-rays.

Chemistry NETHERLANDS
Jacobus Van't Hof: Laws of chemical dynamics and osmotic pressure.

Medicine GERMANY
Emil von Behring: Work on serum therapy.

1902

Physics NETHERLANDS
Hendrik Lorentz, Pieter Zeeman: Investigation of the influence of magnetism on the phenomena of radiation.

Chemistry GERMANY
Emil Fischer: Work on sugar and purine syntheses.

Emil Fischer.

Medicine UK
Sir Ronald Ross: Discovery of how malaria enters an organism.

1903

Physics FRANCE
Antoine Henri Becquerel, Pierre Curie, Marie Curie:

Joint work concerning investigations of the radiation phenomena discovered by A.H. Becquerel.

Chemistry SWEDEN
Svante Arrhenius: Theory of electrolytic dissociation.

Medicine DENMARK
Niels R. Finsen: Treatment of skin diseases with light radiation.

1904

Physics UK
Lord Rayleigh: Discovery of argon.

Chemistry UK
Sir William Ramsay: Discovery of inert gaseous elements and determination of their places in the periodic system.

Medicine RUSSIA
Ivan Pavlov: Work on the physiology of digestion.

1905

Physics GERMANY
Philipp Lenard: Research on cathode rays.

Medicine GERMANY
Robert Koch: Tuberculosis research.

Robert Koch.

Chemistry GERMANY
Adolf von Baeyer: Work on organic dyes and hydroaromatic compounds.

1906

Physics UK
Sir Joseph Thomson: Researches into electrical conductivity of gases.

Chemistry FRANCE
Henri Moissan: Isolation of fluorine; introduction of Moissan furnace.

Medicine ITALY, SPAIN
Camillo Golgi, S. Ramón y Cajal: Work on the structure of the nervous system.

1907

Physics USA
Albert Michelson: Spectroscopic and metrological investigations using precision optical instruments.

Medicine FRANCE
Alphonse Laveran: Discovery of the role of protozoa in diseases.

Alphonse Laveran.

Chemistry GERMANY
Eduard Buchner: Discovery of noncellular fermentation.

1908

Physics FRANCE
Gabriel Lippmann: Photographic reproduction of colors.

Medicine GERMANY
RUSSIA
Paul Ehrlich, Elie Metchnikoff: Work on immunity.

Paul Ehrlich.

Chemistry UK
Lord Rutherford: Investigations into the disintegration of elements and the chemistry of radioactive substances.

1909

Physics ITALY, GERMANY
Guglielmo Marconi, Karl Braun: Development of wireless telegraphy.

Chemistry GERMANY
Wilhelm Ostwald: Pioneer work on catalysis, chemical equilibrium, and reaction velocities.

Medicine SWITZERLAND
Emil Kocher: Physiology, pathology, and surgery of thyroid gland.

1910

Physics NETHERLANDS
J. van der Waals: Research concerning the equation of state of gases and liquids.

Chemistry GERMANY
Otto Wallach: Pioneer work in alicyclic combinations.

Medicine GERMANY
Albrecht Kossel: Researches in cellular chemistry.

1911

Physics GERMANY
Wilhelm Wien: Discoveries regarding laws governing heat radiation.

Chemistry FRANCE
Marie Curie: Discovery of radium and polonium; isolation of radium.

Marie Curie.

Medicine SWEDEN
Allvar Gullstrand: Work on dioptrics of the eye.

Allvar Gullstrand.

1912

Physics SWEDEN
Nils Gustaf Dalén: Invention
of automatic regulators for
lighting coastal beacons and
light buoys during darkness
or other periods of reduced
visibility.

Chemistry FRANCE
Victor Grignard: Discovery
of the so-called Grignard
reagents.

Chemistry FRANCE
Paul Sabatier: Method of
hydrogeneting organic
compounds in the presence of
finely powdered metals.

Medicine FRANCE
Alexis Carrel: Work
on vascular suture;
transplantation of organs and
blood vessels.

Physics NETHERLANDS
H. Kamerlingh Onnes:
Investigation into the
properties of matter at low
temperatures; production of
liquid helium.

1913

Chemistry SWITZERLAND
Alfred Werner: Work on
the linkage of atoms in
molecules.

Medicine FRANCE
Charles Richet: Work on
anaphylaxis.

1914

Medicine AUSTRIA
Robert Bárány: Physiology
and pathology of vestibular
apparatus.

Robert Bárány.

Physics GERMANY
Max von Laue: Discovery
of diffraction of X-rays by
crystals.

Chemistry USA
Theodore Richards: Accurate
determination of the
atomic weights of numerous
elements.

1915

Physics UK
Sir William Bragg, Sir
Lawrence Braff: Analysis of
crystal structure by means of
X-rays.

Chemistry GERMANY
Richard Willstätter: Pioneer
researches on plant
pigments, especially
chlorophyll.

1917

Physics UK
Charles Barkla: Discovery of
characteristic X-radiation
of elements.

1918

Physics GERMANY
Max Planck: Discovery of the
elemental quanta.

Chemistry GERMANY
Fritz Haber: Synthesis of
ammonia from its elements.

1919

Physics GERMANY
Joahannes Stark: Discovery
of the Doppler effect in canal
rays and of the division of
spectral lines in the electric
field.

Jules Bordet.

Medicine BELGIUM
Jules Bordet: Discoveries in
regard to immunity.

1920

Physics SWITZERLAND
Charles Guillaume: Discovery
of anomalies in nickel-steel
alloys.

Chemistry GERMANY
Walther Nernst: Work in
thermochemistry.

Medicine DENMARK
August Krogh: Discovery of
capillary motor regulating
mechanism.

1921

Physics GERMANY,
SWITZERLAND
Albert Einstein: Services
to theoretical physics,
especially discovery of law of
photoelectric effect.

Albert Einstein.

Chemistry UK
Frederick Soddy: Chemistry
of radioactive substances;
occurrence and nature of
isotopes.

1922

Physics DENMARK
Niels Bohr: Investigation
of atomic structure and
radiation.

Chemistry UK
Francis Aston: Work with
mass spectrograph; whole-
number rule.

Medicine UK
Archibald V. Hill: Discovery

relating to heat production in
muscles.

Medicine GERMANY
Otto Meyerhof: Discovery of
correlation between oxygen
consumption and metabolism
of lactic acid in muscles.

1923

Physics USA
Robert Millikan: Work on
elementary electric charge and
the photoelectric effect.

Chemistry AUSTRIA
Fritz Pregl: Method of
microanalysis of organic
substances.

Medicine CANADA, UK
Sir F.G. Banting, J.J.R.
Macleod: Discovery of insulin.

Sir F.G. Banting.

1924

Physics SWEDEN
Karl Siegbahn: Discoveries
and investigations in X-ray
spectroscopy.

Medicine NETHERLANDS
Willem Einthoven: Discovery
of electrocardiogram
mechanism.

1925

Physics GERMANY
James Franck, Gustav
Hertz: Discovery of the laws
governing the impact of an
electron on an atom.

Chemistry AUSTRIA
Richard Zsigmondy:
Elucidation of the
heterogeneous nature
of colloidal solutions.

1926

Physics FRANCE
Jean Baptiste Perrin: Works
on discontinuous structure
of matter, especially the
discovery of the equilibrium
of sedimentation.

Chemistry SWEDEN
Theodor Svedberg: Work on
disperse systems.

Medicine DENMARK
Johannes Fibiger: Discovery of
Spiroptera carcinoma.

1927

Physics USA
Arthur Holly Compton:
Discovery of wave-length
change in diffused X-rays.

Physics UK
Charles Wilson: Method of
making visible the paths of
electrically charged particles
by vapor condensation.

Chemistry GERMANY
Heinrich Wieland: Researches
into the constitution of bile
acids.

Medicine AUSTRIA
J. Wagner von Jauregg:
Discovery of therapeutic
importance of malaria

inoculation in dementia paralytica.

1928

Physics UK
Sir Owen Richardson: Discovery of Richardson's law (the dependency of the emission of electrons on temperature).

Chemistry GERMANY
Adolf Windaus: Constitution of sterols and their connection with vitamins.

Medicine FRANCE
Charles Nicolle: Work on typhus.

1929

Physics FRANCE
Prince Louis de Broglie: Discovery of the wave nature of electrons.

Chemistry UK, SWEDEN
Sir Arthur Harden, H. von Euler-Chelpin: Investigations on the fermentation of sugars and the enzymes acting in this connection.

Medicine NETHERLANDS
Christiaan Eijkmann: Discovery of antineuritic vitamin.

Medicine UK
Sir F. Hopkins: Discovery of growth-stimulating vitamins.

1930

Physics INDIA
Sir C. Raman: Work on light diffusion; discovery of Raman effect.

Chemistry GERMANY
Hans Fischer: Researches into haemin and chlorophyll, and synthesis of haemin.

Medicine USA
Karl Landsteiner: Grouping of human blood.

Karl Landsteiner.

1931

Chemistry GERMANY
Karl Bosch, Friedrich Bergius: Invention and development of chemical high-pressure methods.

Medicine GERMANY
Otto Warburg: Discovery of nature and action of respiratory enzyme.

1932

Physics GERMANY
Werner Heisenberg: Creation of quantum mechanics.

Chemistry USA
Irving Langmuir: Discoveries and investigations in surface chemistry.

Medicine UK
Edgar D. Adrian, Sir C. Sherrington: Discovering functions of neurons.

1933

Physics UK, AUSTRIA
Paul Dirac, Erwin Schrödinger: Discovery of new fruitful forms of atomic energy.

Medicine USA
Thomas Hunt Morgan: Heredity transmission functions of chromosomes.

1934

Chemistry USA
Harold Urey: Discovery of heavy hydrogen.

Medicine USA
George R. Minot, William P. Murphy, George H. Whipple: Discoveries concerning liver therapy against anemia.

1935

Physics UK
Sir James Chadwick: Discovery of neutron.

Chemistry FRANCE
Frédéric Joliot, Irène Joliot-Curie: Synthesis of new radioactive elements.

Medicine GERMANY
Hans Spemann: Organizer effect in embryonic development.

1936

Physics AUSTRIA
Victor Hess: Discovery of cosmic radiation.

Physics USA
Carl Anderson: Discovery of positron.

Chemistry NETHERLANDS
Peter Debye: Studies of dipole

moments and the diffraction of X-rays and electrons in gases.

Medicine UK, GERMANY
Sir H.H. Dale, Otto Loewi: Discoveries relating to the chemical transmission of nerve impulses.

1937

Physics USA, UK
Clinton Davisson, Sir George Thomson: Experimental discovery of the interference phenomenon in crystals irradiated by electrons.

Chemistry UK
Sir Walter Haworth: Research on carbohydrates and vitamin C.

Chemistry SWITZERLAND
Paul Karrer: Research on carotenoids, flavins, and vitamins.

Medicine HUNGARY
Albert Szent-Györgyi: Work on biological combustion.

1938

Physics ITALY
Enrico Fermi: Disclosure of artificial radioactive elements produced by neutron irradiation.

Chemistry GERMANY
Richard Kuhn: Carotenoid and vitamin research (declined).

Medicine BELGIUM
Corneille Heymans: Discovery of role of sinus and aortic mechanism in respiration regulation.

1939

Physics USA
Ernest Lawrence: Invention of the cyclotron.

Chemistry GERMANY
Adolf Butenandt: Work on sexual hormones (declined).

Chemistry SWITZERLAND
Leopold Ruzicka: Work on polymethylenes and higher terpenes.

Medicine GERMANY
Gerhard Domagk: Antibacterial effect of prontosil (declined).

1943

Physics USA
Otto Stern: Discovery of the magnetic moment of the proton.

Chemistry HUNGARY
George de Hevesy: Use of isotopes as traces in chemical research.

Medicine DENMARK
Henrik Dam: Discovery of vitamin K.

Medicine USA
Edward A. Doisy: Discovery of chemical nature of vitamin K.

1944

Physics USA
Isidor Rabi: Resonance method for registration of magnetic properties of atomic nuclei.

Chemistry GERMANY
Otto Hahn: Discovery of the fission of heavy nuclei.

Medicine USA
Joseph Erlanger, Herbert S. Gasser: Researches on differentiated function of single nerve fibers.

1945

Physics AUSTRIA
Wolfgang Pauli: Discovery of the exclusion "Pauli" principle.

Chemistry FINLAND
Artturi Virtanen: Invention of fodder preservation method.

Medicine UK, AUSTRIA
Sir A. Fleming, Ernst Boris Chain, Lord Florey: Discovery of penicillin and its curative value in some infectious diseases.

Sir A. Fleming

Ernst Boris Chain

Lord Florey.

1946

Physics   USA
Percy Bridgman: Discoveries
in the domain of high-
pressure physics.

Chemistry   USA
James Sumner: Discovery of
enzyme crystallization.

Chemistry   USA
John Northrop, Wendell
Stanley: Preparation of
enzymes and virus proteins in
pure form.

Medicine   USA
Hermann J. Muller:
Production of mutations by
X-ray irradiation.

1947

Physics   UK
Sir Edward Appleton:
Discovery of Appleton layer in
upper atmosphere.

Chemistry   UK
Sir Robert Robinson:
Investigations on alkaloids
and other plant products.

Medicine   USA
Carl F. Cori, Gerty T. Cori:
Discovery of how glycogen is
catalytically converted.

Medicine   ARGENTINA
Bernardo Houssay: Pituitary
hormone function in sugar
metabolism.

1948

Physics   UK
Patrick Blackett: Discoveries in
the domain of nuclear physics
and cosmic radiation using
the Wilson cloud chamber.

Chemistry   SWEDEN
Arne Tiselius: Researches
on electrophoresis and
adsorption analysis; researches
on the serum proteins.

Medicine   SWITZERLAND
Paul Müller:
Properties of DDT.

Paul Müller.

1949

Physics   JAPAN
Hideki Yukawa: Prediction of
the existence of mesons.

Chemistry   USA
William Giauque: Behaviors
of substances at extremely low
temperatures.

Medicine   SWITZERLAND
Walter Hess: Discovery of
function of middle brain.

Medicine   PORTUGAL
Antonio Moniz: Therapeutic
value of leucotomy in psychoses.

1950

Physics   UK
Cecil Powell: Photographic
method of studying nuclear
process; discoveries of
mesons.

Chemistry   GERMANY
Otto Diels, Kurt Alder:
Discovery and development of
diene synthesis.

Medicine
USA,   SWITZERLAND
Philip S. Hench, Edward C.
Kendall, Tadeusz Reichstein:
Research on adrenal cortex
hormones, their structure and
biological effects.

1951

Physics   UK, IRELAND
Sir John Cockcroft,
Ernest Walton:
Work on transmutation of
atomic nuclei by artificially
accelerated particles.

Chemistry   USA
Edwin McMillan,
Glenn Seaborg:
Discovery of and research
on transuranium elements.

1951

Medicine SOUTH AFRICA,
                            USA
Max Theiler:
Yellow fever discoveries.

1952

Physics   USA
Felix Bloch, Edward Purcell:
Discovery of nuclear magnetic
resonance in solids.

Chemistry   UK
Archer Martin, Richard
Synge: Method of identifying
and separating chemical
elements by chromatography.

Medicine   USA
Selman Waksman: Discovery
of streptomycin.

1953

Physics   NETHERLANDS
Frits Zernike: Method of
phase-contrast microscopy.

Chemistry   GERMANY
Hermann Staudinger: Work
on macromolecules.

Medicine   GERMANY
Fritz Lipmann, Hans Krebs:
Discovery of the citric acid
cycle and discovery of co-
enzyme A and its importance
for intermediary metabolism.

1954

Physics   UK
Max Born: Statistical studies
on wave functions.

Physics   GERMANY
Walther Bothe:
Invention of studies with
coincidence method.

Chemistry   USA
Linus Carl Pauling: Study of
the nature of the chemical
bond.

Medicine   USA
John Enders, Thomas Weller,
Frederick Robbins: Cultivation
of the poliomyelitis virus in
tissue cultures.

1955

Physics   USA
Willis Lamb Jr.:

Discoveries of magnetic
moment of electron.

Physics   USA
Polykark Kusch: Measurement
of magnetic moment of
electron.

Chemistry   USA
Vincent du Vigneaud: First
synthesis of a polypeptide
hormone.

Medicine   SWEDEN
Hugo Theorell: Nature and
mode of actions of oxidation
enzymes.

Hugo Theorell.

1956

Physics   USA
William Shockely,
John Bardeen, Walter
Brattain: Investigations on
semiconductors and discovery
of the transistor effect.

Chemistry   USSR, UK
Nikolai Semenov,
Sir Cyril Hinshelwood:
Work on the kinetics of
chemical reactions.

Medicine USA, GERMANY
André Cournand,
Dickinson Richards Jr.,
Werner Forssmann:
Discoveries concerning heart

catheterization and circulatory
changes.

1957

Physics   CHINA
Tsung-Dao Lee,
Chen Ning Yang:
Discovery of violations of
the principle of parity
(space reflection symmetry).

Chemistry   UK
Sir Alexander Todd: Work on
nucleotides and nucleotide
co-enzymes.

Medicine   ITALY
Daniel Bovet: Production of
synthetic curare.

1958

Physics   USSR
Pavel Cherenkov, Ilya Frank,
Igor Tamm: Discovery
and interpretation of the
Cherenkov effect (emission
of light waves by electrically
charged particles moving
faster than light).

Chemistry   UK
Frederick Sanger:
Determination of structure of
insulin molecule.

Medicine   USA
George Beadle, Edward
Tatum, Joshua Lederberg:
Genetic regulation of
chemical processes;
genetic recombination;
bacterial genetics.

1959

Physics   USA
Emilio Segrè, Owen
Chamberlain:
Confirmation of the existence
of the anti-proton.

Chemistry
CZECHOSLOVAKIA
Jaroslav Heyrovsky: Discovery and development of polargraphy.

Medicine USA
Severo Ochoa, Arthur Kornberg: Work on producing nucleic acids artificially.

1960

Physics USA
Donald Glaser: Development of the bubble chamber.

Chemistry USA
Williard Libby: Development of radiocarbon dating.

Medicine AUSTRALIA, UK
Sir Macfarlane Burnet, Peter Medawar: Acquired immunity to tissue transplants.

1961

Medicine HUNGARY
Georg von Békésy: Functions of the inner ear.

Georg von Békésy.

Physics USA
Robert Hofstadter: Determination of shape and size of atomic nucleons.

Physics GERMANY
Rudolf Mössbauer: Discovery

of the "Mossbauer effect."

Chemistry USA
Melvin Calvin: Study of chemical steps that take place during photosynthesis.

1962

Physics USSR
Lev D. Landau: Contributions to the understanding of condensed states of matter (superfluidity in liquid helium).

Chemistry UK
John C. Kendrew, Max F. Perutz: Determination of the structure of hemoproteins.

Medicine UK, USA
Francis Crick, Maurice Wilkins, James Watson: Discoveries concerning the molecular structure of deoxyribonucleic acid (DNA).

Francis Crick.

Maurice Wilkins.

James Watson.

1963

Physics GERMANY, USA
J. Hans, D. Jensen, Maria Goeppert Mayer: Development of shell model theory of the structure of atomic nuclei.

Physics USA
Eugene Paul Wigner: Principles governing mechanics and interaction of protons and neutrons in the atomic nucleus.

Chemistry ITALY
GERMANY
Giulio Natta, Karl Ziegler: Structure and synthesis of polymers in the field of plastics.

Medicine UK, AUSTRALIA
Alan Hodgkin, Andrew Huxley, Sir John Eccles: Study of the transmission of impulses along a nerve fiber.

1964

Physics USA, USSR
Charles H. Townes, Niolai G. Basov, Aleksandr M. Prokhorov: Work in quantum electronics leading to construction of

instruments based on maser-laser principles.

Chemistry UK
Dorothy M.C. Hodgkin: Determining the structure of biochemical compounds essential in combating pernicious anemia.

Medicine GERMANY
Konrad Bloch, Feodor Lynen: Discoveries concerning cholesterol and fatty acid metabolism.

1965

Medicine FRANCE
François Jacob, André Lwoff, Jacques Monod: Discoveries concerning regulatory activities of body cells.

François Jacob.

Physics USA, JAPAN
Julian S. Schwinger, Richard P. Feynman, Shin'ichirō Tomonaga: Basic principles of quantum electrodynamics.

Chemistry USA
Robert B. Woodward: Synthesis of sterols, cholorophyll, and other substances once thought to be produced only by living things.

1966

Physics FRANCE
Alfred Kastler: Discovery/development of optical methods for studying Hertzian resonances in atoms.

Chemistry USA
Robert S. Mulliken: Work concerning chemical bonds and the electronic structure of molecules by the molecular orbital method.

Medicine USA
Charles Huggins, Francis Peyton Rous: Research on causes and treatment of cancer.

1967

Physics USA
Hans A. Bethe: Discoveries concerning the energy production of stars.

Chemistry GERMANY, UK
Manfreed Eigen, Ronald G.W. Norrish, George Porter: Studies of extremely fast chemical reactions.

Medicine SWEDEN, USA
Ragnar Granit, Haldan Hartline, George Wald: Discoveries about chemical and physiological visual processes in the eye.

1968

Physics USA
Luis W. Alvarez: Work with elementary particles, including the discovery of resonance states.

Chemistry USA
Lars Onsager: Contributions to the theory of the thermodynamics of irreversible processes.

Medicine USA
Robert Holley, Har Gobind Khorana, Marshall Nirenberg: Deciphering the genetic code.

Robert Holley.

1969

Physics USA
Murray Gell-Mann: Discoveries regarding classification of elementary particles and their interactions.

Chemistry UK, NORWAY
Derek H.R. Barton, Odd Hassel: Work in determining actual three-dimensional shape of certain organic compounds.

Medicine USA
Max Delbrück, A.D. Hershey, Salvadore Luria: Research and discoveries concerning viruses and viral diseases.

1970

Physics SWEDEN, FRANCE
Hannes Alfvén, Louis Néel: Work in magnetohydro-dynamics and in antiferromagetism and ferrimagnetism.

Chemistry ARGENTINA
Luis F. Leloir: Discovery of sugar nucleotides and their

role in the biosynthesis of carbohydrates.

Medicine   UK, SWEDEN, USA
Sir Bernard Katz, Ulf von Euler, Julius Axelrod: Discoveries concerning the chemistry of nerve transmission.

1971

Physics   UK
Dennis Gabor: Invention of holography.

Chemistry   CANADA
Gerhard Herzberg: Research in the structure of molecules.

Medicine   USA
Earl Sutherland Jr.: Action of hormones.

Earl Sutherland.

1972

Physics   USA
John Bardeen, Leon N. Cooper, John R. Schrieffer: Development of the theory of superconductivity.

Chemistry   USA
Christian B. Anfinsen, Stanford Moore, William H. Stein: Fundamental contributions to enzyme chemistry.

Medicine   UK, USA
Rodney Porter, Gerald Edelman: Research on the chemical structure of antibodies.

1973

Physics   JAPAN, USA, UK
Leo Esaki, Ivar Giaever, Brian D. Josephson: Tunneling in semiconductors and superconductors.

Chemistry GERMANY, UK
Ernst Fischer, Geoffrey Wilkinson: Organometallic chemistry.

Medicine   GERMANY, AUSTRIA, UK
Karl von Frisch, Konrad Lorenz, Nikolaas Tinbergen: Discoveries in animal behavior patterns.

Karl von Frisch.

Konard Lorenz.

Nikolaas Tinbergen.

1974

Physics   UK
Sir Martin Ryle, Antony Hewish: Work in radio astronomy.

Chemistry   USA
Paul J. Flory: Studies of long-chain molecules.

Medicine   BELGIUM, ROMANIA/USA
Albert Claude, Christian de Duve, George Palade: Research on structural and functional organization of cells.

1975

Physics   DENMARK, USA
Aage N. Bohr, Ben R. Mottelson, L. James Rainwater: Work on the atomic nucleus.

Chemistry
    UK, SWITZERLAND
John W. Cornforth, Vladimir Prelog: Work in stereochemistry.

Medicine   USA, ITALY
David Baltimore, Howard Temin, Renato Dulbecco: Interaction between tumor viruses and the genetic material of the cell.

1976

Physics USA
Burton Richter, Samuel C.C. Ting: Discovery of new class of elementary particles (psi, or J).

Chemistry USA
William N. Lipscomb: Structure of boranes.

Medicine USA
B.S. Blumberg, D.G. Gajdusek: Studies of origin and spread of infectious diseases.

B.S. Blumberg.

1977

Physics USA, UK
Philip W. Anderson, John H. van Vleck, Sir Nevill F. Mott: Contributions to understanding of the behavior of electrons in magnetic, noncrystalline solids.

Chemistry BELGIUM
Ilya Prigogine: Widening the scope of thermodynamics.

Medicine USA
Roalyn Yalow: Development of radio-immunoassay.

Medicine USA
R. Guillemin, A. Schally: Research on pituitary hormones.

1978

Physics USSR
Pyotr L. Kapitsa: Invention and application of helium liquefier.

Physics USA
Arno A. Penzias, Robert W. Wilson: Discovery of cosmic microwave background radiation, providing support for the big-bang theory.

Chemistry UK
Peter D. Mitchell: Formulation of a theory of energy transfer processes in biological systems.

Medicine SWITZERLAND, USA
W. Arber, D. Nathans, H. Smith: Discovery and application of enzymes that fragment deoxyribonucleic acids.

1979

Physics USA, PAKISTAN
Sheldon Glashow, Steven Weinberg, Abdus Salam: Establishment of analogy between electromagnetism and the "weak" interactions of subatomic particles.

Chemistry USA, GERMANY
Herbert C. Brown, Georg Wittig: Introduction of compounds of boron and phosphorus in the synthesis of organic substances.

Medicine UK, USA
Godfrey Newbold Hounsfield, Allan Mcleod Cormack: Development of the CAT scan, a radiographic diagnostic technique.

1980

Physics USA
James W Cronin, Val Logsdon Fitch: Demonstration of simultaneous violation of both charge-conjugation and parity-inversion symmetries.

Chemistry USA
Paul Berg: First preparation of a hybrid DNA.

Chemistry USA, UK
Walter Gilbert, Frederick Sanger: Development of chemical and biological analyses of DNA structure.

Medicine USA, FRANCE, VENEZUELA
George Snell, Jean Dausset, Barui Benacerraf: Investigations of genetic control of the response of the immunological system to foreign substances.

1981

Physics SWEDEN
Kai M. Siegbahn: Electron spectroscopy for chemical analysis.

Physics USA
Nicolaas Bloembergen, Arthur L. Schawlow: Applications of lasers in spectroscopy.

Chemistry JAPAN, USA
Kenichi Fukui, Roald Hoffmann: Orbital symmetry of chemical reactions.

Medicine USA
Roger Sperry: Functions of the cerebral hemispheres.

Medicine USA, SWEDEN
David Hubel, Torsten Wiesel: Processing of visual information by the brain.

David Hubel.

Torsten Wiesel.

1982

Physics USA
Kenneth G. Wilson: Analysis of continuous phase transition.

Chemistry UK
Aaron Klug: Determination of structure of biological substances.

Medicine SWEDEN, UK
Sune K. Bergström, Bengt I. Samuelsson, John R. Vane:

Biochemistry and physiology of prostaglandins.

1983

Physics USA
Subrahmanyan Chandrasekhar, William A. Fowler: Contributions to understanding of the evolution and devolution of stars.

Chemistry USA
Henry Taube: Study of electron transfer reactions.

Medicine USA
Barbara McClintock: Discovery of mobile plant genes that affect heredity.

1984

Physics ITALY, NETHERLANDS
Carlo Rubbia, Simon van der Meer: Discovery of subatomic particles W and Z, which supports the electro-weak theory.

Chemistry USA
Robert Bruce Merrifield: Development of a method of polypeptide synthesis.

Medicine DENMARK, GERMANY, ARGENTINA, UK
Niels K. Jerne, George Köhler, Cesar Milstein: Theory and development of a technique for producing monoclonal antibodies.

1985

Physics GERMANY
Klaus von Klitzing: Discovery of the quantized Hall effect, permitting exact measurements of electrical resistance.

Chemistry USA
Herbert Hauptman, Jerome Karle: Development of way to map chemical structures of small molecules.

Medicine USA
Michael Brown, Joseph Goldstein: Discovery of cell receptors relating to cholesterol metabolism.

1986

Physics GERMANY, SWITZERLAND
Ernst Ruska, Gerd Binnig, Heinrich Rohrer: Development of special electron microscopes.

Chemistry USA, CANADA
Dudley R. Herschbach, Yuan Lee, John Polanyi: Development of methods for analyzing basic chemical reactions.

Medicine USA
Stanley Cohen, Rita Levi-Montalcini: Discovery of chemical agents that help regulate the growth of cells.

Rita Levi-Montalcini.

1987

Physics SWITZERLAND, GERMANY
Georg Bednorz,
Karl Alax Müller:
Discovery of new super-
conducting materials.

Chemistry USA, FRANCE
Donald J. Cram, Charles J.
Pedersen, Jean-Marie Lehn:
Development of molecules
that can link with other
molecules.

Medicine JAPAN
Susumu Tonegawa: Study of
genetic aspects of antibodies.

Susumu Tonegawa.

1988

Physics USA
Leon Lederman, Melvin
Schwartz, Jack Steinberger:
Research in subatomic particles.

Chemistry GERMANY
Johann Deisenhofer, Robert
Huber, Hartmut Michel:
Discovery of structure
of proteins needed in
photosynthesis.

Medicine UK, USA
James Black, Gertrude
Elion, George Hitchings:
Development of new
classes of drugs for combating
disease.

Johann Deisenhofer.

1989

Physics USA
Norman F. Ramsey:
Development of the atomic
clock.

Physics USA, GERMANY
Hans G. Dehmelt, Wolfgang
Paul: Development of
methods to isolate atoms and
subatomic particles for study.

Chemistry CANADA, USA
Sidney Altman,

J. Michael Bishop.

Harold E. Varmus.

Thomas R. Cech:
Discovery of certain basic
properties of RNA.

Medicine USA
J. Michael Bishop, Harold
E. Varmus: Study of cancer-
causing genes called oncogenes.

1990

Physics USA, CANADA
Jerome I. Friedman,
Henry W. Kendall,
Richard E. Taylor:
Discovery of atomic quarks.

Chemistry USA
Elias James Corey:
Development of "retrosynthetic
analysis" for synthesis of
complex molecules.

Joseph E. Murray.

E. Donnall Thomas.

Medicine USA
Joseph E. Murray,
E. Donnall Thomas:
Development of kidney and
bone-marrow transplants.

1991

Physics   FRANCE
Pierre-Gilles de Gennes:
Discovery of general rules for
behavior of molecules.

Chemistry SWITZERLAND
Richard R. Ernst:
Improvements in nuclear
magnetic resonance
spectroscopy.

Medicine   GERMANY
Erwin Neher,
Bert Sakmann: Discovery of
how cells communicate, as
related to diseases.

Erwin Neher.

Bert Sakmann.

1992

Physics   FRANCE
Georges Charpak: Inventor of
detector that traces subatomic
particles.

Chemistry   USA
Rudolph A. Marcus:
Explanation of how electrons
transfer between molecules.

Medicine   USA
Edmond H. Fischer, Edwin
G. Krebs: Discovery of class of
enzymes called protein kinases.

1993

Physics   USA
Russell A. Hulse, Joseph H.
Taylor Jr.: Identifying binary
pulsars.

Chemistry USA, CANADA
Kary B. Mullis, Michael
Smith: Inventors of
techniques for gene study and
manipulation.

Medicine   UK, USA
Richard J. Roberts, Phillip A.
Sharp: Discovery of "split," or
interrupted, genetic structure.

1994

Physics   CANADA, USA
Bertram N. Brockhouse,
Clifford G. Shull:
Development of neutron-
scattering techniques.

Chemistry   USA
George A. Olah:
Development of techniques to
study hydrocarbon molecules.

Alfred G. Gilman.

Medicine   USA
Alfred G. Gilman, Martin
Rodbell: Discovery of cell
signalers called G-proteins.

1995

Physics   USA
Martin L. Perl:
Discovery of the tau lepton.

Physics   USA
Frederick Reines:
Detection of the neutrino.

Chemistry NETHERLANDS,
MEXICO,
USA
Paul Crutzen, Mario Molina,
F. Sherwood Rowland:
Work in atmospheric
chemistry, particularly
concerning the formation and
decomposition of ozone.

Medicine USA, GERMANY
Edward B. Lewis, Christiane
Nüsslein-Volhard, Eric F.
Wieschaus: Discoveries
concerning the genetic
control of early embryonic
development.

1996

Physics   USA
David M. Lee, Douglas
D. Osheroff, Robert C.
Richardson: Discovery of
superfluidity in helium–3.

Chemistry   USA, UK
Robert F. Curl Jr., Sir Harold
W. Kroto, Richard E. Smalley:
Discovery of fullerenes.

Medicine   AUSTRALIA,
SWITZERLAND
Peter C. Doherty, Rolf M.
Zinkernagel: Discoveries
concerning the specificity of
the cell mediated immune
defense.

Peter C. Doherty.

Rolf M. Zinkernagel.

1997

Physics   USA, FRANCE
Steven Chu, Claude Cohen-Tannoudji, William D. Phillips: Development of methods to cool and trap atoms with laser light.

Chemistry   USA, UK
Paul D. Boyer, John E. Walker: Elucidation of the enzymatic mechanism underlying the synthesis of adenosine triphosphate (ATP).

Chemistry   DENMARK
Jens C. Skou: Discovery of an ion-transporting enzyme, NA+,K+-ATPase.

Medicine   USA
Stanley B. Prusiner: Discovery of Prions—a new biological principle of infection.

1998

Physics   USA
Robert B. Laughlin, Horst L. Störmer, Daniel C. Tsui: Discovery of a new form of quantum fluid with fractionally charged excitations.

Chemistry   USA
Walter Kohn: Development of the density-functional theory.

Chemistry   USA
John A. Pople: Development of computational methods in quantum chemistry.

Medicine   USA
Robert F. Furchgott, Louis J. Ignarro, Ferid Murad: Discoveries concerning nitric oxide as a signaling molecule in the cardiovascular system.

1999

Physics   NETHERLANDS
Gerardus 't Hooft and Martinus J.G. Veltman: Elucidating quantum structure of electroweak interactions in physics.

Chemistry   EGYPT, USA
Ahmed H. Zeweil: Discovering transitional states of chemical reactions using femtosecond spectroscopy.

Gunter Blobel.

Medicine: GERMANY
Gunter Blobel: Discovering origins of the effects of hereditary diseases.

2000

Physics: RUSSIA, GERMANY, USA
Zhores I. Alferov, Herbert Kroemer, Jack S. Kilby: Invention of rapid transistors, laser diodes, and integrated circuits.

Chemistry   USA, JAPAN
Alan J. Heeger, Alan G. MacDiarmid, Hideki Shirakawa: For discovery and development of constructive polymers.

Arvid Carlsson.

Paul Greengard.

Medicine   SWEDEN, USA, AUSTRIA
Arvid Carlsson, Paul Greengard, Eric Kandel:

Eric Kandel.

Discoveries concerning signal transduction in the nervous system.

2001

Physics   USA, GERMANY
Eric A. Cornell, Carl E. Weineman, Wolfang Ketterle: Achievements of Bose-Einstein condensation in dilute gases of alkali atoms for early fundamental studies of the properties of the condensates.

Chemistry   USA, JAPAN
William S. Knowles, K. Barry Sharpless, Ryoji Noyori: Development of catalyctic assymmetric synthesis.

Medicine   USA, UK
Leland Hartwell, Tim Hunt, Paul Nurse: Discovery of key regulators of the cell cycle.

2002

Physics   USA, JAPAN
Raymond Davis, Jr., Riccardo Giacconi, Masatoshi Koshiba: Pioneering contributions to astrophysics, in particular for detection of cosmic neutrinos.

Chemistry   USA, JAPAN, SWITZERLAND
John B. Fenn, Koichi Tanaka,

Kurt Wuthrich: Development of soft desorption ionization methods for mass spectrometric analyses of biological macromolecules.

Medicine   USA, UK
Sydney Brenner, H. Robert Horvitz, John E. Sulstan: Discoveries concerning genetic regulation of organ development and programmed cell death.

2003

Physics   RUSSIA, USA, UK
Alexei A. Abrikosov, Vitaly Ginzburg, Anthony J. Leggett: Pioneering contributions to the theory of superconductors and superfluids.

Chemistry   USA
Peter Agre, Robert MacKinnon: Discoveries concerning channels in cell membranes.

Medicine   USA, UK
Paul C. Lautebur, Peter Mansfield: Discoveries concerning magnetic resonance imaging.

2004

Physics   USA
David J. Gross, H. David Politzer, Frank Wilczek: Discovery of asymptotic freedom in theory of strong interaction.

Chemistry   ISRAEL, USA
Aeron Ciechanover, Avram Hershko, Irwin Rose: Discovery of ubiquitous-medicated protein degradation.

Medicine   USA
Richard Axel, Linda B. Buck:

Discoveries of odorant receptors and organization of the olfactory system.

Richard Axel.

Linda B. Buck.

2005

Physics   USA
Roy J. Glauber: Contribution to quantum theory of optical coherence.

Physics   USA, GERMANY
John L. Hall, Theodor W. Hansch: Contributions to development of laser-based precision spectroscopy including optical frequency comb technique.

Chemistry   FRANCE, USA
Yves Chauvin, Robert H. Grubbs, Richard R Schrock: Development of metathesis method in organ synthesis.

Medicine   AUSTRALIA
Barry J. Marshall,
J. Robin Warren:
Discovery of the bacterium
Hlicobacter pylori and its role
in gastritis and peptic ulcer
disease.

2006

Physics   USA
John C. Mather, George F.
Smoot: The discovery of gene
silencing by double-stranded
RNA.

Chemistry   USA
Roger D. Kronberg:
Studies of molecular basis of
eukaryolic transcription.

Medicine   USA
Andrew Z. Fire, Craig C.
Mello: Discovery of RNA
interference—gene silencing by
double-stranded DNA.

2007

Physics   FRANCE,
GERMANY
Albert Fert, Peter Grunberg:
Discovery of giant
magnetoresistance.

Chemistry   GERMANY
Gerhard Ertl:
Studies of chemical processes
on solid surfaces.

Medicine   USA, UK
Mario R. Capecchi, Oliver
Smithies, Martin J. Eans:
Discoveries of principles for
introducing specific gene
modifications in mice by the
use of embryonic stem cells.

2008

Physics   JAPAN
Yoichiro Nambu:
Discovery of the mechanism of

spontaneous broken symmetry
in subatomic physics.

Physics   JAPAN
Makoto Kobayashi, Toshihide
Maskawa: The discovery
of the origin of the broken
symmetry that predicts the
existence of at least three
families of quarks in nature.

Chemistry   USA
Osamu Shimomura, Martin
Chalfie, Roger Y. Tsien: The
discovery and development of
the green fluorescent protein,
GFP.

Medicine   GERMANY
Harald zur Hausen: Discovery
of human papilloma viruses
causing cervical cancer.

Medicine   FRANCE
Françoise Barré-Sinoussi,
Luc Montagnier: Discovery
of human immunodeficiency
virus.

Luc Montagnier.

2009

Physics   CHINA
Charles K. Kao: Achievements
concerning the transmission
of light in fibers for optical
communication.

Physics   CANADA, USA
Willard S. Boyle, George
E. Smith: Invention of the
CCD sensor, an imaging
semiconductor circuit.

Chemistry   USA, ISRAEL
Venkatraman Ramakrishnan,
Thomas A. Steitz, Ada E.
Yonath: Studies of the structure
and function of the ribosome.

Medicine   USA
Elizabeth H. Blackburn, Carol
W. Greider, Jack W. Szostak:
Discovery of the protection
of chromosomes by telomeres
and the enzyme telomerase.

2010

Physics   RUSSIA, UK
Andre Geim, Konstantin
Novoselov: Experiments
regarding the two-dimensional
material graphene.

Chemistry   USA, CHINA,
JAPAN
Richard F. Heck, Ei-ichi
Negishi, Akira Suzuki: For
palladium-catalyzed cross-
couplings in organic synthesis.

Medicine   UK
Robert G. Edwards:
Development of in vitro
fertilization.

These facts extracted from the Timechart are, for reasons of space, necessarily limited, especially in recent decades when there have been so many developments. While they cannot, therefore, reflect the entire medical history of any nation, it is hoped they will act as a useful source of data.

ANCIENT ASSYRIANS AND BABYLONIANS
BCE
2000 Used distillation, "essences" of cedar, and volatile oils
1948–05 Earliest known regulations of medical practice, Code of Hammurabi: Includes laws relating to medical practice
1900–1800 Assyrians and Babylonians see liver as seat of life • Custom to lay the sick in street so that passers-by can offer advice • Herodotus says every Babylonian was an amateur physician!

ANCIENT CHINESE SKILLS
BCE
3494 Legendary emperor Shennong discovers herbal medicine
3000–2700 Stone acupuncture needles used to treat pain
2,698–2,598 Huang-ti's *Nei Ching*, medical compendium
2,000–1,000 Treat disease by balance, harmony of elements, and between opposing forces of Yin and Yang • Traditional medicine develops
551–479 K'ung Fu-tzu's (Confucius) work is based on the elements of life: Water, fire, wood, metal, and earth
479–300 Revised *Nei Ching* manual of physic describes acupuncture
c. 280 Ts'ang Kung studies medicine: Writes 25 case histories
200 Doctor Zhang Zhongjjing's massive medical book contains all remedies and treatments known

CE
190–265 Physician and famous surgeon, Hua Tuo pioneers abdominal surgery and use of anesthesia. Surgical advances halt after this time, when ancient Confucian interdict on mutilation of body becomes dominant
c. 168–196 Chang Chung-ching, Hippocrates of China, writes 16-volume classic clinical work on disease
280 Wang Shu-ho composes 12-volume *Mei Ching* (*Book of Pulse*). Believes body's pulses act like musical chords
400 Pharmacists hand down vast knowledge: Belief in medical powers of precious stones and ginseng root
1522–78 52-volume *Great Herbal* by Li Shi-chen contains 1,900 prescriptions

ANCIENT EGYPT
BCE
10,000–2,000 Ancient texts provide evidence of medicine
5,000–2,500 Belief in magic: Priestly medicine
2,900–2,750 Dentistry evidence
2,800 Imhotep, doctor to Pharaoh Zoser • Pulse-taking
2,500 Evidence of surgery • Knowledge of anatomy through mummification • Ptolemaic period lifts ban on dissection • Doctors many and specialized • Use animal and plant extracts, more than 500 substances • Anubis: Conductor of the dead and patron god of embalmers • Surgery depicted on tombs
1660 Mummy of Rameses V has smallpox scars
1600 Ebers Papyrus and Edwin Smith Papyrus—earliest known surgical texts
1500 Physician's Tomb, Saqquara: Paintings of manipulating feet and hands
535 Imhotep given full status as a god. Greeks adopt him as Imouthes—identified with Asklepios

ANCIENT GREECE & ROME
BCE
2000–500 Medicine is described as noble art in Homer's *Iliad*
639–544 Thales of Miletos: 1st Greek scientist/philosopher
580–489 Pythagoras: School at Croton • Alcmaeon of Croton
509 Etruscans: Skilled dentists
500–428 Anaxagoras: Particles theory
500–420 Hippocrates, Father of Western Medicine. His school of medicine flourishes
460–377 Hippocratic Oath
c. 460 Empedocles' teaching and theory of 4 elements

430–27 Great Plague, Athens
400 Thucydides describes Athenian epidemic
384–22 Aristotle founds scientific study
370–286 Theophrastus of Eresos: *The History of Plants*
330–260 Herophilus of Chalcedon: 1st true anatomist
300–200 Alexandria: Library founded by Ptolemy I
234–149 Cato collects medical "recipes"
c. 200 Archagathus, 1st Greek doctor in Rome, founds 1st European pharmacy
219 He is granted a public surgery and citizenship
120–70 Asclepiades of Bithynia, physician, introduces humane treatment of mentally ill
116–28 Marcus Terentius Varro recommends draining marshes
100 Julius Caesar supposedly delivered by Caesarean section
80 Mithridates VI experiments with poison antidotes
48 Alexandria: Library partially destroyed by fire
46 Julius Caesar grants citizenship to doctors in Rome
23 Antonius Musa cures emperor with cold water treatment • Doctors granted immunity from taxes

CE
14–37 Celsus's *De Medicina*, earliest Latin scientific medical work describes Roman surgical/medical practice
23–79 Pliny the Elder's *Natural History* describes many drugs
40–90 Dioscorides describes 600 plant medicines • Vespasian frees doctors from military service
54 Theriac, universal antidote, invented by Nero's physician, Andromarchos
79 Vesuvius erupts • Plague • 200 different medical instruments found, Pompeii
96 Aqueducts and good water systems: Latrines, baths, drains, canals
c. 98–117 Rufus of Ephesus writes about medicine
c. 98–138 Soranus of Ephesus, 1st great obstetrician: His text is used for 15 centuries
131–201 Galen, famous surgeon, writes much on anatomy, physiology, and medicine— stresses humoral theory and Hippocratic doctrine
165–69 Plague of Antoninus
200 Medical licensing introduced
c. 300 Guilds send texts to military forts: Medical knowledge spreads
302 Eusebius describes Syrian smallpox epidemic
325–403 Oribasius: Writes on fractures, traction, and pulley systems • Also medical and surgical encyclopaedia
357–77 1st great Christian hospital at Caesarea
375 Plague Hospital, Edessa
c. 397 Fabiola founds 1st hospital in Western Europe
502–75 Aetius of Amida describes ligatures, aneurysms, diphtheria
525–605 Alexander of Tralles: Physician and author
625–90 Paul of Aegina discusses surgical procedures

ANCIENT INDIA
BCE
2,500–1,500 Magic important element, but sorcerers become practitioners and scholars
1,500 to 600 *Charaka Samhita* and *Susruta Samhita*, two basic texts of early Ayurvedic medicine. *Susruta* describes plastic surgery, 121 surgical instruments, 760 medical plants
1500 Aryan invasion: Sanskrit writings about herbs, instruments, surgery
400 Surgery extensive
300–275 Hospitals for people and animals established
274 Trained doctors from Taxila and Benaras schools work with physician priests

CE
800–1000 Brahminic medicine
664 Muslim conquest of India: Arab medicine arrives
1000 Ayurvedic medicine achieves modern form

AFRICA
BACKGROUND The north of the continent is home to many highly developed civilizations. The Arab world, in particular, plays a large part in the advance of medicine. However, in the

interior, primitive medicine is practiced for centuries. Drugs and the smearing of skin with plant substances are implemented to reduce pain during surgical procedures. Witch doctors, sometimes in a state of trance, consult gods as to causes of disease. Treatment might involve elaborate ceremonies, and there remains today a great belief in magic, charms, and fetishes.

Western medicine is introduced as explorers and missionaries penetrate Africa. The western coast, however, is called the "white man's grave," as so many Westerners suffer from exposure to malaria—a perennial problem in Africa—and other tropical diseases.

1284 Mausuri hospital founded in Cairo

1348 Black Death outbreak in Egypt

1600s Slave trade increases spread of tropical diseases to other areas of the world

1755 Smallpox outbreak in Cape Town: Spreads inland

1882 British control Egypt. Cultivating cash crops and new irrigation schemes mean greater exposure to water: Cases of bilharzia increase

1886 Laveran, French army surgeon working in Algeria, discovers malaria parasites

1889 South African (Boer) War: Voluntary inoculation of soldiers against typhoid

1913 Dr. Albert Schweizer, Alsatian philosopher, doctor, and missionary, begins his great work in French Equatorial Africa. In due course, he will build hospitals with his own hands, then equip and maintain them with money from his book royalties, plus gifts from all around the world. In **1924** Schweizer returns to Africa to continue his work, creating a larger hospital and helping some 150 lepers in a leper colony (established near the hospital village that developed), using the new drugs now available

1940s HIV virus responsible for AIDS probably appears in humans

1940 South of Cairo, 5 percent of population infected with S. *haematobium* in areas of basin irrigation; 60 percent where perennial irrigation

1967 1st heart transplant performed by Christiaan Barnard at Cape Town. Patient dies 18 days later

1971 1st combined heart and lung transplant

1980s HIV virus identified

1990s AIDS becomes pandemic. Its incidence in Africa is especially high

1996 In Gabon, 10 people die of Ebola virus after eating a chimpanzee

2000 Out of 36 million HIV-positive people in the world, almost 25 million are in sub-Saharan Africa

2001 16 West African states renew their commitment to eradicating polio with a massive immunization campaign launched by WHO, UNICEF, and Rotary International

2007 A WHO-UNAIDS publication on AIDS recommends male circumcision in Africa, as it can offer partial protection against AIDS

2011 Polio outbreak in the Republic of Congo causes at least 179 deaths.

AUSTRALIA

1906 Bancroft demonstrates dengue transmitted by mosquito bites

1912 1st ante-natal clinic in Sydney

1928 Flying doctor service set up in Queensland

1976 Shannon develops bionic artificial arm

1981 World's 1st test-tube twins born in Melbourne

1983 1st woman to give birth after receiving donated egg

1984 1st baby from a frozen embryo born in Melbourne

1995–96 World's 1st law permitting voluntary euthanasia. 1st man dies under the legislation

2003 Influenza B-Brisbane, a new strain of flu, discovered by Queensland scientists

2011 New drugs that target BRAF gene mutations successfully shrink up to 80 percent of secondary melanomas.

AUSTRALIA/USA

2010 Genetic mutations giving high risk of developing ovarian cancer identified, Researchers shrink tumors of cancers caused by genes known as microRNAs by applying a microRNA inhibitor

AUSTRIA

1365 Rudoph IV founds University of Vienna. By **1399** it has a Faculty of Medicine

1401 1st public dissection

1586 University of Graz
1672 University of Innsbruck • *Theatrum anatomicum*, Vienna
1754 Van Swieten organizes clinical instruction, Vienna
1761 Auenbrugger's *Inventum novum* published
1762 Von Plencisz's theory of *contagium animatum*
1776 Plenck's classification of skin diseases
1777–78 Frank's statistics establish importance of public health measures
1783 Austria separates surgeons from barbers
1791 University of Innsbruck restored to rank
1810–19 Gall and Spurzheim's treatise on nervous system and skull shapes gives rise to pseudoscience of phrenology
1839 Skoda's treatise on percussion and auscultation lays groundwork for diagnostic process
1844 Rokitansky demonstrates tubercular nature of Pott's disease.
1847 Semmelweis shows septicemia causes puerperal fever • Royal Academy of Sciences, Vienna
1862 1st hydropathic establishment at Vienna
1865 Mendel publishes experiments that form basis of genetic science
1873 Billroth excises larynx
1874 Cholera conference
1895 Freud and Breuer publish work on "unconscious mind"
1879 Nitze devises electric light cystoscopy in Vienna
1899 Gärtner's tonometer
1900 Freud publishes *The Interpretation of Dreams*
1901 Three major blood cell groups described by Landsteiner • Safer methods of transfusion develop
1906 Bárány's pointing test: Nobel Prize, 1914
1907 Von Pirquet introduces skin test for TB
1940 Landsteiner and Wiener find Rh antigen in blood

BELGIUM
1424 1st recorded regulations for midwives
1426 University of Louvain
1514–1564 Vesalius founds the "new anatomy"
1605 Verhoeven publishes the 1st ever newspaper
1620 Van Helmont's *Conservation of Matter*; he founds biochemistry. In 1648 he writes *Ortus medicinae*

1816 University of Ghent founded 1817 University of Liège founded 1834 University of Brussels 1852
1876 International Congresses of Hygiene
1897 Bordet discovers bacterial hemolysis; with Gengou, he discovers bacillus of whooping cough.
1906 School of Tropical Medicine, Brussels
1920 1st Congress of Medical History (Antwerp)

BRITAIN
1345 1st apothecary shop in London • English pepperers, grocers, and apothecaries unite in Guild of St. Anthony
1349 The Black Death
1376 Board of medical examiners in London
1460–1524 Linacre trains at Oxford and Padua: Becomes kings' physician
1485 Sweating sickness
1500–99 Institutions for insane appear
1505 Royal College of Surgeons of Edinburgh
1518 Royal College of Physicians
1540 Company of the Barber Surgeons • Henry VIII allows 4 dissections a year
1543 English apothecaries legalized
1547 "Bedlam," asylum established at St. Mary of Bethlehem, London
1562 Witchcraft made capital offense
1563 Witchcraft a capital crime in Scotland
1565 Elizabeth I permits dissection of executed criminals
1578 William Harvey born 1616 Harvey lectures on circulation of blood
1617 Woodall says lemon or lime juice prevents scurvy • Society of Apothecaries
1620 Bacon's *Novum Organum*
1624 Thomas Sydenham, "English Hippocrates," born
1628 Harvey publishes *De Motu Cordis* describing circulation of blood
1643 Typhus affects armies in English Civil War
1651 Harvey's treatise on generations of animals
1652 Thomas Culpepper's *Herbal*
1653 Glisson describes anatomy of liver
1656–67 Boyle, Wren, and Lower experiment with blood transfusion in animals
1660 Willis describes puerperal fever
1661 Scarlatina, or scarlet fever, outbreak
1662 Charles II charters Royal Society • John Graunt founds medical statistics

1664 *Cerebri anatome* by Willis, illustrated by Wren

1665 Great Plague of London

1665 Hooke describes plant cells, with microscopic drawings and in 1667 shows true function of lungs

1668–72 Dysentery epidemic

1668 Lower shows change of color in blood to do with uptake of substance from air

1675 Sydenham distinguishes scarlatina from measles and discusses gout

1689 Harris publishes work on children's diseases.

1690 Locke's *Essay on the Human Understanding*
 • Floyer counts the pulse by using a watch and in 1700–1710 invents special pulse watch

1693–94 Queen Mary II dies of smallpox in a plague that sweeps Europe

1703 Apothecaries authorized to prescribe drugs

1714 Turner's treatise on skin diseases founds British dermatology

1718 Lady Mary Wortley Montagu has son inoculated with smallpox

1723 Yellow fever, London

1725 Guy's Hospital opens • 1st British school of midwifery

1726 Hales measures blood pressure • 1st chair of midwifery at Edinburgh

1730 Forceps introduced • 1st tracheotomy

1735 Witchcraft laws repealed

1745 Barbers separated from barber surgeons

1750 Sea Bathing Infirmary at Margate: 1st British hospital for treatment of TB

1752 Smellie's obstetric forceps and midwifery treatise

1743 Sir John Pringle's work on army disease

1753 Lind's book *A Treatise on the Scurvy*

1757 William Hunter describes arterio-venous aneurysm
 • Lind's treatise on naval hygiene
 • Brocklesby improves military conditions and sanitation

1766 Cavendish discovers hydrogen

1768 Lind's treatise on tropical medicine

1770 William Hunter founds school of anatomy

1771 Priestley and Scheele isolate oxygen
 • John Hunter's treatise on teeth and lectures on surgery

1772 Priestley discovers nitrous oxide. Observations on different kinds of air

1773 White urges cleanliness in midwifery to prevent puerperal fever; he pioneers asepsis

1774 William Hunter's fine anatomical atlas published with life-size plates of human uterus
 • Dorset farmer vaccinates wife and sons with cowpox
 • Priestley discovers ammonia

1777 Howard's investigations of prisons and hospitals

1779 Pott describes Pott's disease of the spine

1785 John Hunter discovers collateral circulation and introduces proximal ligation
 • Blane's work on naval medicine

1786 Withering's treatise on the foxglove
 • John Hunter's treatise on VD

1791 Soemmerring publishes 1st volume of anatomy

1794 John Hunter's treatises on blood, inflammation, gunshot wounds, and animal tissue transplantation

1796 Jenner vaccinates boy with cowpox

1798 Jenner's *Inquiry*
 • Willan's treatise on skin diseases

1799 Jennerian vaccination on Continent and Asia
 • Hodgkin defines disease named after him

1800 Royal College of Surgeons
 • Sir Humphry Davy discovers anesthetic effect of nitrous oxide

1803 Percival's code of medical ethics

1811 Bell's work on spinal nerve-roots and brain anatomy

1812 Miranda Stewart Barry qualifies as Doctor James Barrie at Edinburgh

1817 Parkinson describes Parkinson's disease

1827 Richard Bright describes "Bright's disease"

1830 Lister perfects achromatic microscope

1832 British Medical Association founded
 • Thomas Hodgkin describes Hodgkin's disease

1837 Registration of deaths

1840s Public Health Acts mean cleaner water and mains drainage

1841 Pharmaceutical Society of Great Britain and in 1842 its School of Pharmacy

1847 Simpson uses chloroform

1848 Public Health Act

1849 Addison describes Addison's anemia and Addison's disease

1851 Great Ormond Street Hospital for Sick Children

1853 Queen Victoria has chloroform during childbirth

1853–56 Crimean War. Nightingale reforms nursing

1854 Cholera in London. John Snow proves drinking water source of infection

1858 Medical Act: Registration of doctors

1863 Harrington invents clockwork dental drill

1864 Parkes' *Manual of Practical Hygiene*

1865 Elizabeth Garrett Anderson obtains Diploma of Society of Apothecaries

1867 Lister operation using antiseptics • Clinical Society

1874 London School of Medicine for Women

1874–79 Tait: Performs 1st successful hysterectomy, and cholecsytectomy

1875 Public Health Act

1877 Manson shows mosquitoes transmit infective diseases

1880 Balfour's treatise on embryology

• Gower's work helps found modern neurology

• London Association of Medical Women

1883 Tait operates for ectopic pregnancy

1886 Midwifery training given to doctors

1888 MacEwan improves understanding of epilepsy

1889 Infectious Diseases Notification Act

1890s Halsted uses rubber gloves in surgery

1890 Infectious Diseases Prevention Act

1891 Lister Institute for Preventive Medicine

1894 Lane introduces pinning of fractures

1897 Ross discovers parasite responsible for malaria.

1900 Manson's experiments prove mosquito responsible for carrying malaria

• Surgical caps and masks introduced by W. Hunter

1901 Dutton and Forde identify cause of sleeping sickness

• First-ever hospital prenatal care

• King Edward VII suffers appendicitis and focuses attention of abdominal surgeons on this illness

1902 Imperial Cancer Research Fund

• Bayliss and Starling discover hormones

1903 Bruce and Nabarro show sleeping sickness transmitted by tsetse fly

• Smith perfects new operation for eye cataracts

• Royal Army Medical College

1914–18 Plastic surgery is developed by Gillies

1915 Tetanus antitoxin for wounded soldiers

1919 British Ministry of Health

1920s Marie Stopes: 1st birth control clinic

1924–25 London University issues external degrees for pharmacy

1925 Insulin treatment

1928 Fleming discovers penicillin, 1st antibiotic

• Vaccine against yellow fever

1938 Synthetic estrogen

1947 All medical schools accept women

1948 National Health Service

1953 Crick and Watson discover structure of DNA

1963 Human kidney transplant

1967 Hospice care for the terminally ill

1968 Successful heart transplant

1969 Test-tube fertilization of human eggs

1970 Pacemaker driven by a nuclear battery

1972 Kidney and pancreatic tissue transplant

1978 The world's 1st test-tube baby is born

1986 World's 1st triple heart, lungs, and liver transplant

1997 Five-day-old baby given a new liver

• Ban on the sale of beef to prevent spread of BSE, or "mad cow disease"

• Cloning of sheep

1998 A 60-year-old woman has a baby son

1999 Meningitis C: Vaccination campaign

2000 Stephen Westaby installs the first permanent artificial heart

2002 According to the *British Journal of Psychiatry*, thioridazine, a common drug used in the treatment of some psychoses, is now linked to sudden unexplained death

2004 The first international standard for common genetic tests identifies Factor V Leiden, a genetic predisposition that induces defects in the body's natural anti-coagulation system • The world's first stem cell bank in Hertfordshire. It is responsible for storing, characterizing, and supplying ethically approved, quality controlled stem cell lines from embryonic, fetal, and adult tissues

2010 Study shows that small doses of aspirin taken for several years can lower risk of death from several cancers • Doctors at Cancer Genome Project announce a new drug that treats tumors by targeting gene mutations • Researchers at the Juvenile Diabetes Research Foundation, Cambridge University, create an insulin pump that continually measures blood sugar and automatically delivers the correct amount of insulin

2011 Surgeons at the Royal County Hospital, Guildford, use special glasses to gain a 3D image inside a body and conduct remote keyhole surgery

CANADA

1639 1st hospital
1644 Hôtel Dieu, Montréal
1746 Princeton College
1821 McGill College and University founded, Montréal
1895 Chiropractic manipulation of joints introduced by Palmer
1906 Surgeons perform kidney operations on animals to prove human transplants possible
1921 Insulin treatment for diabetes developed by Banting and Best
2011 University of Montréal's Department of Biochemistry show that PML molecules, present in benign cancer cells, can suppress certain proteins needed for the cell to multiply, whereas malignant cancer cells continue to replicate themselves

CHINA

1997 The influenza A H5N1 virus (commonly known as "bird flu") first crosses from birds to humans.
2009 Scientists succeed in breeding laboratory mice through reprogramming of adult skin cells

CZECHOSLOVAKIA

1161 Jewish physicians burned at Prague on charge of "poisoning wells"
1348 Clement VI charters University of Prague
1657 Comenius publishes *Orbis pictus*
1745 Ambulatory clinic, Prague
1860 Czermak introduces rhinoscopy
1867 Rokitansky performs nearly 60,000 autopsies in 50 years
1884 Carl Koller uses cocaine in eye surgery
1910 Jansky demonstrates 4 main blood groups: A, B, AB, & O

DENMARK

1475 Copenhagen University
1652 Bartholin describes lymphatic system
1661 Stensen discovers duct of parotid gland

1868 Meyer describes adenoid vegetations
1893 Niels Ryberg Finsen, founder of phototherapy, demonstrates therapeutic value of actinee and ultraviolet rays on skin diseases: **1903** Wins Nobel Prize

EGYPT

2001 The *Middle East Fertility Society Journal* reports that in an opinion poll among members of APART—an international association of assisted reproductive technology centers—three-quarters of the respondents express willingness to provide human cloning for patients in clinically indicated cases
1011–21 Ibn al-Haytham (Alhazen), ground-breaking work on optics and scientific method

FRANCE

542 Nosocomia hospitals founded at Lyons and Arles
581 Gregory of Tours describes smallpox epidemic
590 Pandemic of St. Anthony's fire (ergotism)
651 Hôtel-Dieu founded
738 School of Montpellier
962 Hospice of Great St. Bernard
1131 Council of Rheims stops monks practicing medicine for money
1180 University of Montpellier founded:**1181** it becomes a free school of medicine **1289** It is chartered by Nicholas IV
c. **1200** University of Paris
1223–26 2000 lazar houses
1257 Sorbonne founded
c. **1260** Arnold of Villanova translates Galen and Avicenna
1295 Lanfranch's treatise on surgery, *Cyrugia Magna*
1300–68 Guy de Chauliac, great surgeon and leader
1304 Henri de Mondeville teaches anatomy at Montpellier **1306** He writes his *Cyrurgia*. Develops 1st proper French surgery
1348–50 Black Death. Guy de Chauliac helps victims. In 1363 publishes his *Chirurgia magna*
1497–1588 Jean Fernel: Introduces division of medicine into standard disciplines of physiology and pathology; 1st to describe appendicitis accurately
1510–90 Paré, army doctor and renowned

master surgeon: 1st to introduce ligatures in amputation

1514 Pierre Brissot revives Hippocratic teaching: Bloodletting near lesions

1532 Rabelais publishes 1st Latin version of the aphorisms of Hippocrates

1536 Paré's 1st excision of elbow joint. In **1545** he improves amputation and gunshot wound treatment

1551 Anatomical theaters at Paris and Montpellier

1554 Writings by Aretaeus of Cappodocia printed

1561 Paré founds orthopedics. A *Universal Surgery* published

1564 Estienne and De Gorris's two medical dictionaries

1567 Fernel's *Universa Medicinia*—includes a section on therapeutics

1575 Paré introduces massage and artificial eyes

1578 De Baillou describes whooping cough

1596 Descartes born. In **1637** he shows visual accommodation depends on change in form of lens. In **1644** he describes reflex action and publishes treatise on dioptrics. In **1662** 1st treatise on physiology

1609 Louise Bourgeois publishes her observations on midwifery

1656 Lazar houses abolished

1667 Jean Baptiste Denis of Paris transfuses blood from lamb to man

1674 More's tourniquet for stopping hemorrhage

1678–1761 Fauchard, known as "father of dentistry." Writes *The Surgeon Dentist, A Treatise on Teeth*, describing oral anatomy and pathology, plus dental techniques

1679 De Blegny publishes 1st medical periodical *Nouvelles découvertes*

1683 Duverney's 1st treatise on otology

1705 Brisseau and Maitre Jan show cataract is a clouded lens

1713 Anel catheterizes tear ducts. **1714** He invents fine point syringe

1715 Petit differentiates between compression and concussion of brain

1720–21 Plague in Marseilles

• Palfyn's obstetric forceps

1724 De Moivre publishes memoir *Annuities Upon Lives*

• Guyot of Versailles attempts catheterization of Eustachian tubes

1728 Fauchard's *Le chirurgien dentiste*

1730 Réamur introduces 80-degree thermometer

1731 Hoffmann describes chlorosis

• 1st Academy of Surgeons

1736 Petit 1st to open mastoid and perform a cholecystectomy

1739 Morand makes 1st excision of hip joint

1741 André calls study of bones orthopedics

1745 Deparcieux's idea of "mean expectation of life"

1749 Buffon's *Natural History*

• Senac's treatise on the heart

1752 Réaumur's experiments on digestion in birds

1753 Daviel's modern method of cataract extraction

1764 Louis claims to introduce digital compression for hemorrhage

1766 Desault's bandage for fractures

1770 Abbé de l'Épée invents sign language for deaf-mutes

1771–1802 Bichat shows how individual tissue can be diseased • *Anatomie générale, apliquée à la physiologie et à médicine* is one of medicine's most important books

1777 Lavoisier describes exchange of gases in respiration

1779 Mesmer's memoir on animal magnetism

1783 Marschal excises prolapsed cancerous uterus

1786 Moreau excises elbow joint

1793 Larrey introduces *ambulances volantes*

1794 Lavoisier guillotined

1800s Dupuytren: Important in anatomy and pathology; performs daring surgery; devises new instruments

1800–01 Seen as founding modern histology and tissue pathology, Bichat's *Traité des membranes* and *Anatomie générale*. He revolutionizes descriptive anatomy

• Cuvier's *Comparative Anatomy*

• Pinel's psychiatric treatise. He reforms treatment of insane

1812 Larrey 1st to use local anesthesia by freezing limbs before amputation. His care for patients will form basis of Red Cross

1815–19 Laënnec invents stethoscope

1818 Pelletier and Caventou isolate strychnine and quinine

1820 Coindet uses iodine in goiter treatment

1821 Itard's treatise on otology

1822–40 Magendie pioneers physiology and

pharmacology; studies spinal canal and nervous system; demonstrates Bell's law of the spinal nerve roots; analyzes drug action

1823 Chevreul investigates animal fats

1824 Flouren works on cerebral physiology

1825 Bouillaud describes and localizes aphasia

1825–93 Charcot researches epilepsy and other neurological diseases. Works at Salpêtrière Hospital in Paris

1826 Laënnec gives classical description of bronchitis and other thoracic diseases

1827 Seglas invents endoscope

1829 Braille introduces printing for the blind

1831 Soubeiran discovers chloroform

1834 Dumas obtains and names pure chloroform

1835 Louis founds medical statistics

• Cruveilhier describes multiple sclerosis

1840s A founder of endocrinology, Brown-Séquard demonstrates function of suprenal gland: 1st scientist to work out physiology of spinal card and to discover hormones

1846–49 Bernard describes digestive function of pancreas, and glycogenic function of liver in sugar metabolism; produces diabetes by puncturing 4th ventricle

• Magendie pioneers physiology and pharmacology

1851–54 Bernard describes vasomotor function of sympathetic nervous system: Discovers function of vasodilator nerves

1858 Marey: 1st to show vagus tone increases with increase of blood pressure, so can assess absolute pressure of blood in a human artery

• Bernard discovers vasoconstrictor and extended vasodilator nerves

1860 Ménière describes aural vertigo, severe giddiness (Ménière's disease)

1861 Pasteur discovers anerobic bacteria

• Broca says speech control located in brain's left frontal lobe

1863 Pasteur discovers bacteria destroyed by heat; invents pasteurization; investigates silkworm disease

1865 Villemin demonstrates TB due to specific agent he calls a "germ"

1867 Bernard establishes principle of homeostasis

1869–72 Universities accept female medical students

1874 *Loi Roussel* enacted for protection of infants

1878 International Congress of Hygiene

1880–81 Pasteur isolates streptococcus, staphylococcus, and pneumococcus

• Laveran discovers malarial fever parasite

1883–6 Pasteur vaccinates against anthrax; makes 1st effective vaccine against rabies, *Méthode pour prévenir la rage*

1886 Neurologist Pierre Marie describes gigantism due to pituitary gland disease

1887 D'Arsonval introduces high frequency currents

1888 Institut Pasteur founded

• Roux and Yersin investigate diphtheria toxins

1894 Kitasato and Yersin discover plague bacillus

1896 Becquerel discovers radioactivity in uranium

• Widal and Sicard introduce agglutination test for typhoid fever

1898 Pierre and Marie Curie discover radium

1900 Widal and Ravaut introduce cytodiagnosis

1902 Carre introduces vascular anastomosis and transplantation of tissues

1903 Metchnikoff inoculates higher apes with syphilis

1905 Psychologist Binet develops way of testing brain's ability to reason

1907 Laveran awarded Nobel Prize

• Calmette devises conjunctival test for TB

• In Paris, doctors announce discovery of a serum to cure dysentery

1910 Victor Henri and others introduce ultraviolet sterilization of water

• Gattefossé studies therapeutic actions of plant oils

• Marie Curie's treatise on radiography

1911 Carrel investigates extravital culture and rejuvenation of tissues

1912 Dastre pioneers cornea graft to restore eyesight

• Odin claims isolation and cultivation of cancer microbe

1913 De Sandfort devises ambrine (paraffin-resin solution) treatment for burns

1914–18 Carrel and Dakin improve treatment of infected wounds

1921 Development of TB vaccine from living non-virulent bovine bacilli by Calmette and Guérin; **1924** introduced as BCG preventive vaccination

1926 Pasteur Institute announces discovery of anti-tetanus serum

1950 Küss and colleagues transplant kidneys from deceased to living patients

1998 1st arm transplant operation

2001 Establishment of the Meningitis Vaccine Project with the objective to eliminate epidemic meningitis in sub-Saharan Africa

2008 On the basis of a study, drug company Sanofi-aventis approves the use of nasal spray Nasacort AQ (triamcinolone acetonide), for even 2- to 5-year-old children, in treating seasonal and perennial allergic rhinitis

2010 World's reputedly first full-face transplant performed at Paris by Laurent Lantieri

GERMANY

1163 Abbess Hildegard von Bingen writes on holistic healing and natural history

1193–1280 Albertus Magnus, dominant in science learning

1316 City surgeon at Lübeck earns a salary of 16 marks per year

1440 Printing press: Gutenberg uses movable type for 1st time

1457 Tutenberg Purgation-Calendar 1st medical publication

1469–78 Da Grado's *Practica* and Mondino's *Anathomia*

1484 Schhöffer's herbal *Latin Herbarius* 1485 German *Herbarius*

1493 Smallpox outbreak

1513 Rösslin's *Roszgarten*—earliest printed text book for midwives

1517 Fugitive anatomical plates published by Schott of Mainz

• Gersdorff's *Field-Book of Wound-Surgery*

1518 Nuremberg ordinance regulating sale of food

1522 Doctor Wertt of Hamburg burned at stake for impersonating a midwife

1530 Brunfels' atlas of plants, *Herbarium vivae eicones*

1542 Fuchs's *Herbal* classifies medical plants

1546 Cordus's pharmacopeia

• Bock's *Kräuterbuch*

1560–1634 Father of German Surgery, Wilhelm Fabry, amputates with red-hot knife to reduce hemorrhage and through healthy tissue above gangrenous parts (rather than into gangrene)

1583 Bartisch's *Augendienst* 1st book on eye surgery

1604 Kepler shows inversion of optic image on retina

1619 Scheiner's *Oculus*

1640 Rolfink revives dissecting ("rolfinken")

1642 Wirsung discovers pancreatic duct named after him

1653–55 Scultetus's *Armamentarium chirurgicum* shows graphic representation of breast amputation

1660 Schneider shows nasal secretion not from pituitary body

1680 Plague hospital in Magdeburg

1690 Siegemundin's treatise on midwifery

1698 Stahl's treatise on diseases of the portal system: In 1702 he states phlogiston theory

1713 *Theatrum anatomicum*, Berlin

1714 Fahrenheit makes 212-degree mercury thermometer

1716 Surgeon General appointed in German Army at a salary of 900 marks per year

1719 Heister's work on surgery—founder of German scientific surgery

1721 General Holtzendorff creates "Collegium medico-chirurgicum" at Berlin

1738 Lieberkühn invents reflector microscope

1740 Hoffman describes rubella

1745 Kratzenstein uses electrotherapy

1751 Royal Society of Sciences at Göttingen founded by Haller

1754 1st woman with medical doctorate, at Halle

1755–1843 Samuel Hahnemann; he becomes founder of homeopathy

1756 Frederick the Great's dentist, Pfaff, describes making plaster models from wax impressions

1757 Halle's *Elementa physiologiae corporis humani et causis morborum*

1762 Roederer and Wagler describe typhoid fever

1768 Wolff's classic on chick's intestine embryology

1778 Von Siebold performs symphysiotomy

1781 Kant's *Critique of Pure Reason*

1791 Soemmering publishes 1st volume of his anatomy work

1795 Frank's 7 volumes *De curandis hominum morbis epitome*

1805–06 Sertürner isolates morphine

1807 Compulsory vaccination introduced in Bavaria and Hesse

1828 Forerunner of organic chemistry, Wöhler, synthesizes urea

1830 Kopp describes thymus death
1831–32 Von Liebig discovers chloroform, analyzes acetone, and discovers chloral
1833 Müller's physiology treatise
1836 Schwann discovers pepsin in stomach. In 1841 he shows bile essential for digestion. Great work on nerves and muscles
1837 Henle describes epithelial tissues of skin and intestine. Contributes greatly to microscopic anatomy • Schönlein publishes *Peliosis Rheumatica*, describing skin condition of purpura known by his name • Schwann discovers yeast cell and founds a germ theory
1838 Schleiden describes plant cells
• Johannes Müller's treatise on tumors
1839 Schwann publishes treatise on cell theory
1840s Wunderlich uses a clinical thermometer
1841 Henle's *Allgemeine Anatomie* contains many of his discoveries
1842 Wöhler describes synthesis of hippuric from benzoic acid.
• Dieffenback's treatise on strabismus
1843 Ludwig investigates urinary secretion mechanism
1845–58 Creator of modern pathology, Virchow, discovers much about human cells, and with Bennett, describes leukemia. He shows embolism is cause of pyemia
• Langenbeck detects actinomyces
1846 Weber brothers discover inhibitory effect of vagus nerve
1848–51 Helmholtz locates source of animal heat in muscles; measures velocity of nerve current; invents ophthalmoscope for examination of eye interior
• Du Bois-Reymond's treatise on animal electricity
1854 Virchow describes neuroglia
1857 Graefe introduces operation for strabismus
1854 Virchow's *Die Cellular Pathologie*: Founds cellular pathology
• Niemann isolates cocaine
1859 Kirchhoff and Bunsen develop recording spectroscope
• Kolbe synthesizes salicylic acid
1861 Max Schultze defines protoplasm and cell
1862 F. Hoppe Seyler discovers hemoglobin
1863 Preparation of barbituric acid by Van Baeyer

• Helmholtz's *Tonempfindungen*
• Voit and Pettenkofer's investigations of metabolism in respiration
1866 Voit establishes 1st hygienic laboratory, Munich
1867 Helmholtz's treatise on physiological optics
1868 Haeckel's *Natürliche Schöpfungsgeschichte*
• Wunderlich's work on temperature in disease; founds clinical thermometer
1869 Esmarch introduces india rubber bandage to provide bloodless field for limb surgery
• Virchow urges medical inspection of schools
1869–72 Universities accept female medical students
1870 Simon reports successful planned removal of kidney
1871 Weigert stains bacteria with carmine
1872 Abbe introduces optical instruments and oil immersion lenses • Billroth excises larynx • Revaccination compulsory • Obermeier discovers spirillum of relapsing fever
1874 Ehrlich introduces dried blood smears and improves stain methods
1875 Lösch discovers *Entamolba histolytica*, infective agent of amoebic dysentery • Meat inspection compulsory • Landois discovers hemolysis
1876 Imperial Board of Health founded, Berlin • Koch grows anthrax bacilli on artificial medium and isolates salicylic acid
1877 Cohnheim: successful inoculation of TB in rabbit's eye • Nitze introduces cystoscopy
1878 Von Volkmann successfully removes a rectum cancer • Freund excises cancerous uterus • Koch discovers causes of traumatic infections
1879 Neisser discovers gonococcus • German food law passed
1881–82 Billroth resects pylorus • Koch introduces plate cultures and discovers tubercle bacillus • Flemming studies cell division
1883–84 Klebs discovers diphtheria bacillus • Koch discovers cholera bacillus
1885 Weismann's memoir on continuity of germ plasm • Weigert begins hematoxylin staining of nerve fibers
1886 Von Bergmann begins steam sterilization in surgery

1887 Flick invents glass contact lenses
1889–90 Von Behring discovers antitoxins •
Buchner discovers alexins • Von Mering
and Minkowski produce experimental
pancreatic diabetes • Von Behring and
Kitasato discover diphtheria and tetanus
antitoxins and provide basis for serotherapy
• Von Behring treats diphtheria with
antitoxin • Koch introduces tuberculin •
Weigert stains neurolglia with methyl violet
1891 Institute for Infectious Diseases, Berlin,
under Koch • Waldeyer founds neuron
theory • Quinke uses lumbar puncture
1892 Cholera epidemic in Hamburg • Kossel
and Neumann discover pentose
1893 Aspirin marketed to treat rheumatism •
International Cholera Conference, Dresden
1895 Röntgen discovers X-rays; takes 1st
X-ray of his wife's hand • His reforms of
anatomical nomenclature
1897 Fischer synthesizes caffeine,
theobromine, xanthin, guanin, and adenin
1898 Löffler and Frosch investigate filtrable
viruses • Fishcer isolates purin nucleus of
uric acid compounds • Heroin and aspirin
used in medicine
1899 Einhorn synthesis of procaine
(novocaine) • Ehrlich's Institute for
Serology and Serum Testing becomes
Royal Institute for Experimental Therapy
at Frankfurt. Ehrlich's work there founds
chemotherapy
1900 Wertheim introduces radical operation
for uterine cancer
1901 Koch states that bubonic plague
may have been due solely to rats •
Röntgen wins Nobel Prize
1902 Barbituric acid formula patented
1903 Fischer and Von Mering introduce
veronal • Bier introduces artificial
hyperemia in surgery
1904 Sauerbruch designs negative pressure
chamber for surgery of chest
1905 Schaudinn discovers spirochaete of
syphilis • Koch studies African fever
1907 Wassermann introduces sero diagnostic
test for syphilis
1909 Ehrlich introduces Salvarsan. In 1911 he
tests it in the treatment of syphilis—seen as
the birth of chemotherapy
1912 Sudhoff opposes theory of American
origin of syphilis, believing it existed in
Europe pre-Columbus

1917 Von Economo describes experimental
transmission of encephalitis lethargica
1928 Ascheim and Zondek introduce 1st
usable pregnancy test
1932 Anti-malarial drug, atebrin, synthesized by
Mietzsch, Mauss, and Kirkuth • Evipan, a
barbiturate anesthetic, introduced by Weese
and Scharpff • 1st electron microscope
1935 Domagh finds that pronotosil protects
mice against fatal doses of striptococel
1979 1st human liver transplant
2000 Researchers decode all the genes of the
meningitis bacterium, Neisseria meningitis,
associated with epidemics of the disease,
especially in developing countries
2008 "Bionic" microchips for the blind are
successfully pioneered

HAITI
2010 A disastrous earthquake is followed by a
cholera outbreak, killing more than 1,000
people

IRELAND
675 Monastic records of smallpox
1593 University of Dublin (Trinity College)
founded
1770 Rutty describes relapsing fever
1784 Royal College of Surgeons in Ireland
1785 Chair of anatomy in University of
Dublin
1827 Adams describes heartblock
1832 Corrigan describes aortic insufficiency
1835 Graves urges use of healthy nutritious
foods. Gives classic account of
exuphthalmic goiter now known as Graves
disease
1837 Colles states law of maternal immunity
in syphilis
1845 Rynd invents instrument to give
hypodermic infusions • Potato famine—
thousands emigrate

ISRAEL
2007 Preliminary findings indicate that oral
antisense oligonucleotide effectively and
safely reduces neuromuscular disease
severity by 46 percent and improves muscle
function and swallowing time in patients
2008 ReWalk, a robotic suit developed by
Argo Medical Technologies, Ltd., helps
people paralyzed from the waist down to
stand, walk, and climb stairs

ITALY

848–56 Hospital from which School of Salerno will develop by 10th century, with female professors. The best known is Trotula, a gynecologist, who publishes a book on midwifery

1020–87 Constantinus the African. Medieval medical scholar translates Greek and Arabic works into Latin

1025 University of Parma

1080–1200 School of Salerno a center of knowledge. Five-year courses of study. Anatomical dissection on animals

1140 Roger II of Sicily restricts medical practice to licentiates

1150–58 Medical school and University of Bologna

1170 Roger of Palermo completes *Cyrurgia Rogerii*

1180 Roger of Parma's *Practica chirurgiae*

1201–77 Saliceto: Surgeon, writes many books

1221 Frederick II decrees no one to practice medicine unless approved by masters of Salerno. In **1224** he issues law regulating study of medicine; founds Naples and Messina universities **1231** Authorizes a quinquennial dissection at Salerno **1240–41** Makes regulations—to separate pharmacy from medicine; institute government supervision of pharmacy; oblige pharmacists to take an oath to prepare drugs reliably: encourages dissection

1250 Roland of Parma edits Roger of Salerno's work

1260 De Mondeville, surgeon to Philip the Fair, advises cleanliness and describes surgical procedures

1266 Borgognoni or Theodeoric teaches new treatment of wounds

1267 Council of Venice forbids Jews to practice medicine among Christians

1270 Spectacles introduced by Venetian glassmakers

1275 Saliceto completes treatise on regional surgical anatomy; advocates knife rather than usual cautery

1295 Lanfranchi's treatise on surgery, *Cyrugia Magna*

1302 1st judicial postmortem, at Bologna

1315 Anatomical dissection by De Luzzi at Bologna

1316 Mondino writes 1st "modern" textbook on anatomy, *Anathomia*

1317 Bull against alchemy and other magical practices

1345 *Anatomica* by Guido de Vigrevano tries to improve status of surgeons

1400s Boards of Health at Venice and Milan

1450 Krebs suggests timing pulse and weighing of blood and urine

1472 Bagellardo's treatise on pediatrics

1474–78 Saliceto's *Cyrurgia* (work on surgery) and 1st edition of work of Celsus printed: 1st medical author printed in movable type

1497 Aldine edition of *Theophrastus* printed

1498 Florentine *Ricettario* (1st official pharmacopeia)

1500 Da Carpi treats syphilis with mercury

1507 Benivieni's collection of postmortem sections printed

1510 Leonardo da Vinci's fine drawings of human body

1521–23 Da Carpi publishes anatomical treatises

1523–62 Fallopius teaches at Padua, writes on anatomy, studies reproductive system, and inner ear. Fallopian tubes are named after him

1526 1st (Aldine) Greek translation of Hippocrates

1530 Fracastorius's poem on syphilis published

1535 Mariano Santo di Barletta: 1st account of median lithotomy

1537 Dryander's *Anatomia*

1537–1619 Fabricius ab Aquapedente discovers much about valves in veins

1538 Vesalius publishes his *Tabulae anatomicae sex*

1540 Mattioli: Internal use of mercury for syphilis

1543 Vesalius founds modern anatomy: *De Humani Corporus Fabrica*

1546 Fracastoro publishes work on contagious illnesses

1549 Anatomy theater, Padua

1558 Cornaro's treatise on personal hygiene

1559 Comuno describes pulmonary circulation

1561 Fallopius (Fallopio) *Observationes anatonmicae*, greatly extends knowledge of anatomy, especially female reproductive system, inner ear, cerebral arteries, nerves, eye muscles, tissues

1564 Galileo born. Develops careful measurements in medicine, microscope, and telescope • Eustachius discovers abducens nerve thoracic duct and suprarenal glands

1567 Paracelsus's account of miners' phthisis

1572 Mercuriale's systematic treatise on skin diseases

1576 Paracelsus's tract on mineral waters

1580 Alpino introduces moxabustion from Orient

1586 Della Porta's *De humana physiognomia* pioneers physiogynomy

1594 1st permanent operating theater at Padua

1595 Quercetanus uses purgative, calomel • Mercurio's *La Comare o Raccoglitrice (The Midwife)*

1597 Tagliacozzi's treatise on plastic surgery

1603 Fabricus ab Aquapendente's *De Venarium Ostiolis* suggests to Harvey the circulation of the blood

1609 Clinical thermometer invented by Sanctorius

1610 Galileo's microscope

1622 Aselli discovers lacteal vessels

1626 Sanctorius Santonio records use of clinical thermometer and pulse clock

1629 Severino makes 1st resection of wrist

1633–1717 Ramazzini: Writes 1st full-scale treatise on occupational health

1640 Severino creates local anesthesia with snow and ice

1648 Kircher describes ear trumpet • Redi disproves spontaneous generation theory

1654–1720 Maria discusses idea that malaria might be caused by mosquito bites

1658 Kircher attributes plague to *contagium animatum*

1659–61 Malpighi outlines lymphadenoma; discovers capilliary anastomosis; describes histology of lungs

1662 Bellini discovers kidneys' excretory ducts

1666 Malpighi's treatise on viscera. **1670** He discovers Malpighian bodies in spleen and kidneys. **1673** He describes chick development. **1675** Publishes *Anatome plantarum*

1680–81 Borelli studies mechanics and "physical laws" of the body; publishes *De motu animalium*

1682–1771 Examination of dead body developed by pathologist Morgagni

1700 Ramazzini's treatise on occupational diseases

1704 Valsalva describes Valsalva's maneuver

1710 Santorini's muscle in larynx discovered

1719 Morgagni describes syphilis of cerebral arteries

1761 Morgagni's *De sedibus*

1770 Cotugno demonstrates albumen in urine

1772 Scarpa discovers ear labyrinth

1784 Cotugno discovers cerebro-spinal fluid

1787 Mascagni publishes atlas of lymphatics

1794 Scarpa's *Tabulae nevrologicae* shows his work on heart nerves. In **1804** he describes arteriosclerosis

1827 Amici and Cuthbert invent reflecting microscope

1876 Lombroso inaugurates doctrine of "criminal type"

1916 Vanghetti introduces cineplasty

2005 Only 1 out of 4 Italians vote in the referendum to modify the country's law on assisted reproduction

2006 The world's first unmanned robotic surgery

2008 The Moli-sani Project reports that one small square of dark chocolate consumed two or three times a week can reduce blood inflammation, and therefore the chances of cardiovascular disease

2010 Discovery of a 16th-century Latin book by surgeon Gaspare Tagliacozzi explaining one of the world's first known "nose jobs"

JAPAN

1868 University of Tokyo

1890 Kitasato and Von Behring discover diphtheria and tetanus antitoxins

1894 Kitasato and Yersin discover plague bacillus

1897 Shiga discovers dysentery bacillus

1909 Noguchi improves the Wassermann reaction **1911** Introduces luetin reaction **1913** Demonstrates *Spirochaete pallida* in brains of syphilitic patients suffering from paresis **1920** Discovers leptospira in yellow fever **1928** Dies of yellow fever in Ghana

1914–15 Inada and others describe cause, method of infection, and treatment of spirochaetal jaundice

1916 Futaki and others discover a spirillum in cases of ratbite fever

1920 Naito's artificial blood

MEXICO

2009-10 "Swine flu" first identified; causes pandemic; virus developed in 2009

NETHERLANDS

1590 Invention of compound microscope by Hans and Zacharia Janssen

1621 Drebbel improves microscope

1638 Drebbel improves thermometer

1642–45 Cholera 1st studied by Bonitus, who also describes beriberi in his book *De medicina Indorum*

1646 Diemerbroek publishes monograph on plague

1658 Swammerdam describes red blood-corpuscles

1662 De Graaf shows that ova arise in the ovary

1663 Sylvius describes digestion as a fermentation

1664 Swammerdam discovers valves of lymphatics • De Graaf examines pancreatic juice and its importance in digestion of food. In **1667** he describes docimiasia of fetal lungs

1670 Swammerdam discovers muscle-tonus

1672 De Graaf describes Graafian follicles in ovary

1673 Leeuwenhoek makes microscopes and describes red blood cells. In **1683** he describes bacteria • Discoveries: **1674** sperm; **1675** protozoa; **1679** striped muscle; **1680** yeast plant; **1689** rods in retina and finer anatomy of cornea; **1703** parthenogenesis of plant lice

1732 Boerhaave's *Elementa chemiae*

1738 Lieberkühn invents reflector microscope

1758 De Haën uses thermometer in clinical work

1860 Donders introduces cylindrical and prismatic spectacles for astigmatism. In **1862** he publishes studies on astigmatism and presbyopia

1869–72 Universities accept female medical students

1901 De Vries's mutation theory

1903 Einthoven invents string galvanometer, 1st practical electrocardiograph (ECG) • Rocci invents sphygmomanometer for measuring blood pressure

1910 Worldwide organization Féderation Internationale Pharmaceutique begins

1924 Einthoven wins Nobel Prize

1930 Debye uses X-rays to investigate molecule structure • 1st kidney dialysis machine developed by Kolff in secret for Dutch resistance

2000 First country in the world to decriminalize voluntary euthanasia

RUSSIA

1755 University of Moscow

1798 Imperial Medico-Military Academy, St. Petersburg

1819 University of St Petersburg

1852 Pirogoff uses frozen sections in his *Anatome topigraphica*

1867 Pavlov, famous for his dogs, helps understanding of conditioned reflexes

1892 Ivanovsky describes mosaic tobacco disease and discovers viruses

1937 Artificial heart by Demikhov

1970 Balloon surgery

SOUTH AMERICA

Earliest times Pre-Columbian medicine is a mix of religious and magical practice. Tropical forests remain a source of many drugs

1508 Guaiac from West Indies and tropical America used as wood or resin for syphilis, dropsy, and gout

1524 Cortes erects 1st hospital in city of Mexico

1530s Sarsaparilla—dried roots of several tropical American plants—used as an emetic, to treat psoriasis, and as flavoring

1609 Jalap, a purgative from the fibrous roots of a climbing plant, brought to Europe from Mexico

1721 Universidad Central de Venezuela, Caracas

1743 University of Santiago founded in Chile

1808 Medical Faculty at Rio de Janeiro, Brazil

1901 Instituto Oswaldo Cruz, Rio de Janeiro, Brazil

SOUTH KOREA

2010 "Superbug" bacterium resistant to antibiotics found in two patients in Seoul

SPAIN AND PORTUGAL

580 Hospital at Merida founded by Bishop Masona

936 Albucasis, Muslim surgeon, writes 1st illustrated book on surgery and introduces the use of red hot iron to cauterize wounds

1094–1162 Ibn Zuhr, Arab physician born in Seville. Writes treatise on clinical medicine

1309 University of Coimbra chartered by

King Diniz of Portugal (reconstituted, 1772). An important school of medicine

1391 University of Lerida permitted to dissect a body every 3 years • 1st dissection recorded in Spain

1400s Gold leaf used as a dental filling material

1409 Insane asylum at Seville; and **1425** Insane asylum, Saragossa

1450 University of Barcelona **1501** University of Valencia **1504** University of Santiago **1505** University of Seville

1508 University of Madrid

1531 University of Granada

1537 Dryander's *Anatomia*

1548 Charles V declares surgery honorable

1553 Servede, 1st to suggest transit of blood through lungs, burned at stake in Geneva because of his revolutionary ideas

1571 Bravo describes Spanish typhus

1583–1600 Diphtheria (garotillo) epidemic

1590 D'Acosta describes mountain sickness

1611 Real and Vilius describe diphtheria (garotillo) epidemic

1638 Acuna, Portuguese monk, uses oil of capaiva

1640 Malaria arrives • Del Vigo introduces cinchona, a substitute from Peruvian bark associated with quinine and a cure for fevers

1935 1st pre-frontal leucotomy by Moniz to treat some psychoses

2008 The European Study of Human Genetics announces the discovery of genetic mutations in 8 new areas. This is expected to help in addressing intestinal disorders and shed new light on a range of autoimmune and inflammatory diseases

SWEDEN

1735 Linnaeus's *Systema naturae*

1742 Celsius invents 100 degree thermometer • Linnaeus describes aphasia and then, in **1763**, publishes his classification of disease, *Genera morborum*

1764 Von Rosenstein of Uppsala's book on children's diseases and treatment begins modern pediatrics

1774 Scheele discovers chlorine. In 1776 with Bergmann, he discovers uric acid in bladder stones

1808 Swedish Medical Society

1869–72 Universities accept female medical students

1880 Sandström describes parathyroid gland

1911 Gullstrand wins Nobel Prize for optical researches

1958 Ake Senning implants 1st internal heart pacemaker

1956 Fijoe and Levan state 46 normal human chromosomes exist. Leads to discovery of Down syndrome

SWITZERLAND

1460 University of Basel founded by citizens of city

1493–1551 Paracelsus: Questions classics and defies tradition; advocates chemical therapies, called the "father of pharmacology." In 1527 he publishes his revolutionary ideas, promises to free medicine from its worst errors, and burns books by Galen and Avicenna

1537 Vesalius graduates, Basel

1554 Rueff's *De Conceptu*; becomes popular handbook for midwives

1570 Platter, one of 1st to distinguish between various mental disorders, urges psychic treatment of insane

1588 Anatomy theater, Basel

1602 Platter publishes 1st attempt at classification of diseases. He dissects more than 300 bodies

1623 Medical faculty added to University of Altdorf

1658 Wepfer demonstrates lesion of brain in apoplexy

1677 Peyer describes lymphoid follicles in small intestine, Peyer's patches

1682 Brunner describes duodenal glands, which were found in **1679** by his father-in-law, Wepfer

1708–77 Von Haller, writer, botanist, physiologist, who studies nervous system. In **1736** he points out function of bile in digestion of fats

1739 Royal Swedish Academy of Medicine

1744 Trembley describes regeneration of tissues in hydrozoa

1747 Haller's *Primae lineae physiologiae*, 1st textbook on physiology

1749 Meyer orders phthisical patients to mountain areas

1752 Haller publishes memoir of specific irritability of tissues. **1757** Publishes *his Elementa physiologiae corporis humani et causis morborium*

1805 Vieusseux describes cerebro-spinal meningitis

1832 University of Zurich **1834** University of Bern

1846 Kölliker describes smooth muscle. In **1852** his *Handbuch der Gwewbelenhre* is 1st systematic treatise on histology

1865 Universities accept female medical students

1911 Bleuler proposes term "schizophrenia"

1948 World Health Organization forms, Geneva

1972 Borel discovers cyclosporin-A from a mushroom suppresses immune system and helps transplants to take

2007 Installation of the world's 1st BSD 500 hyperthermia cancer therapy system at Aarau. Hyperthermia is delivered here through microwave energy • The 1st extra-cranial stereotactic treatment done in Berne on a lung cancer patient. Three highly focused radiotherapy doses are delivered to destroy a tumor, which reportedly shrinks

TAIWAN
2004 First International Symposium on Tibetan medicine

USA
1636 Harvard College founded by act of General Court of Massachusetts • Assembly of Virginia passes act regulating surgeons' fees

1638 Assembly of Maryland act regulates surgeons' fees

1639 Virginia Assembly's law regulates medical practice

1646 Syphilis in Boston

1647 Yellow fever in Barbados spreads through American ports • Firmin lectures on anatomy in Massachusetts

1649 Act regulates medical practice in Massachusetts

1659 Diphtheria at Roxbury, Massachusetts

1663 1st hospital in American colonies (Long Island, N.Y.)

1666 Coroners appointed for each county of Maryland

1668 Yellow fever, New York

1677 A broadside printed during a smallpox epidemic in Boston becomes the first medical publication printed in the American colonies.

1685 Bidloo's *Anatomia* • Vieussens's *Nevrographia* on brain, spinal cord, and nerves. Best illustrated 17th-century work on subject

1691 Autopsy of Governor Slaughter in New York • Yellow fever in Boston

1692 Salem witchcraft trials

1699 Infectious diseases act in Massachusetts

1703–1850 Devastating epidemics of yellow fever in tropical/subtropical zones

1716 New York City issues ordinance for midwives

1717 Hospital for infectious diseases, Boston

1721 Boylston inoculates for smallpox in Boston

1730–31 Cadwalader teaches anatomy in Philadelphia

1735 Scarlatina appears

1760 W. Shippen Jr. lectures on anatomy in Philadelphia • Act regulates medical practice in New York

1762 1st medical library in USA (Pennsylvania Hospital) • Shippen's private maternity hospital, Philadelphia

1765 John Morgan founds 1st medical school in USA at College of Pennsylvania

1768 Medical School Kings College, New York

1770 1st medical degree in USA conferred by King's College on Robert Tucker • Pennsylvania quarantine act

1772 New Jersey act regulates medical practice

1773 1st insane asylum in USA, Williamsburg, Virginia

1774 Chovet teaches anatomy in Philadelphia

1777 William Shippen: Director General of American Army Medical Department

1778 Brown publishes 1st USA pharmacopeia *Pharmacopoeia simpliciorum et efficaciorum* • Yellow fever, Memphis

1780 Benjamin Franklin invents bifocal lenses • Dengue fever at Philadelphia

1782 Medical Department of Harvard University founded

1787 College of Physicians of Philadelphia

1791–99 Baynham operates for extra-uterine pregnancy

1796 Yellow fever in Boston • Wright Post successfully ligates femoral artery

1797 Medical Repository (New York) published

1797–99 Yellow fever in Philadelphia

1798 Medical and Chirurgical Faculty of Maryland founded

1800 Waterhouse introduces Jennerian vaccination in New England

1809 Famous surgeon, McDowell of Kentucky, performs ovariotomy

1810 Yale Medical School

1812 *Medical inquiries & observations upon the diseases of the mind* by Rush, 1st American book on psychiatry • Bellevue Hospital, New York

1817 Plantson invents dental plate

1821 Philadelphia College of Pharmacy, 1st in USA

1825 Fever hospital, New York City

1828–1917 Dr. Andrew Taylor Still founds osteopathy

1831 Guthrie discovers chloroform

1831–1915 Black reforms dentistry—devises foot engine so dentists can keep both hands free when powering drill. Notes densely matted coating on teeth and suggests dental caries and periodontal disease infections brought about by bacteria. Scientific evidence confirms this—but not until 1960s!

1832 Cholera: 3 major outbreaks during century • Boston Lying-in Hospital

1833 Beaumont publishes experiments on digestion

1839–40 Baltimore College of Dental Surgery is 1st dental school in world

1842 Long operates with ether anesthesia

1843 Holmes writes *Contagiousness of puerperal fever*—a medical classic

1846 Morton uses ether to put patient to sleep during dental operation • J. Marion Sims invents a vaginal speculum

1847 1st school for mentally retarded, in Massachusetts

1847 American Medical Association • New York Academy of Medicine

1849 1st English woman to graduate as a doctor: Elizabeth Blackwell, at the Geneva Medical School, New York • J.M. Sims operates for vesico-vaginal fistula

1850 Detmold opens abscess of brain

1852 American Pharmaceutical Association

1853 Sims's treatise on vesico-vaginal fistula. In 1855 founds Hospital for Women's Diseases, New York

1861 Wollcott (Milwaukee) 1st to excise renal tumor

1861–65 American Civil War. Many outbreaks of communicable disease • Beaumont treats war patient's close shotgun blast: He survives with permanent exterior opening to stomach

1865 Chicago Hospital for Women

1866 Sims's *Clinical Notes on Uterine Surgery*

1875 Silas Weir Mitchell's rest cure for nervous diseases • Boston Medical Library

1876 Johns Hopkins University: Many forward-thinking investigative and innovative policies

1880 American Surgical Association founded

1884 Koller uses cocaine in eye surgery

1886 Fitz describes pathology of appendicitis

1889 Johns Hopkins Hospital (Baltimore) opens

1890 Halsted introduces rubber gloves for surgery at Johns Hopkins

1892 Welsh and Nuttall discover gas gangrene bacillus • Halsted ligates subclavian artery in 1st portion

1897 Cannon's solution of radio-opaque bismuth acts as diagnostic meal to outline stomach • Murphy: 1st to successfully repair gunshot wound of a major artery

1897–98 Cannon discovers barium suspensions show alimentary canal on x-ray plate

1898 Pathologist T. Smith differentiates between bovine and human tubercle bacilli

1899 Reed, Carroll, Simoni, and Lazear establish transmission of yellow fever by mosquito

1899 Loeb produces chemical activation of sea urchin egg

1901 Rockefeller Institute for Medical Research, New York

1902 North and South America establish International Sanitary Bureau

1903 Henry Phipps Institute for Tuberculosis, Baltimore • Porcelain fillings

1904 Atwater invents respiration calorimeter

1906 Nutrition Laboratory, Boston • "Typhoid Mary," famous typhoid carrier, discovered • Food and Drugs Act

1907 Immigrant's health checks to ensure free of contagious diseases; card given to signify clean bill of health; unfit immigrants may be sent home

1910 Harrison demonstrates nerve-fiber outgrowth extravitality • Flexner produces poliomyelitis experimentally • Ricketts shows woodtick is vector of Rocky Mountain spotted fever, which he differentiates from typhus • X-ray machine guides a surgeon to remove a nail from a boy's lung

1911 1st prenatal clinic, Boston • Peyton Rous transmits a malignant tumor as a filterable virus • Cushing describes dyspituitarism

1912 Children's Bureau established, Washington, DC • Public Health Services • Cushing describes pituitary disorders

1913 Supreme Court denies "rights" of individuals if inimical to public welfare • American College of Surgeons

1915 Fitzgerald introduces "zone therapy" to alleviate certain symptoms and induce numbness

1917–18 American Commission investigates trench fever

1922 McCollum and others identify vitamin D

1928 Iron lung used for the 1st time in the USA

1932 Development of 1st vaccine against yellow fever

1933 Anti-beriberi vitamin identified by R. Williams and colleagues; produced synthetically in **1936**

1934 Mixter and Barr demonstrate role of intervertebral disc herniation in sciatica

1938 New York is 1st state to pass law requiring medical tests for marriage licenses

1943 Waksman discovers streptomycin, 1st antibiotic effective against TB

1944 1st eye bank, New York • 1st successful heart operation on a newborn baby • Waksman discovers antibiotic streptomycin

1945 World's 1st fluoridated water supply, Michigan • Vaccine against virus A and B influenza used on U.S. Army • Benadryl developed to treat common allergies

1946 Dr. Spock's book *Baby* and *Child Care*

1947 Gerty Cori: 1st woman wins Nobel Prize in medicine

1949 Gross does resection of waretation of aorta

1950 Green grows skin for grafting from a newborn baby • 1st human kidney transplant by R.H. Lawler • Murray and colleagues transplant 1st kidneys from deceased to living patients

1952 Artificial heart 1st used in an operation at Pennsylvania Hospital • Operations and hormone treatment change a man's sex

1953 Virologist Dr. Salk successfully tests a polio vaccine

1955 Pincus and others invent contraceptive pill

1956 1st successful kidney transplant between identical twins by Merrill and others

1960 Enders and others develop attennated measles virus vaccine

1966 Artificial blood invented by Clark and Gollan

1972 Syphilis scandal in Alabama

1976 1st artificial functioning gene

1981 AIDS recognized in New York and Los Angeles

1982 1st operation to implant artificial heart

1984 AIDS virus discovered

1987 Prozac licensed

1992 Baboon liver transplant

1995 Cancer supergun may help body's immune system fight tumors

1997 1st surviving septuplets born

1998 Viagra, anti-impotence treatment, approved • 1st surviving octuplets born

1999 New skin patch test for diabetes • Leech neurones used in a "living" computer • Cloning of 1st human embryo

2000 Human Genome Project scientists sequence 90 percent of the human genome • National Institute of Health officially recognizes for the first time that stress reduction is important to alleviate mental and physical disease caused by modern lifestyles • *Time* magazine recognizes Siemens Biograph as one of the inventions of the year • Bill and Melinda Gates Foundation announces new global health grants of $28.5 million to eradicate guinea worm disease, caused by drinking infected water

2001 16.9 million nuclear medicine procedures performed • St. Jude's Medical, Inc., announces the first implant of its new invention, the dual-chamber pacemaker, designed to better manage pacemaker patients suffering from atrial fibrillation, the most common cardiac arrhythmia • Researchers from the Universities of Chicago and Michigan identify the first genetic abnormality: Mutations of gene Nod2 that increases susceptibility to Crohn's Disease

2003 Human genome sequencing complete. The accuracy is expected to be at least 99.9 percent • The first biotech pet, genetically modified zebrafish, available commercially • A new MRI scanner provides real-time updates during surgery and detects any part of a tumor that may have been overlooked

2004 Advances in CT, MRI imaging, and ultrasound enable Johns Hopkins surgeons to prolong the lives of cancer patients by 30 to 50 percent

2005 The Shang Shung Institute in Massachusetts offers a four-year Traditional Tibetan Medicine Program, the only one of its kind anywhere in the West • New research at Oregon State University comes closer to explaining how vitamin C can prevent cancer and heart disease by getting rid of toxic byproducts of fat metabolism • Researchers at Harvard School of Public Health awarded a five-year, $30 million grant to study the long-term effects on children of antiretroviral drug exposure

2006 New surgery for morbid obesity through transoval endoscopic surgical technique at the American College of Gastroenterology • Alberto Ascherio's study at Harvard School of Public Health reveals that high vitamin D levels in the body may decrease risks of multiple sclerosis • Researchers at Mayo identify Complex Sleep Apnea, wherein the patient stops breathing 20 to 30 times per hour each night. The Continuous Airway Pressure device, used in obstructive and central sleep apnea cases, is ineffective in its treatment

2007 Special issue of *Science Times*, an associated publication of the *New York Times*, examines a cascade of research into the science of sleep • Triphala, a well known Indian herbal supplement, is reported to have cancer fighting properties

2008 The first hybrid PET/MRI system for humans, installed by Siemens. PET evaluates metabolic aspects of disease, while MRI provides high-resolution anatomical information • A study at the University of Texas and National Institutes of Health shows the Chinese herb *Tripterygium wilfordii Hook F* (TWHF) to be effective in the treatment of rheumatoid arthritis • Research at the University of Alabama shows that the investigational drug triphendial kills malignant cells in pancreatic and bile duct carcinoma • Pharma company Genentech, supported by the FDA, announces that cancer drug Tarceva (erlotinib) can lead to liver problems and fatalities • Advances in plastic surgery toward repairing facial injuries of soldiers wounded in the war in Iraq is to be made available to civilian victims of urban violence • Research indicates that palmitoleate, a newly identified hormone, can combat diabetes and conditions related to obesity • The EndoBarrier Gastrointestinal Liner, a new non-invasive devise inserted endoscopically into the small intestine through the mouth, could promote blood sugar control and weight loss • Scientists at Northwestern University report that people with chronic backaches have brains that are 11 percent smaller than non-sufferers, perhaps due to the stress of having to live with the condition • Researchers from Massachusetts General Institute of Neurodegenerative Disease and Harvard School of Public Health, claim that elevated levels of urate, a normal antioxidant in the blood, may slow progression of Parkinson's disease in men • American *Journal of Epidemiology* reports that drinking alcohol in the first three months of pregnancy results in an increased risk of producing infants with cleft lip and cleft palate deformity • OvaSure, a new blood test, is developed at Yale for early detection of ovarian cancer. It is yet to be validated • Dr. Gail Rebovic's oncoplastic surgery for breast cancer incorporates surgery and cosmetic reconstruction simultaneously. By minimizing the number of times patients have to go under the knife, it counters poor insurance reimbursements for plastic surgery • A link between the lack of protein MeCP2, associated with Rett syndrome, and certain behavioral disorders is revealed • New research at the University of Michigan on how the protein HIV-1 Nef keeps immune cells from doing their normal work of detecting and killing infected cells • The protein Npas4, the first known "master switch" in brain cells, essential for proper brain function, is identified at the Children's Hospital, Boston. It regulates more than 200 genes that calm down overexcited cells, thereby restoring balance in neurological disorders • The Archives of International Medicine reports that a diet restricted in calories does not cause bone loss in young, overweight adults, provided adequate amount of calcium and other nutrients are maintained • Identification of three phospatases enzymes by researchers at Baylor College of Medicine could be the beginning of a new treatment for prostate cancer • Researchers at NYC Cancer Institute and the Ronald O. Perelman Department of Dermatology identify mebandozole, a drug used globally to treat parasite infections, as a new agent for treating chemotherapy-resistant malignant melanoma • American Heart Association achieves goal of reducing coronary heart disease and stroke risk by 25 percent since 2000

2009 Ban on federal funding of embryonic stem cell reseach is lifted • First signs of a potential AIDS vaccination • A study suggests that regular screening and early detection of prostate cancer does not lower death rate from the cancer • A genetic clue to autism is discovered • Three separate genes linked to late-onset Alzheimer's disease identified

2010 HAART (highly active anti-retroviral drug therapy) gives persons with AIDS a life expectancy of 69 years • Trials for screening heavy smokers for lung cancer with spiral CT scans decrease deaths from lung cancer by about 20 percent • Biological indicators or biomarkers for Alzheimer's disease are identified; will be able to detect very early sign of the disease • Health care reform bill passed, giving health care coverage to about 95 percent of Americans

2011 Indianapolis researchers announce a new, accurate, and simple method of identifying individuals who are pre-diabetic and who could take preventive measures to avoid developing diabetes

VIETNAM

2003 Carlo Urbani sounds alarm to the possibility of a SARS (severe acute respiratory syndrome) epidemic, thus enabling a timely, effective response. Urbani himself dies of the disease a few weeks later

The former residence of Thomas Nelson Page in Washington, D.C., currently serves as headquarters of the American Institute for Cancer Research.

GLOSSARY

anesthetic A drug or gas administered before surgery and used to produce a loss of the sense of pain in a patient.

antibiotic Destroying or inhibiting the growth of bacteria and other microorganisms.

antiseptic Preventing infection and decay by inhibiting the action of microorganisms.

bacteria One-celled organisms that have no chlorophyll, multiply by simple division, and are microscopic. Some bacteria cause disease.

diphtheria An infectious disease caused by a bacterium and characterized by weakness, high fever, and the formation of tough, membrane-like obstructions in the patient's air passages, making breathing very difficult.

epidemic When a disease is prevalent and spreading rapidly among many individuals in a community at the same time; widespread.

hepatitis An inflammation of the liver.

hospice A home for the sick or poor.

husbandry Farming; management of domestic affairs and resources. Animal husbandry is the care and raising of domesticated animals such as cattle, sheep, goats, pigs, and horses.

immunity Resistance to or protection against a specific disease; the power to resist infection.

influenza A contagious and infectious disease caused by any of a group of viruses and characterized by inflammation of the respiratory tract, fever, and muscular pain; the "flu."

microbe A microscopic organism, such as a disease-causing bacterium; a germ.

microorganism Any microscopic animal or vegetable organism, including bacteria and viruses.

pandemic A disease that is prevalent over a whole area, region, or country; an epidemic over a large region.

pathogen Any microorganism or virus that can cause disease.

pathology The branch of medicine that deals with the nature of disease, especially with the structural and functional changes caused by disease; all the conditions, processes, or results of a particular disease.

pestilence Any deadly contagious or infectious disease, especially one of epidemic proportions.

physiology The branch of biology dealing with the functions and vital processes of living organisms or their parts and organs; the functions and vital processes of an organism or of an organ or system of organs.

plague Any contagious epidemic disease that is deadly; often refers to the bubonic plague (the "Black Death") specifically.

post-mortem A detailed examination or evaluation of an organism performed after its death.

pox Any of various diseases characterized by skin eruptions, such as smallpox or chickenpox; was also once a slang term for the venereal disease syphilis.

putrefaction The decomposition of organic matter by bacteria, fungi, and oxidation, resulting in the formation of foul-smelling products; a rotting.

rhinovirus Any of a large subclass of viruses that are among the chief infectious agents that cause the common cold.

sepsis A poisoned state caused by the absorption of disease-causing microorganisms and their products into the bloodstream.

virus Ultramicroscopic or submicroscopic infective agents that cause various diseases in plants and animals; they are both living organisms and complex proteins.

FOR MORE INFORMATION

American Council on Science and Health
1995 Broadway, 2nd Floor
New York, NY 10023-5860
(212) 362-7044
Web site: http://www.acsh.org
The American Council on Science and Health is a group of consumer education advocates that includes doctors, scientists, and policymakers.

American Public Health Association
800 I Street NW
Washington, DC 20001
(202) 777-2742
Web site: http://www.apha.org
The American Public Health Association is an organization of health professionals dedicated to improving public health.

Centers for Disease Control and Prevention
1600 Clifton Road
Atlanta, GA 30333
(800) 232-4636
Web site: http://www.cdc.gov
The Centers for Disease Control and Prevention is an organization that provides the public with reliable information about disease and health-related topics.

Health Canada
Health Canada Address Locator 0900C2
Ottawa, ON K1A 0K9
Canada
(866) 225-0709
Web site: http://www.hc-sc.gc.ca
Health Canada is the federal department responsible for helping Canadians maintain and improve their health. Health Canada's goal is for Canada to be among the countries with the healthiest people in the world.

Health Museum
John P. McGovern Museum of Health and Medical Science
1515 Hermann Drive
Houston, TX 77004
(713) 521-1515
Web site: http://www.mhms.org
The John P. McGovern Museum of Health & Medical Science, also known as the Health Museum, is Houston's most interactive science learning center and a member institution of the world-renowned Texas Medical Center. The Health Museum encourages growing interest and regard for healthier lifestyles, fitness, and good physical, mental, and spiritual health. The Health Museum is committed to excellence in innovative and interactive health and science educational experiences.

Mütter Museum
College of Physicians of Philadelphia
19 South 22nd Street
Philadelphia, PA 19103-3097
(215) 563-3737

The College of Physicians of Philadelphia, founded in 1787, is the oldest professional medical organization in the country. The college is home to the Mütter Museum and the Historical Medical Library. The Mütter Museum is dedicated to improving the health of the public through its education programs, services, and resources. A visit to the museum offers a unique environment to learn more about health and medicine.

National Museum of Health and Medicine
6900 Georgia Avenue NW, Building 54
Washington, DC 20307
(202) 782-2200
Web site: http://nmhm.washingtondc.museum
The National Museum of Health and Medicine was established during the Civil War as the Army Medical Museum, a center for the collection of specimens for research in military medicine and surgery. By World War II, research at the museum focused increasingly on pathology; in 1946 the museum became a division of the new Army Institute of Pathology (AIP), which became the Armed Forces Institute of Pathology (AFIP) in 1949. The museum's library and part of its archives were transferred to the National Library of Medicine when it was created in 1956. The Army Medical Museum became the Medical Museum of the AFIP in 1949, the Armed Forces Medical Museum in 1974, and the National Museum of Health and Medicine in 1989.

Public Health Agency of Canada
1015 Arlington Street
Winnipeg, MB R3E 3R2
Canada
(204) 789-2000
Web site: http://www.phac-aspc.gc.ca
The Public Health Agency of Canada is a government organization that promotes health and helps people to prevent and control diseases, injuries, and infections.

World Health Organization
Avenue Appia 20
1211 Geneva 27, Switzerland
Phone: + 41 22 791 21 11
Web site: http://www.who.int
The World Health Organization is part of the United Nations. It provides health leadership for the world and monitors health trends worldwide.

WEB SITES
Due to the changing nature of Internet links, Rosen Publishing has developed an online list of Web sites related to the subject of this book. This site is updated regularly. Please use this link to access the list:

http://www.rosenlinks.com/ht/med

Abram, Ruth
Send Us a Lady Physician: Women Doctors in America, 1835–1920
W.W. Norton & Co., 1985

Achterberg, Jeanne
Woman as Healer
Shambhala Publications, 1991

Ackerknecht, Erwin Heinz
A Short History of Medicine
Johns Hopkins University Press, 1982

Ackerman, Evelyn Bernette
Health Care in the Parisian Countryside, 1800–1914
Rutgers University Press, 1990

Adams, Annmarie
Architecture in the Family Way: Doctors, Houses and Women, 1870–1900
McGill Queens University Press, 1996

Aidan, Francis;
Cardinal, Gasquet
The Black Death of 1348 and 1349
AMS Press, 1977

Allbutt, Sir Thomas Clifford
The Historical Relations of Medicine and Surgery to the End of the 16th Century
AMS Press, 1978

Alphen, J. Van (Editor); et al
Oriental Medicine: An Illustrated Guide to the Asian Arts of Healing
Shambhala Publications, 1997

Alton, Geoff
Contemporary Accounts of the Great Plague of London
Tressell Publications, 1985

American Medical Association Family Medical Guide
American Medical Association, 2004

American Medical Association
Caring for the Country: A History and Celebration of the First 150 Years of the American Medical Association
Random House, 1997

Andreski, Stanislav
Syphilis, Puritanism, and Witch Hunts: Historical Explanations in the Light of Medicine and Psychoanalysis with a Forecast about AIDS
St. Martins Press, 1990

Armstrong, David; Armstrong, Elizabeth Metzger
The Great American Medicine Show
Prentice Hall, 1991

Baas, J.H.
History of Medicine
R.E. Krieger Pub. Co., 1971

Baly, Monica E.
Florence Nightingale and the Nursing Legacy, 2nd edition: **Building the Foundations of Modern Nursing and Midwifery**
Bain Bridge Books, 1998

Beinfield, Harriet; Korngold, Efrem
Between Heaven and Earth: A Guide to Chinese Medicine
Ballantine Books, 1992

Bell, E.M.
Storming the Citadel: The Rise of the Woman Doctor
Constable & Co., 1953

Bendiner, Jessica;
Bendiner, Elmer (Contributor)
Biographical Dictionary of Medicine
Facts on File, Inc., 1990

Berge, Ann L.A.;
Feingold, Mordechai (Editor)
French Medical Culture in the Nineteenth Century
Rodopi BV Editions, 1994

Binneveld, J.M.W.;
Binneveld, Hans
From Shell Shock to Combat Stress: A Comparative History of Military Psychiatry
Amsterdam University Press, 1998

Bishop, W.J.
The Early History of Surgery, Oldbourne, 1960

Blake, J.B.
Education in the History of Medicine
Hafner Publishing Co., 1968

Bliss, Michael
The Discovery of Insulin
McClelland & Stewart, 1996

Blustein, Bonnie Ellen
Preserve Your Love for Science (Life of William Hammond, American Neurologist)
Cambridge University Press, 1992

Bondeson, Jan (Preface)
A Cabinet of Medical Curiosities
Cornell University Press, 1999

Bourdillon, Hilary
Women as Healers: A History of Women and Medicine
Cambridge University Press, 1989

Bousell, Patrice; Bonnemain, Henri; Bové, Frank
History of Pharmacy and the Pharmaceutical Industry, Asklepios Press, 1982

British Medical Association Complete Home Medical Guide
Dorling Kindersley, 2010

British Medical Association
Complementary Medicine: New Approaches to Good Practice
BMA, 1993

Brockington, C.F.
The Theory and Practice of Public Health
Oxford University Press, 1975

Brooke, Elisabeth
Medicine Women: A Pictorial History of Women Healers
Quest Books, 1997

Brooke, Elisabeth
Women Healers: Portraits of Herbalists, Physicians, and Midwives
Inner Traditions Int., Ltd., 1995

Bryan, Jenny
The History of Health and Medicine
(Science Discovery)
Thomson Learning, 1996

Bryder, Linda
Below the Magic Mountain: A Social History of Tuberculosis in Twentieth-Century Britain
(Oxford Historical Monographs)
Oxford University Press, 1988

Bullough, V.L.
The Development of Medicine as a Profession
S.Karger, 1966

Bunn, Howard Franklin; Aster, Jon C.
Pathophysiology of Blood Disorders
Lange, 2011

Busvine, James R.
Disease Transmission by Insects: Its Discovery and 90 Years of Effort to Prevent It
Spring Verlag, 1993

Bynum, W.F. (Editor);
Porter, Roy (Editor)
Companion Encyclopedia of the History of Medicine
Routledge, 1997

Cameron, M.L.
Anglo-Saxon Medicine
(Cambridge Studies in Anglo-Saxon England, Vol 7), Cambridge University Press, 1993

Campbell, Donald
Arabian Medicine and Its Influence on the Middle Ages
Kegan Paul, Trench, Trüber & Co., 1926

Campbell, Sheila; et al.
Health, Disease, and Healing in Medieval Culture
St. Martins Press, 1991

Cartwright, F.
The Development of Modern Surgery
Arthur Baker, Ltd., 1967

Cassedy, James H.
American Medicine and Statistical Thinking,1800–1860
Harvard University Press, 1984

Cassedy, James H.
Medicine in America: A Short History
(The American Moment)
Johns Hopkins University Press, 1991

Cochrane, Jennifer
An Illustrated History of Medicine
Tiger Books International, 1996

Cod, F.E.G.
Illustrated History of Tropical Diseases
Wellcome Trust, 1996

Cohen, Mark Nathan
Health and the Rise of Civilization
Yale University Press, 1991

Coleman, Vernon
The Story of Medicine
Robert Hale, 1985

**The Concise Human Body Book: An
Illustrated Guide to Its Structure, Function,
and Disorders**
Dorling Kindersley, 2009

Conrad, L.I.; et al.
**The Western Medical Tradition 800 BC to
AD1800**
Cambridge University Press, 1995

Cook, Harold J.
**Matters of Exchange: Commerce, Medicine,
and Science in the Dutch Golden Age**
Yale University Press, 2007

Coward, R.
**The Whole Truth: The Myth of Alternative
Medicine** Faber & Faber, 1989

Craft, Naomi
The Little Book of Medical Breakthroughs
New Holland, 2008

Cravens, Hamilton (Editor)
**Technical Knowledge in American Culture:
Science, Technology, and Medicine Since the
Early 1800s**
University of Alabama Press, 1996

Crellin, J.K.; Philpott, J.
Herbal Medicine of Past and Present
Duke University Press, 1997

Crissey, John T.
**Dermatology and Syphilology of the
Nineteenth Century**
Praeger Pub. Text, 1981

Cule, John
**A Doctor for the People:
2000 Years of General Practice in Britain**
Update Books, 1980

Cule, John
**Wales and Medicine: A Source List for
Printed Books and Papers Showing the
History of Medicine in Relation to Wales
and Welshmen**
National Library of Wales, 1980

Cumston, C.G.
**History of Medicine—
The History of Civilization**
Routledge, 1997

D'Estaing, Valérie-Anne Giscard
The Book of Inventions and Discoveries
Queen Anne Press, 1991

Digby, Anne
**The Evolution of British General Practice
1850–1948**
Oxford University Press, 1999

Drake, Ellen
Sloane's Medical Word Book
Saunders, 2011

Duffy, John
**From Humors to Medical Science: A History
of American Medicine**
University of Illinois Press, 1993

Duin, Nancy; Sutcliffe, Jenny
A History of Medicine
Simon & Schuster, 1992

Duke, Martin
**The Development of Medical Techniques
and Treatments: From Leeches to Heart
Surgery**
International Universities Press, 1991

Dunlop, Robert H.;
Williams, David J., (Contributor)
Veterinary Medicine: An Illustrated History
Mosby Year Book, 1995

Eagle, R.
A Guide to Alternative Medicine
British Broadcasting Corporation, 1980

Eberson, Frederick
Early Physicians of the West
Valkyrie Pub. House, 1979

Edelstein, Ludwig; et al.
Ancient Medicine: Selected Papers of Ludwig Edelstein
Johns Hopkins University Press, 1989

Edwards, Owen Dudleys
Burke and Hare
Laurier Books, Ltd., 1994

Ehrenreich, Barbara; English, Deirdre
Witches, Midwives, and Nurses: A History of Women Healers
Feminist Press, 1973

Ellis, H.
Operations That Made History
Greenwich Medical Publications, 1996

Ellis, H.
Surgical Case Histories from the Past
Royal Society of Medicine Press, 1994

Emmerson, Joan S. (Editor)
Catalogue of the Pybus Collection of Medical Books, Letters and Engravings: 15th –20th Centuries
Manchester University Press, 1983

Encyclopaedia Britannica

Fee, Elizabeth (Editor); Fox, Daniel M. (Editor)
AIDS: The Making of a Chronic Disease
University California Press, 1992

Feldberg, Georgina D.
Disease and Class: Tuberculosis and the Shaping of Modern North American Society (Health and Medicine in American Society)
Rutgers University Press, 1995

Finnane, Mark
Insanity and the Insane in Post-Famine Ireland
Barnes & Noble, 1981

Fischer, Stuart
The Book of Medical Emergencies
Carlton Books, 2006

Freemon, Frank R.
Gangrene and Glory: Medical Care During the American Civil War
Fairleigh Dickinson University Press, 1998

French, Roger (Editor); et al.
Medicine from the Black Death to the French Disease (History of Medicine in Context)
Ashgate Publishing Co., 1998

French, Roger;
Wear, Andrew (Editor)
British Medicine in an Age of Reform (Wellcome Institute Series in the History of Medicine)
Routledge, 1992

Friedman, Meyer;
Friedman, Gerald W.
Medicine's 10 Greatest Discoveries
Yale University Press, 1998

Furst, Lilian R. (Editor)
Women Healers and Physicians: Climbing a Long Hill
University Press of Kentucky, 1997

Gabriel, Richard A.;
Metz, Karen S.
A History of Military Medicine
Greenwood Publishing Group, 1992

Garza, Hedda; Green, Robert
Women in Medicine (Women Then-Women Now)
Franklin Watts, Inc., 1996

Gentilcore, David
Healers and Healing in Early Modern Italy (Social and Cultural Values in Early Modern Europe)
Manchester University Press, 1998

Getz, Faye
Healing and Society in Medieval England: A Middle English Translation of the Pharmaceutical Writings of Gilbertus Anglicus
University of Wisconsin Press, 1991

Getz, Faye
Medicine in the English Middle Ages
Princeton University Press, 1998

Giblin, James Cross; Frampton, David
(Illustrator)
When Plague Strikes:
The Black Death, Smallpox, AIDS
Harper Collins Children's Books, 1997

Gilman, Sander L.
Sexuality: An Illustrated History:
Representing the Sexual in Medicine and
Culture from the Middle Ages to the Age of
AIDS
John Wiley & Sons, 1989

Goldie, Sue M. (Editor)
'I Have Done My Duty': Florence
Nightingale in the Crimean War, 1854–58
University of Iowa, 1988

Gordon, L.
A Country Herbal
Mayflower Books, 1980

Gordon, Richard
An Alarming History of Famous and
Difficult Patients: Amusing Medical
Anecdotes from Typhoid Mary to FDR
St. Martins Press, 1997

Gordon, Richard
The Alarming History of
Medicine: Amusing Anecdotes
from Hippocrates to
Heart Transplants
St. Martins Press, 1994

Greene, Rebecca (Editor)
History of Medicine
Hamworth PR, 1988

Grmek, Mirko Drazen (Editor); et al.
Western Medical Thought from
Antiquity to the Middle Ages
Harvard University Press, 1999

Guthrie, Douglas
A History of Medicine
J.B. Lippincott Co., 1946

Hamilton, David (Introduction)
The Healers: A History of Medicine in
Scotland (The Little Books Series)
Pelican Pub. Co., 1999

Hamlin, Christopher
Public Health in the Age of Chadwick
(Britain, 1800–1854)
Cambridge University Press, 1998

Hanaway, Joseph;
Cruess, Richard (Contributor)
McGill Medicine: The First Half Century
1829–1885
McGill Queens University Press, 1996

Hanlon, J.J.
Public Health: Administration and Practice
C.V. Mosby Co., 1974

Henderson, Beverley; Dorsey, Jennifer Lee
Medical Terminology for Dummies
Wiley, 2008

Hicks, A.
Principles of Chinese Medicine
Thorson, 1996

Hooper, Tony
Breakthrough Surgery
Simon & Schuster Young Books, 1992

Hope, Tony
Medical Ethics: A Very Short Introduction
Oxford University Press, 2004

Horacio, J.R. Fabrega
Evolution of Sickness and Healing
University California Press, 1997

Horrox, Rosemary (Translator)
The Black Death (Manchester Medieval
Sources)
Manchester University Press, 1994

Howson, Mark; et al.
Practice and How It Fits with the Medicine
of the West Henry Holt, 1990

Hudson, Robert P.
Disease and Its Control: The Shaping of
Modern Thought
Greenwood Press, 1983

Hunt, T.
The Medieval Surgery
The Boydell Press, 1992

Hunter, Lynette (Editor); Hutton, Sarah (Editor)
Women, Science, and Medicine, 1500–1700: Mothers and Sisters of the Royal Society
Sutton Publishing, 1997

Hurb-Mead, Kate Campbell
A History of Women in Medicine from the Earliest Times to the Beginning of the Nineteenth Century
AMS Press, 1977

Isaacs, Ronald H.
Judaism, Medicine, and Healing
Jason Aronson, 1998

Jackson, Ralph
Doctors and Diseases in the Roman Empire
University of Oklahoma Press, 1988

Johnson, R.W.
Disease and Medicine
B.T. Batsford, 1967

Jones, Helen
Health and Society in Twentieth-Century Britain (Themes in British Social History)
Longman Group UK, 1994

Jones, Peter Murray
Medieval Medicine in Illuminated Manuscripts
British Library Publications, 1999

Jordanova, Ludmilla
Sexual Visions: Images of Gender in Science and Medicine Between the Eighteenth and Twentieth Centuries
University of Wisconsin Press, 1993

Jouanna, Jacques; et al.
Hippocrates (Medicine and Culture)
Johns Hopkins University Press, 1999

Kaptchuk, T.; Croucher M.
The Healing Arts: A Journey Through the Faces of Medicine
BBC, 1986

Kaufman, Sharon R.
The Healer's Tale: Transforming Medicine and Culture
University of Wisconsin Press, 1995

Kett, Joseph F.
The Formation of the American Medical Profession
Greenwood Publishing Group, 1980

King, Roger
Making of the Dentiste, 1650–1780
Ashgate Publishing, Ltd., 1998

Kiple, Kenneth, F. (Editor)
The Cambridge World History of Human Disease
Cambridge University Press, 1993

Kiple, Kenneth
Plague, Pox, and Pestilence
Weidenfeld & Nicolson, 1997

Knapp, Vincent J.
Disease and Its Impact on Modern European History (Studies in Health and Human Services, Vol. 10)
Edwin Mellen Press, 1989

Kremers, E.; Urdang, G.
History of Pharmacy
J.B.Lippincott Co., 1976

Kumar, Parveen; Clark, Michael L.
Kumar and Clark's Clinical Medicine
Elsevier, 2009

Lawrence, Christopher
Medical Theory, Surgical Practice
Routledge, 1992

Leathard, Audrey
Health Care Provision: Past, Present, and Future
Chapman & Hall, 1990

Leavitt, Judith Walzer
Typhoid Mary: Captive to the Public's Health
Beacon Press, 1997

Lipp, Martin R.
Medical Landmarks USA: A Travel Guide to Historic Sites, Architectural Gems, Remarkable Museums and Libraries, and Other Places Health-Related
McGraw-Hill, 1990

Lisowski, F.P.; Ho, P.Y.
Brief History of Chinese Medicine
World Scientific Pub. Co., 1996

Lloyd, Wyndham E.B.
A Hundred Years of Medicine
Gerald Duckworth & Co., Ltd., 1968

Longrigg, James (Editor)
**Greek Medicine: From the Heroic to the
Hellenistic Age: A Source Book**
Routledge, 1998

Longmore, Murray; Wilkinson, Ian;
Davidson, Edward; Foulkes, Alexander
Oxford Handbook of Clinical Medicine
Oxford University Press, 2010

Loudon, Irvine (Editor)
Western Medicine: An Illustrated History
Oxford University Press, 1997

Loudon, Irvine (Editor); et al.
**General Practice Under the
National Health Service,
1948–1997**
Clarendon Press, 1998

Lu, Henry C.
Chinese System of Natural Cures
Sterling Publications, 1994

Luchetti, Cathy
**Medicine Women: The Story of Early
American Women Doctors**
Crown Publications, 1998

Lyons, A.S.; Petrucelli, R.J.
Medicine: An Illustrated History
Abradale Press, Harry N. Abrams, Inc.,
Publishers, 1987

Magner, Lois N.
A History of Medicine
Marcel Dekker, 1992

Major, Ralph H.
A History of Medicine
Blackwell, 1954

Marcuse, Peter M.
Disease: In Search of Remedy
University of Illinois Press, 1996

Margotta, Roberto
The Hamlyn History of Medicine
Reed International, 1996

Mayer, Robert G.
Embalming: History, Theory, and Practice
Appleton & Lange, 1996

McGowen, Tom
The Black Death (First Books)
Franklin Watts, Inc., 1995

McGregor, Deborah Kuhn
**From Midwives to Medicine:
The Birth of American Gynecology**
Rutgers University Press, 1998

Mettler, Cecelia
History of Medicine
Blakiston Co., 1947

Meyer, Clarence
American Folk Medicine
Meyer Books, 1985

Michell, A.R. (Editor)
**The Advancement of Veterinary Science:
History of the Healing Professions: Parallels
Between Veterinary and Medical History**
Cabi Publishing, 1993

Miller, Jonathan
The Body in Question
Jonathan Cape, 1978

Miller, Timothy S.
**The Birth of the Hospital in the Byzantine
Empire**
Johns Hopkins University Press, 1997

Morton, L.T.; Moore, R.J.
**A Chronology of Medicine and Related
Sciences**
Scolar Press, 1997

Moscucci, Ornella
**The Science of Woman: Gynaecology and
Gender in England, 1800–1929**
Cambridge University Press, 1993

Newman, Art
The Illustrated Treasury of Medical Curiosa
McGraw-Hill, 1988

Nuland, Sherwin B.
Medicine: The Art of Healing
Hugh Lauter Levin Associates, Inc., 1992

Numbers, Ronald L. (Editor); Amundsen,
Darrel W. (Editor)
Caring and Curing:
Health and Medicine in the Western
Religious Traditions
Johns Hopkins University Press, 1998

Nunn, John F.
Ancient Egyptian Medicine
University of Oklahoma Press, 1996

Nutton, V.; Porter, Roy
Murders and Miracles:
Lay Attitudes Towards Medicine in Classical
Antiquity
Cambridge University Press, 1985

O'Boyle, Cornelius
The Art of Medicine:
Medical Teaching at the University of Paris,
1250–1400
Brill Academic Publishers, 1998

100 Greatest Medical Discoveries
Grolier Educational Corp., 1997

Orme, N.; Webster, M.
The English Hospital, 1070–1570
Yale University Press, 1995

Peters, Ann
British Medical Association Illustrated
Medical Dictionary
Dorling Kindersley, 2007

Peters, Michael
British Medical Association A–Z Family
Medical Encyclopedia
Dorling Kindersley, 2008

Phillips, E.D.
Aspects of Greek Medicine
The Charles Press, Publishers, 1987

Pick, Christopher;
Murphy, Dervla
Embassy to Constantinople: The Travels of
Lady Mary Worley Montagu
Century, 1988

Pickstone, John V. (Editor)
Medical Innovations in Historical
Perspective
St. Martins Press, 1992

Porter, Dorothy
Health, Civilization, and the State: A
History of Public Health from Ancient to
Modern Times
Routledge, 1999

Porter, Dorothy;
Porter, Roy (Editor)
Doctors, Politics, and Society: Historical
Essays
Rodopi BV Editions, 1993

Porter, Dorothy;
Porter, Roy
Patient's Progress
Polity Press (Blackwell Publishing), 1989

Porter, Roy (Editor)
The Cambridge Illustrated History of
Medicine
Cambridge University Press, 1996

Porter, Roy
Disease, Medicine, and Society in England,
1550–1860
Cambridge University Press, 1996

Porter, Roy
Doctor of Society: Thomas Beddoes and the
Sick Trade in Late Enlightenment England
Routledge, 1992

Porter, Roy
The Greatest Benefit to Mankind:
A Medical History of Humanity
W.W. Norton & Co., 1998

Porter, Roy
Health for Sale:
Quackery in England, 1660–1850
Manchester University Press, 1989

Porter, Roy
London: A Social History
Harvard University Press, 1998

Porter, Roy (Editor)
Medicine: A History of Healing:

Ancient Traditions to Modern Practices
Michael O'Mara Books, 1997

Porter, Roy
Mind Forg'd Manacles: Madness in England from Restoration to the Regency
Harvard University Press, 1988

Porter, Roy; Porter, Dorothy
**In Sickness and in Health: The British Experience,
1650–1850**
Blackwell Pub., 1989

Pouchelle, Marie-Christine
The Body and Surgery in the Middle Ages
Rutgers University Press, 1990

Powell, J.H.; et al.
**Bring Out Your Dead:
The Great Plague of Yellow Fever in Philadelphia in 1793**
University of Pennsylvania Press, 1993

Poynter, F.N.L.
Medicine and Culture
Wellcome Institute for the History of Medicine, 1969

Preuss, Julius;
Rosner, Fred (Translator)
Biblical and Talmudic Medicine
Jason Aronson, 1994

Prioreschi, Plinio
A History of Medicine: Greek Medicine
(Mellen History of Medicine)
Edwin Mellen Press, 1994

Prioreschi, Plinio
The History of Medicine: Primitive and Ancient Medicine
(Mellen History of Medicine, Vol.1)
Edwin Mellen Press, 1991

Proctor, Robert N.
The Nazi War on Cancer
Princeton University Press, 1999

Rawcliffe, Carole
Medicine and Society in Later Medieval England
Sutton Publishing, 1998

Reader's Digest Family Guide to Alternative Medicine
The Reader's Digest Association, Ltd., 1991

Reagan, Leslie J.
When Abortion Was a Crime: Women, Medicine, and Law in the United States, 1867–1973
University of California Press, 1998

Repp, Kevin
Timelines of World History
Bramley Books, 1998

Reynolds, Brenda M.
**History of Medicine:
Reference and Research Subject Analysis with Bibliography**
ABBE Publishers Association of Washington, DC, 1984

Reynolds, Moira Davison
How Pasteur Changed History: The Story of Louis Pasteur and the Pasteur Institute
McGuinn & McGuire, 1994

Rhodes, Philip
An Outline History of Medicine
Butterworth, 1985

Riddle, J.M.
Dioscordies on Pharmacy and Medicine
University of Texas Press, 1985

Riley, James C.
The Eighteenth-Century Campaign to Avoid Disease
St. Martins Press, 1987

Roberts, Charlotte; Manchester, Keith
(Contributor)
The Archaeology of Disease
Cornell University Press, 1997

Roberts, Shirley
Sophia Jex-Blake: A Woman Pioneer in Nineteenth-Century Medical Reform
Routledge, 1993
Roccatagliata, Guieppe A.
History of Ancient Psychiatry
Greenwood Publishing Group, 1986

Root-Bernstein, Robert; et al.

Honey, Mud, Maggots, and Other Medical
Marvels: The Science Behind Folk Remedies
and Old Wives' Tales
Mariner Books, 1998

Rose, Jeanne
A History of Herbs and Herbalism: A
Chronology from 10,000 BCE to the Present
Herbal Studies Course, 1988

Rosenberg, Charles E.
Explaining Epidemics:
And Other Studies in the History of
Medicine
Cambridge University Press, 1992

Rosenberg, C.E.; Golden, J.
Framing Disease: Studies in Cultural
History (Health and Medicine in American
Society)
Rutgers University Press, 1992

Rosenfeld, Louis
Thomas Hodgkin: Morbid Anatomist and
Social Activist
Madison Books, 1993

Rosner, Lisa
Medical Education in the
Age of Improvement:
Edinburgh Students and
Apprentices, 1760–1826
Edinburgh University Press, 1991

Rothstein, William G.
American Physicians in the
Nineteenth Century:
From Sects to Science
Johns Hopkins University Press, 1992

Rousselot, Jean
Medicine in Art: A Cultural History
McGraw-Hill, 1967

Rushton, Alan R.
Genetics and Medicine in the United States,
1800 to 1922
Johns Hopkins University Press, 1994
Saks, Mike (Editor)
Alternative Medicine in Britain
Clarendon Press, 1991

Schlefman, Arthur

History of Medicine: Reference and
Research Subject Analysis with
Bibliography
ABBE Publishers Association of Washington,
DC, 1986

Scott, Henry H.
A History of Tropical Medicine
AMS Press, 1939

Selin, Helain (Editor)
Encyclopaedia of the History of Science,
Technology, and Medicine in Non-Western
Cultures
Kluwer Academic Press, 1997

Sharma, U.
Complementary Medicine Today:
Practitioners and Patients
Routledge, 1992

Shelton, Herbert M.
The Myth of Medicine
Cool Hand Communications, Inc., 1995

Shorter, Edward
Bedside Manners:
The Troubled History of Doctors and
Patients
Simon & Schuster, 1985

Shultz, Suzanne M.
Body Snatching: The Robbing of Graves
for the Education of Physicians in Early
Nineteenth-Century America
McFarland & Company, 1992

Siegfried, Donna Rae
Anatomy and Physiology for Dummies
Wiley, 2002

Sigerist, Henry E.
The Great Doctors: A Biographical History
of Medicine W.W. Norton, 1933
Sigerist, Henry Ernest
A History of Medicine: Early Greek, Hindu,
and Persian Medicine
Oxford University Press, 1987

Sigerist, Henry Ernest
A History of Medicine:
Primitive and Archaic Medicine
Oxford University Press, 1987

Singer, Charles J.
Greek Biology and Greek Medicine
AMS Press, 1985

Siraisi, N.G.
**Medieval and Early Renaissance Medicine:
An Introduction to Knowledge and Practice**
The University of Chicago Press, 1990

Slack, Paul
**The Impact of Plague in Tudor and Stuart
England**
Clarendon Press, 1991

Sournia, Jean-Charles
Illustrated History of Medicine
AMER College of Physicians, 1997

Stetter, Cornelius
**The Secret Medicine of the Pharaohs:
Ancient Egyptian Healing**
Edition Q, 1993

Stevens, Rosemary
**American Medicine and the
Public Interest**
University California Press, 1998

Stevenson, Lloyd G.
A Celebration of Medical History
Johns Hopkins University Press, 1982

Storr, David
Medicine in History
Wayland Publishers, Ltd., 1985

The Human Body
Time-Life Books, 1990

Tiner, John Hudson
The History of Medicine
Master Books, 1999
Travers, Bridget (Editor); Freiman, Fran
Locher (Editor)
**Medical Discoveries: Medical Breakthroughs
and the People Who Developed Them**
Gale Research, 1996

Tuve, Jeanette
First Russian Women Physicians
Oriental Research Partners, 1981

Unschuld, Paul U.
Medicine in China: A History of Ideas
University of California Press, 1985

Unschuld, Paul U.;
Wiseman, Nigel (Translator)
Chinese Medicine
Paradigm Publications, 1998

Van Der Zee, Barbara; et al.
**Green Pharmacy:
The History and Evolution of Western
Herbal Medicine**
Inner Traditions Intl., Ltd., 1997

Van Hartesveldt, Fred R. (Editor)
**The 1918–1919 Pandemic of Influenza:
The Urban Experience in the Western World**
Edwin Mellen Press, 1993

van Zandt, Eleanor
Twenty Names in Medicine
Wayland Publishers, Ltd., 1987

Voel, Virgil L.
American Indian Medicine
University of Oklahoma Press, 1970

Waserman, Manfred (Editor); Kottek, Samuel
S. (Editor)
**Health and Disease in the Holy Land:
Studies in the History and Sociology of
Medicine from Ancient Times to the Present**
Edwin Mellen Press, 1996

Watts, Sheldon
**Epidemics and History: Disease, Power, and
Imperialism** Yale University Press, 1998

Wear, Andrew (Editor)
Medicine in Society
Cambridge University Press, 1992
Wear, Delese (Editor); Conley, Frances K.
**Women in Medical Education:
An Anthology of Experience**
State University of New York Press, 1996

Webster, C.
**Health, Medicine, and Mortality in the
Sixteenth Century**
Cambridge University Press, 1979

Weir's Guide to
Medical Museums in Britain
RSM, Press 1996

Werner, D.
History of the Red Cross Cassell & Co., 1941

Wilbur, C. Keith
Civil War Medicine, 1861–1865
Globe Pequot Press, 1998

Wilbur, C. Keith
Revolutionary Medicine, 1700–1800
(Illustrated Living History Series)
Chelsea House Publishing, 1997

Williams, Guy R.
The Age of Agony: The Art of Healing,
1700–1800
Academy Chicago Pub., 1995

Wilson, Philip K.
Childbirth, Changing Ideas and
Practices in Britain and America, 1600
to the Present (5 volumes)
Garland Publishing, Inc., 1996

Woodham, Anne; Peters, Dr. David
Encyclopedia of Complementary Medicine
Dorling Kindersley, 1997

Woodward, J.; Richards, D.
Health Care and Popular Medicine in
Nineteenth-Century England
Homes & Meier Pub., Inc., 1977

Young, J.H.
Medical Messiahs: A Social History of
Medical Quackery in the Twentieth
Century
Princeton University Press, 1967

Zhenguo, W.; Peiping, X.
History and Development of Traditional
Chinese Medicine
IOS Press, 1998

Zigrosser, C.
Medicine and the Artist
Dover Publications, 1970

Zilboorg, G.; Henry, G.W.
A History of Medical Psychology
W.W. Norton & Co., 1941

Zimmeman, L.M.; Veith, I.
Great Ideas in the History of Surgery
Dover Publications, 1967

Ziyin, Shen; Zelin, Chen (Contributor)
The Basis of Traditional Chinese Medicine
Shambhala Publications, 1996

Zysk, Kenneth G.
Religious Medicine (The History and
Evolution of Indian Medicine)
Transaction Publishing, 1900

MUSEUMS AND INSTITUTIONS

AUSTRALIA
Medical History Museum
Brownless Medical Library,
University of Melbourne
Museum of Human Disease,
New South Wales
University of Melbourne Medical
History Museum, Western
Australia Medical Museum

BELARUS
Musée d'Histoire de la Médecine
de Biélarus, Minsk

CANADA
Banting Museum, London,
Ontario
Medical History Museum of
Nova Scotia, Nova Scotia
Museum of Contraception,
Toronto

CHANNEL ISLANDS
German Military Underground
Museum,
St. Andrew's, Guernsey
The German Underground
Hospital,
St. Lawrence, Jersey

DENMARK
Medicinsk historisk Museum,
Bredgade 62, Köbenhavn
Steno Museum [Danish Museum
for the History of Science and
Medicine], Aarhus

FRANCE
Centre Hospitalier de Tonnerre,
Tonnerre
Cité des Sciences et de
l'Industrie, Paris
Le Musée Pierre Marly des
Lunettes et Lorgnettes, Paris
Musée Armenien de France,
Paris
Musée d'Anatomie Delmas-
Orfila-Rouviere, Paris
Musée d'Histoire de la
Medecine, Paris
Musée de l'Assistance Publique-
Hopitaux de Paris, Paris
Musée des Arts Forains -

Collection Jean-Paul Favand,
Paris
Musée des Collections
Historiques de la Prefecture de
Police, Paris
Musée Dupuytren, Paris
Musée national des Arts et
Traditions Populaires Paris
Musée Pasteur, Paris
Musée Pierre Fauchard, Musée
d'Art Dentaire, Paris

GERMANY
Deutsches Hygiene Museum,
Dresden
Deutsches Medizinhistorisches
Museum, Ingolstadt
Julius Maximillians-Universität,
Würzburg
Martin von Wagner-Museum,
Würzburg
Krankenhaus-Museum, Bremen
Museum und Archiv zur
Geschichte der urologie, klinik
für Urologie und Kinder
urologie, Düren
Optisches Museum der Ernst-
Abbe-Stiftung, Jena
Universitätsbibliothek Erlangen,
Erlangen

ITALY
Faculta di Medicina e Chirurgia,
Milan
Institute and Museum of History
of Science, Florence
University Museums, Bologna
Vatican Library - Medicine and
Biology, Vatican City

JAPAN
Kawaski Medical University
Museum of Modern Medical
Education Kurashiki, City
Okayama

LATVIA
Paul Stradin Museum of the
History of Medicine, Riga
LITHUANIA
Museums of History of
Lithuanian Medicine and
Pharmacy, Kaunas

NETHERLANDS
Museum Boerhaave, Leiden
Universiteitsmuseum, Utrecht

NEW ZEALAND
Anatomy Museum, Department
of Anatomy and Structural
Biology, University of Otago,
Dunedin

RUSSIA
Scientific Research Center
Medical Museum, Russian
Academy of Medical Sciences,
Moscow

SOUTH AFRICA
Adler Museum of the History
of Medicine, University of the
Witwatersrand, Johannesburg

SPAIN
Fundacio-Museu d'Historia
de la Medicina de Catalunya,
Barcelona
Museo Hispano de Ciencia y
Technologia, Madrid

SWEDEN
Medicinhistoriska Museet,
Göteborg

SWITZERLAND
Medizinhistorisches Institut und
Museum der Universitat Zurich,
Zürich

UK
Alexander Fleming Laboratory
Museum, St. Mary's Hospital,
London
B.O.C. Museum, The
Association of Anaesthetists
of Great Britain and Ireland,
London
Beamish, The North of England
Open Air Museum, Beamish
Hall, Durham
Bethlem Royal Hospital Archives
and Museum, The Bethlem Royal
Hospital, Beckenham, Kent
British Dental Association

Museum, London
British Museum, London
British Optical Association
Collection, The College of
Optometrists, London
British Red Cross Museum and
Archive, London
Chelsea Physic Garden, London
Department of Anatomy,
University of Glasgow
Dinorwig Quarry Hospital,
Llanberis, Gwynedd, Wales
Dorset County Museum,
Dorchester, Dorset
Flambards Victorian Village,
Helston, Cornwall
Florence Nightingale Museum,
London
Freud Museum, London
Glenside Hospital Museum,
Blackberry Hill Hospital,
Stapleton, Bristol
Green Dragon Museum,
Stockton-on-Tees, Cleveland
Hunterian Museum, University
of Glasgow
Jenner Museum and Conference
Centre, Berkeley, Gloucestershire
Keeler Museum and Library,
Windsor, Berkshire
Main Library, University of
Wales College of Medicine,
Cardiff, Wales
Medical Tours, London
Monica Britton Exhibition Hall
of Medical History, Frenchay
Hospital, Bristol
Museum of London, London
Wall, London
Museum of the History of
Science, Oxford
Museum of the Order of St.
John, London
Museum of the Royal
Pharmaceutical Society, London
Museums of the Royal College of
Surgeons, London
Old Operating Theatre Museum
and Herb Garret, London
People's Palace, Glasgow
Queen Alexandra's Royal Army
Nursing Corps Museum + Royal
Army Dental Corps Museum

+ Royal Army Medical Corps
Museum, Aldershot, Hampshire
Royal College of Obstetricians &
Gynaecologists, London
Royal College of Surgeons of
England includes Hunterian
Museum, Odontological
Museum, Wellcome Museum of
Pathology, Wellcome Museum
of Anatomy, The Historian
Instrument Collection, Lincoln's
Inn Fields, London
Royal Infirmary History
Museum, Leicester, Leicestershire
Royal London Hospital Archives
and Museum, London
Royal Museum of Scotland,
Edinburgh
St. Bartholomew's Hospital
Archives & Museum, London
Sir Jules Thorn Historical
Museum, The Royal College of
Surgeons, Edinburgh
Science Museum, London
Stephen Beaumont Museum,
Wakefield, West Yorkshire
Sue Ryder Museum, Cavendish,
Sudbury, Suffolk
Thackray Medical Museum,
Leeds
University College, University of
London, London
Wellcome Centre for Medical
Science and History, London
Wellcome Museum of the
History of Medicine, The Science
Museum London
Whipple Museum of the History
of Science, Cambridge

USA
Alabama Museum of the Health
Sciences, Birmingham, Alabama
Alan Mason Chesney Medical
Archives of The Johns Hopkins
Medical Institutions, Baltimore
American Museum of Natural
History, New York
Bakken Library and Museum,
Minneapolis, Minnesota
College of Physicians of
Philadelphia, Philadelphia,
Pennsylvania

Dittrick Museum of Medical
History, Cleveland, Ohio
DNA Learning Center, New York
Hall of Health, Berkeley,
California
Health Adventure, Asheville
Health Museum of Cleveland
History of Pharmacy Museum,
University of Arizona, Tucson,
Arizona
Houston Museum of Health and
Medical Science, Houston
Indiana Medical History
Museum, Indiana
International Museum of
Surgical Science, Chicago
Lloyd Library, Cincinnati, Ohio
Medical Leech Museum,
Charleston, South Carolina
Michigan Digital Historical
Initiative in the Health Sciences,
Michigan
Museum of Health and Medical
Science, Houston, Texas
Museum of Ophthalmology,
American Academy of
Ophthalmology, San Francisco
Museum of Questionable
Medical Devices, Minneapolis,
Minnesota
Museum of the History of
Psychological Instrumentation,
Montclair State University, New
Jersey
National Museum of American
History, Division of Science,
Medicine & Society, Washington,
DC
National Museum of Civil War
Medicine, Frederick, Maryland
National Museum of Dentistry,
Baltimore, Maryland
National Museum of Health and
Medicine, Washington, DC
Public Health Museum,
Massachusetts
Stetten Museum, Bethesda
University of Iowa Medical
Museum, Iowa
Wood Library-Museum of
Anesthesiology, Park Ridge,
Illinois